Y0-BEJ-301

OMNIVM
LVX
CIVIVM
MDCCCLII
MDCCC
LXXVIII
BOSTON
PUBLIC
LIBRARY

HEINE

THE TRAGIC SATIRIST

BY THE SAME AUTHOR

German Lyric Poetry (Routledge and Kegan Paul)
Heine's *Buch der Lieder* (Edward Arnold)
Mörike und seine Leser (Ernst Klett Verlag)

HEINE

THE TRAGIC SATIRIST

A Study of the Later Poetry
1827–1856

BY

S. S. PRAWER
Senior Lecturer in German Language and Literature,
University of Birmingham

CAMBRIDGE
AT THE UNIVERSITY PRESS
1961

PUBLISHED BY
THE SYNDICS OF THE CAMBRIDGE UNIVERSITY PRESS

Bentley House, 200 Euston Road, London, N.W. 1
American Branch: 32 East 57th Street, New York 22, N.Y.
West African Office: P.O. Box 33, Ibadan, Nigeria

Printed in Great Britain at the University Press, Cambridge
(Brooke Crutchley, University Printer)

FOR

PROFESSOR ROY PASCAL

CONTENTS

PREFACE

THERE has been no comprehensive critical survey of Heine's poetry since Jules Legras published his *Henri Heine, Poète* in 1897. Since then many important studies of individual works and problems have appeared—I would single out particularly the work of R. M. Meyer, Helene Herrmann, Friedrich Hirth, Barker Fairley, William Rose, Kurt Weinberg, Walter Höllerer and Walther Killy; much new light has been thrown on biographical as well as literary problems; and many libraries—the Düsseldorf Landes- und Stadtbibliothek, the Goethe and Schiller archives of Weimar, Harvard University Library and many others—have acquired and made available for study many important manuscripts. The time seems therefore ripe for a re-examination of Heine's poetry. The present book seeks to undertake this; it deals briefly with the *Buch der Lieder* (of which I have recently published a separate study) and fully with *Neue Gedichte*, *Atta Troll*, *Deutschland. Ein Wintermärchen*, *Romanzero*, *Gedichte 1853 und 1854*, and the poems which appeared in the posthumous *Letzte Gedichte und Gedanken* of 1869.

The text of the poems quoted is always (unless definite indications to the contrary are given) that of the last version corrected by Heine himself. I have modernised spelling, but retained Heine's punctuation; following the practice of Jonas Fränkel in the admirable 'Insel Verlag' edition of Heine I have, however, omitted apostrophes wherever words are self-explanatory without them.

In order to reduce notes to a minimum, quotations from Heine's poems and letters have usually been identified in the text. Only for passages from prose works, which cannot be easily identified in this way, and for manuscript and early versions of the poems, are references given in the notes.

All poems are quoted in the original German—for the kind of analysis that is here attempted translations would hardly serve;

but prose quotations have been translated into English. Exact references make it possible for the interested reader to turn up the German originals with little loss of time. My translations are occasionally based on existing versions.

My thanks are due to Professor William Rose, Professor Eudo C. Mason, Dr Brian Rowley and many other scholars, in England, Germany and the United States, who have discussed Heine's poetry with me: to Dr Eberhard Galley, director of the Heine archives of the Landes- und Stadtbibliothek Düsseldorf, for permission to quote from unpublished manuscripts; to Professor Stuart Atkins and the editors of the *Harvard Library Bulletin* for permission to quote from a manuscript of *Für die Mouche*; to the editors of *The Germanic Review*, *German Life and Letters* and the *Proceedings of the English Goethe Society* for permission to use material already published in those journals; and to the University of Birmingham for a generous research grant. I am grateful, above all, for the constant help and advice of the teacher and friend to whom this book is dedicated.

S. S. P.

BIRMINGHAM
1960

ABBREVIATIONS USED IN THE NOTES

Briefe	F. Hirth (ed.), *Heinrich Heine: Briefe*
Gespräche	H. H. Houben (ed.), *Gespräche mit Heine*
SW	E. Elster (ed.), *Heinrich Heines Sämtliche Werke*

Der Ernst tritt um so gewaltiger hervor,
wenn der Spaß ihn angekündigt.

HEINE: *Englische Fragmente*

INTRODUCTION

THE POET OF THE 'BUCH DER LIEDER'

Who in Devil's name ever thought of reading poetry for any political or practical purpose till these Devil's times that we live in?

COLERIDGE

HEINE'S *Buch der Lieder* has become a 'book of songs' in a sense other than that intended by its author. Ever since Schubert, at the very end of his life, discovered *Die Heimkehr* and Schumann, after his long courtship of Clara Wieck, turned to *Lyrisches Intermezzo*, Heine's earlier poems have served the masters of the German Lied as a seemingly inexhaustible reservoir of texts. What attracted these composers to Heine is not difficult to see. His preference for simple strophic metres, his simple language and vivid though sparing imagery, whose import could reach an audience even when the words were sung, his terseness, which would prevent the song from going on too long, his penchant for suggesting certain attitudes and emotions without talking about them directly, which leaves scope for the piano accompaniment; and last but not least, the melodiousness of his language, that 'Singen und Klingen' of his words of which he himself was so proud—such things as these commended his poems to Schubert and Schumann, to Mendelssohn, Franz and Silcher, to Brahms, to Richard Strauss and to a host of other composers in Germany and abroad. They saw above all the Byronically tragic or the romantically 'innig' poet; even *Dichterliebe*, for all its complexity, gives us more of Florestan and Eusebius—Schumann's impetuous and his dreamy self—than of Heine. One may perhaps be forgiven for feeling, with Theodor Adorno,[1] that the nearest musical 'equivalent' of this poetry is to be found, not in the five thousand or so extant Heine settings, but in the work of a man who never set a single one of his poems: in

[1] Theodor Adorno, *Noten zur Literatur* (Berlin and Frankfurt, 1958), p. 150.

the folk-song compositions, the scherzos and the funeral marches of Gustav Mahler.

Among the most powerful of Heine settings proper is Schubert's *Der Doppelgänger*, which Richard Capell has called, with some justification, 'the finest of all achievements in the matching of music and verse'.[1] To this setting of the twentieth poem of *Die Heimkehr* the German Lied owes a new and some might feel a dangerous departure; for it was with *Der Doppelgänger* that Schubert, in the last year of his life, took the decisive step on that road towards the 'declamatory' or 'recitative' song which ought to bear (as has been well said) a warning sign: 'For the genius only.'[2] Inspired by the stark greatness of the poem, Schubert suppressed his natural inclination towards generously flowing melody and produced a song in which the accompaniment is reduced to a tolling *basso ostinato*, while the vocal line (a set of variations, in the main, of one slight opening phrase) follows the natural rhythm of the verse with astonishing faithfulness. Sung by a Gerhardt or a Schlusnus or a Hotter or a Fischer-Dieskau, this song can make the most overwhelming impression in the concert-hall.

In *Der Doppelgänger* Schubert re-embodied in music what may fairly be called the key-poem of the *Buch der Lieder* and a key-figure of Heine's poetry as a whole. This was not the first time a 'second self' had appeared in Heine's writings. One of his earliest letters presents a double, a pale fellow sitting on a chair in the same room and adding to the letter words the poet himself would rather disown.

I have seen her again,

> Dem Teufel meine Seele,
> Dem Henker sei der Leib,
> Doch ich allein erwähle
> Für mich das schöne Weib.

Hu! Are you not shuddering, Christian? Well may you shudder. I am shuddering too.—Burn this letter. God have mercy on my soul.

[1] Richard Capell, *Schubert's Songs* (London, 1928), p. 257.

[2] Maurice J. E. Brown, *Schubert. A Critical Biography* (London, 1958), p. 305.

—I did not write these words.—A pale man sat on a chair, it was he who wrote these words. That's because it is midnight....

(Letter to Christian Sethe, 27 October 1816)

That hovers characteristically between melodrama and parody. Melodrama is in full command, however, when the double appears again, pervasively, in Heine's verse play *William Ratcliff*, where the second self is the wraith of the hero's father and embodies, in the manner of E. T. A. Hoffmann and the German 'Fate' drama, a destiny that interferes with love, a hereditary curse that saps the will. 'Cursed double', Ratcliff exclaims,

> Verdammter Doppelgänger,[1] Nebelmensch,
> Anglotze mich nicht mit den stieren Augen—
> Mit deinen Augen saugst du aus mein Blut,
> Erstarren machst du mich, Eiswasser gießt du
> In meine glühnden Adern, machst mich selbst
> Zum toten Nachtgespenst....[2]

This address to the 'Doppelgänger' has everything: the image of the vampire sucking ghastly nourishment from the living body, that of the hypnotist willing his subject into rigidity, of the spectre freezing the blood, of living men transformed into zombies or ghosts—and because it has everything it has, in the end, nothing. It collects together the trappings of the novel of terror and the 'Fate' drama, overloads the experience to be communicated, and like those films called *Brides of Dracula* or *The Curse of Frankenstein*, it makes us laugh where we ought to have shuddered.

It is in the *Buch der Lieder* that the 'Doppelgänger' image comes, at last, into its own. Throughout that collection Heine speaks to his readers in many guises: as a bold or despairing lover, as a Byronic hero, as a poet conscious of his immortality who can afford to smile down on the Philistine—even, with characteristic blasphemy, as 'der liebe Gott' himself. But all these *personae*, all

[1] This is the form in which the word appears in the edition of 1852; the young Heine invariably wrote 'Doppeltgänger'—throughout *Ratcliff*, in *Tragödien nebst einem lyrischen Intermezzo* (Berlin, 1823) and in all editions of *Die Heimkehr* (see p. 4 below).

[2] *Heinrich Heines Sämtliche Werke*, ed. E. Elster (1887–90), II, 335. (This edition is henceforth cited as *SW*.)

these idealisations and stylisations of his historical self, seem attended by a strange shadow:

Ich und mein Schatten selbander,
Wir wandelten schweigend einher.

(*Lyrisches Intermezzo* 38)

Nor does the shadow always keep his silence: he soon turns into a second self that derides the posturings of the first.

Teurer Freund, du bist verliebt,
Und dich quälen neue Schmerzen;
Dunkler wird es dir im Kopf,
Heller wird es dir im Herzen....

(*Die Heimkehr* 54)

In these poems in which a second self addresses the first as 'Teurer Freund', derision can raise a smile; but elsewhere it brings a start of horror.

Still ist die Nacht, es ruhen die Gassen,
In diesem Hause wohnte mein Schatz;
Sie hat schon längst die Stadt verlassen,
Doch steht noch das Haus auf demselben Platz.

Da steht auch ein Mensch und starrt in die Höhe,
Und ringt die Hände, vor Schmerzensgewalt;
Mir graust es, wenn ich sein Antlitz sehe, —
Der Mond zeigt mir meine eigne Gestalt.

Du Doppeltgänger! du bleicher Geselle!
Was äffst du nach mein Liebesleid,
Das mich gequält auf dieser Stelle,
So manche Nacht, in alter Zeit? (*Die Heimkehr* 20)

Here the 'Doppelgänger' is a spectre of the past arising to confront the present and ape its grief. Through mockery of sorrow ('äffen' and 'quälen' are linked by more than assonance!) the double transforms the 'lyric I' into a watcher, a knowing one, who has lost the ability to respond unequivocally to love and to sorrow, because it has all happened before; who is forced, not only to suffer, but to be an ironic spectator of his own suffering.

In *Die Heimkehr* the figure of the 'Doppelgänger' is more than just a literary device—he is a powerful symbol for that loss of simplicity, for that division into an acting and a watching self, which constitute a central problem of Romantic and post-Romantic art. Nor is his presentation now 'literary' in a pejorative sense. The rant, the obvious gratification of suppressed wishes, the easy rhetoric, the trappings of the novel of terror which characterised *William Ratcliff* have all disappeared, and Heine has learnt to make his effects with few and simple elements: stillness, darkness, a house deserted by its loved inhabitant, a 'man outside'. His lines move slowly—yet within them may be felt an agitation the more powerful for being restrained, an agitation that appears in sudden checks, irregular alternation of stressed and unstressed syllables, the cry of the *ei* assonance in the last line of stanza 2, the intrusion of the polysyllabic 'Schmerzensgewalt' into a predominantly monosyllabic passage, and the change from statement to direct address at the opening of the final stanza. When we are moved by Schubert's *Der Doppelgänger*, we are responding not only to great music but also to great poetry.

The 'Doppelgänger', aping the *personae* assumed by the poet, is responsible for the dissonances that disturb many readers of the *Buch der Lieder*. He calls in question the pretensions of every idealised self, challenges the seriousness with which the lover or Byronic hero takes himself and his grief, and suggests, like Poseidon in *Die Nordsee*, that one man's 'I' may not, after all, be so very important.

> Fürchte dich nicht, Poetlein!
> Ich will nicht im geringsten gefährden
> Dein armes Schiffchen,
> Und nicht dein liebes Leben beängstgen
> Mit allzu bedenklichem Schaukeln.
> Denn du, Poetlein, hast mich nie erzürnt,
> Du hast kein einziges Türmchen verletzt
> An Priamos' heiliger Feste,
> Kein einziges Härchen hast du versengt
> Am Aug meines Sohns Polyphemos,
> Und dich hat niemals ratend beschützt
> Die Göttin der Klugheit, Pallas Athene.
>
> (*Die Nordsee* I, 5)

What is more: he whispers that the pangs of despised love—that constant theme of the *Buch der Lieder*—may not really be worth the unremitting attention the poet gives them; that he has concerns and affections that transcend them in importance.

> Teurer Freund! Was soll es nützen,
> Stets das alte Lied zu leiern?
> Willst du ewig brütend sitzen
> Auf den alten Liebes-Eiern? (*Die Heimkehr* 42)

It needs no hindsight to perceive that Heine could never have rested content with the bitter-sweet love-poetry that made his name and exercised, from the first, so baleful an influence on German poetry. Sooner or later, he had to assume a poetic self different from that so often mocked by his uncomfortable 'Doppelgänger'.

> Doch Lieder und Sterne und Blümelein,
> Und Äuglein und Mondglanz und Sonnenschein,
> So sehr das Zeug auch gefällt,
> So macht's doch noch lang keine Welt.
> (*Junge Leiden — Romanzen* 20)

The contemptuous attitude implicit, even in this early poem, in the words 'das Zeug' made it inevitable that Heine would sooner or later turn away from the poetry of love and nature which had made him famous.

When the *Buch der Lieder* appeared in 1827, Heine had in fact already exhibited himself to his German public in a new guise—he had done so, however, not in his verse, but in the prose of his earliest *Reisebilder*. The traveller of *Die Harzreise*, for all his amorousness and occasional accesses of sentimentality, sees more of the world and responds more fully to what he sees than the lovers and knights of the *Lyrisches Intermezzo*. He combines the irreverence of a seventeenth-century *picaro* with the openness to impressions of a 'sentimental traveller' of the eighteenth century, who mingled his own reflections with accounts of natural scenery, topography and institutions. Heine was here able to draw on a tradition going back both to the picaresque novel and to Laurence

Sterne; a tradition carried on in Germany by Bode and Jacoby, by Hermes and Thümmel, by Jean Paul and Tieck. With Sterne especially Heine was later to claim kinship—for his portrait of Sterne in *Die romantische Schule* could hardly fail to be recognised as a self-portrait by anyone who had read the *Buch der Lieder*.

And since then Sterne's heart and his lips contradicted each other strangely: sometimes, when his heart is tragically moved and he wants to express its deepest feelings, there flutter from his lips—to his own great astonishment—the most merry and amusing words.[1]

'Pauvre Yorick!' the French version[2] adds, in an access of self-pity.

In his *Reisebilder* Heine found a form that would allow him to express aspects of his personality, and point to features of the life he knew, which had been deliberately suppressed or ignored in his lyric poetry. It is true that even the *Buch der Lieder* had thrown malicious sidelights on German academic life and on the affectations of a society whose real god was the golden calf; but nowhere in his verse had Heine felt free to comment on so many aspects of German social and political life.

Two passages especially in *Die Harzreise* pointed the way Heine's genius was to take. One is the amusing tale of the appearance of Dr Saul Ascher's ghost at Goslar—the spectre of a rationalist, a 'personified straight line', who even beyond the grave is still concerned to demonstrate the impossibility of ghosts. 'Do not be afraid', he reassures the frightened traveller,

'and do not believe I am a ghost. It is a trick of your imagination to think you are seeing me as a ghost. What is a ghost? Give me a definition. Show me the conditions under which a ghost could be possible. What link would such an apparition have with reason? Reason—I say reason....'

And now the ghost proceeded to an analysis of reason, quoted Kant's *Critique of Pure Reason*, part two, first section, second book, third chapter, about the distinction between phenomena and noumena, then construed the problematical belief in ghosts, piled one syllogism on top of the other and ended with the logical conclusion that ghosts had no

[1] *SW*, v, 332. [2] *SW*, v, 550.

existence at all. I, meanwhile, felt the cold sweat running down my back, my teeth rattled like castanets; in fear of my soul I nodded absolute agreement to every sentence with which the spectral doctor reduced my fear of ghosts to absurdity; and he was so absorbed in his demonstration that once, instead of a gold watch, he pulled a handful of worms out of his watch-pocket and, noticing his error, pushed them back again with comically anxious haste. 'Reason is the highest...'—then the clock struck one, and the ghost disappeared.[1]

The strength of this passage lies in the intensity with which even the most fantastic detail is visualised. Where, even in the works of E. T. A. Hoffmann, could one hope to match that sentence about the worms mistaken for a watch? Only *Peter Schlemihl*—that greatest and deepest of all romantic tales—offers similar felicities. But beyond this, the strength of Heine's story of the encounter at Goslar lies in the precision with which it exposes contemporary failures of sensibility, the arid rationalism and materialism of 'enlightened' Berlin. In passages such as this Heine found his truest voice: the voice of a man who cocks a snook at authority; who summons up ghosts to laugh at them; who commands a clear and penetrating reason without blocking up those unconscious springs on which the life of literature depends. Here he found a way of transforming into myths the chance encounters of his life—for Dr Ascher was a real person whose acquaintance he had made in Berlin; and while Dr Ascher and his like have been forgotten, the myths into which Heine transformed them have not lost their meaning even in our own day.

What startled and delighted Heine's contemporaries even more than this ghost-story was the explanation, furnished by the traveller of *Die Harzreise* to an ingenuous young man, of the political significance of the ballet at the Royal Opera House of Berlin. The German passion for theatrical spectacle in the years of the Metternich system had often been ridiculed—Börne's *Henriette Sonntag* [*sic*] *in Frankfurt* is a once celebrated example; and it was generally recognised, among liberal writers, that this

[1] *SW*, III, 41–2.

excessive interest in the theatre and its personalities was a direct consequence of enforced political inactivity. Heine, with superb irony, appears to commend such interests. He pretends to see in the ballet a reflection of German political life, and in contemporary curiosity about the doings of the dancer Hoguet and his ballerinas a potential source of political instruction.

Least of all could the young man grasp the significance of the ballet. With great difficulty I proved to him that there is more policy in Hoguet's feet than in Buchholz's head, that all his figures signified diplomatic negotiations and all his movements had a diplomatic import. When he leans forward, for instance, with a languishing air and outstretched hands, he means our Prussian cabinet; when he pirouettes round and round on one toe without advancing an inch, he means the German Diet; when he trips about as if his legs were tied together, he represents the petty German princes; when he sways backwards and forwards as though he were drunk he means the balance of power; arms crossed and interlaced mean a congress; and lastly, when he gradually stretches to his full height, rests for a moment in this attitude and then indulges in a series of terrifying leaps, he is depicting our all-too-powerful friend in the East. To my young friend all this was a revelation. He saw for the first time why it is that dancers are better paid than great poets, why the ballet is an inexhaustible topic of conversation with the diplomatic corps, and why a minister so often has private interviews with a beautiful ballerina—no doubt he labours night and day to make her receptive to his own little political system. By Apis! how great is the number of exoteric and how small that of esoteric theatre-goers! There they stand and gape, admire capers and turns, study anatomy in the poses of Lemière, applaud the entrechats of Röhnisch and talk of grace, harmony and legs—and no one realises that he has before his eyes, in a danced cypher, the fate of the German fatherland![1]

That is political satire whose lightness, grace and deadly accuracy have no peer in German literature before Heine. Its appearance in the 1820's, a time of oppressive censorship and political apathy, was something of a miracle.

Die Harzreise had a deserved success and encouraged Heine to persevere in the mode he had there inaugurated. Four volumes of

[1] *SW*, III, 60.

Reisebilder appeared between 1826 and 1831, including the overtly autobiographical *Buch LeGrand*, the scandalous *Bäder von Lucca* and the violently prejudiced *Englische Fragmente*—but the interests which informed these prose works were obstinately kept out of Heine's writings in *verse* form.[1] For Heine, as for his contemporaries, lyric poetry was not a medium in which feelings and thoughts about social and political matters could properly be conveyed. Unlike their predecessors of 1813–15, the liberal writers of the 1830's—Börne, Wienbarg, Gutzkow, Laube, Mundt and the rest—wrote pamphlets, novels and dramas but left the lyric to the Swabians they despised. For all these writers of the 'Jung Deutschland' movement, as for Heine, lyric poetry remained what it had been for the Goethe of the Sesenheim period: an expression of individual, personal experience, induced by love or delight in the natural scene, which attained its general validity by inducing something analogous to that experience in suitably attuned readers. True, the experiences Heine had to communicate differed from those of Goethe. His lyrics tended to convey, not the eternal within the moment, but the fleeting moment itself, nuances of feeling whose full significance could be appreciated only in the context of a whole collection of poems in which they could be seen in relation to other moments, other nuances. But in subject-matter Heine remained bound by the great tradition the early Goethe had inaugurated. The proper subjects of lyric poetry were 'Love' and 'Nature'.[2] Political and social questions, however deeply they might concern the poet, had no overt place in it. They might enter into the novel or the drama—but the lyric had better keep free of them.

The result was a division between Heine's writings in verse and

[1] There is an attempt at synthesis in the (now almost unreadable) verse dramas Heine produced in the 1820's: *Almansor* deals obliquely with the position of Jews in a Christian society, and *Ratcliff* skirts what Heine liked to call 'die große Suppenfrage'—the war of the poor against the rich.

[2] This is true of the early Heine, but not altogether true of the 'main line' of German lyric poetry in which he stands; cf. L. W. Forster's Introduction to *The Penguin Book of German Verse* (Harmondsworth, 1957), p. xl: 'The chief themes on which German lyric poetry of high quality has been written are dusk, night, peace of mind, death and God.'

in prose. Heine came to believe that the most important relations of man were political and religious[1]—and these he could define best in prose accounts of journeys, art exhibitions and trends in literature and philosophy. But they concerned him so deeply that to keep them out of his poetry meant keeping out the most important part of himself. The self that wrote the poems of the *Buch der Lieder* had to be reconciled with the self that wrote the political and social satire of the *Reisebilder*.

The story of Heine's 'middle years' is the story of that reconciliation.

[1] '...die zwei wichtigsten Verhältnisse des Menschen, das politische und das religiöse...' (*SW*, v, 284).

I

THE MIDDLE YEARS

Rome's quoting, praising, singing out my verses,
In every hand and pocket there's my book:
A chap there blushes, blenches, coughs and curses—
That's how I want my rhymes to make 'em look!

STUART PIGGOTT (after MARTIAL)

---

1. FALSE SPRING

Mein erbarmte sich noch keiner
Von den Frühlingen der Erde.

BRENTANO

THE year 1827, which saw the publication of the *Buch der Lieder*, was marked for Heine by an event which seemed to confirm that his future lay in political journalism rather than in lyric poetry. In this year the publisher Cotta appointed him editor of a newly founded journal which was to be named *Neue Allgemeine Politische Annalen* and was to have its head-quarters in Munich. It is true that Heine saw in this appointment only a stepping-stone to a professorship of literature at Munich university and that he left most of the work connected with Cotta's journal to his co-editor Lindner; but he became more and more convinced that he had exhausted his *Buch der Lieder* mode and that he ought now to give up writing verse. 'I will always know the proper time to stop writing', he proudly informs his friend Moses Moser on 30 May 1829, 'when in some genre I cannot produce something which will surpass my previous achievements'. Again and again he confesses that his poetic quiver is empty—'I cannot find among my papers any poems that equal in value those of my earlier years', he writes to Heinrich Stieglitz on 20 June 1829; and by 1830 he despairs of ever writing verse again. 'Poetry, it seems, is at an end. Let us hope that for that I will live all the longer in prose!' (to Varnhagen von Ense, 27 February 1830). The characteristic works of his last years in Germany were therefore the later volumes of *Reisebilder*; and when, finding that his hopes of obtaining an appointment in Germany were vain, Heine migrated to Paris in 1831, he continued to write in prose rather than in verse.

> I had long realised that I could no longer get on so well with verse and therefore turned to good prose. But since in prose fine weather, spring sun, the delights of May, violets and plum-trees are not enough, I had to find new subject-matter for my new form.
>
> (*Über den Denunzianten*)[1]

The result is the commentary on social, political and intellectual life embodied in the four volumes of *Der Salon*.

Just before leaving Germany Heine did, however, feel tempted to return once more to his well-known and much imitated lyric mode. A composer he had once met and liked in Hamburg, one Albert Methfessel, asked him for a cycle of unpublished poems that might be set to music; and Heine, contrary to his usual practice in face of such requests, complied by supplying, in a very short time, thirty-six new poems. Twenty-four of these were then published, in 1831, in Cotta's *Morgenblatt für gebildete Stände*; the whole cycle, augmented by some earlier poems, made its bow before the public in the second edition of *Reisebilder II*; and part of the cycle was reprinted yet again in the second volume of *Der Salon*, where its main function was to swell the book to a size which would obviate submission to a German censor. (Only short books were subject to censorship before publication!) It then made its positively last appearance at the opening of *Neue Gedichte*—a volume which sought to present the poems written between 1830 and 1844 in the same biographically meaningful sequence in which the *Buch der Lieder* had presented those of an earlier period.

The title—*Neuer Frühling*—is at once hopeful and ironic. Written for the most part in winter and at a time of disappointed

[1] *SW*, IV, 305.

expectations and gloomy prospects, these poems are to recall a happier past and look forward to a better future.

A new spring will come, and to enable me to savour it fully I am now writing the poems that go with it. I have written three dozen of them in these bitter times.

(Letter to Varnhagen von Ense, 30 November 1830)

'The nature of spring', Heine was later to write in his introduction to the first volume of *Der Salon*, 'can best be recognised in winter, and the best songs of May are written behind the stove'.[1] But the letters written at the time of the inception of *Neuer Frühling* amply demonstrate that Heine was unable, in those years, to use the very word 'Spring' without a tinge of irony and bitterness. Either it brought to mind youthful hopes doomed to disappointment:

The spring-flowers would be glad to blossom in comfort, but from above a cold wind of reason blows into their cups, so that they anxiously close again; (Letter to Friederike Robert, May 1829)

or else it conjured up images of Philistine complacency and recalled the poet painfully to his own wintry prospects:

Never do I feel the need for solitude more than in the early springtime, when the awakening of nature is reflected in the faces of urban Philistines and produces there intolerably complacent expressions. How much more dignified and simple is the behaviour of the trees, who quietly clothe themselves with verdure and know exactly what they want!—I also know what I want, but not much seems to come of it.... (To Varnhagen von Ense, 5 April 1830)

There could be no question, then, in this *Neuer Frühling* of 1830, of simple, unequivocal songs of the joys of spring.

In its original form the cycle begins with an account of a miracle. 'Unterm weißen Baume sitzend' presents a dejected man sitting under a snow-covered tree in a cheerless winter landscape; he sees white flakes fall upon him and finds, as he looks up, that the landscape has changed; the tree is now bedecked with spring-blossoms instead of snow.

[1] *SW*, IV, 19.

Welch ein schauersüßer Zauber!
Winter wandelt sich in Maie,
Schnee verwandelt sich in Blüten,
Und dein Herz es liebt aufs neue.

It is not hard to see the connection between 'Unterm weißen Baume sitzend' and the situation described in Heine's letter to Varnhagen von Ense—quoted above—of 30 November 1830. The poem is proleptic, it embodies, in a myth of the seasons, an obvious wish-dream. Yet all too soon, in the midst of all this imagined love and warmth, a strange longing for winter once more supervenes:

'Doch du lächelst, wie verloren
In entfernten Sehnsuchtträumen—
Sprich, Geliebter, welche Wünsche
Dir im lieben Herzen keimen?'

Ach, ich will es dir, Geliebte,
Gern bekennen, ach, ich möchte,
Daß ein kalter Nordwind plötzlich
Weißes Schneegestöber brächte....

(*Neuer Frühling* 31)

No permanent satisfaction is to be found in this imagined vernal world of love—a world whose insufficiency had already been explored in the *Buch der Lieder*. A longing for winter represents a longing for truth. It is almost a relief, like that of stepping out of a hothouse into the cool air outside, when the final poem of the cycle reverses the opening miracle, and spring and summer fade into the greyest, most cheerless, most un-Keatsian of autumns.

The sense of relief experienced at the end of *Neuer Frühling* is due in part to the undoubted fact that this cycle contains some of the weakest and falsest poems Heine was ever to write. He seems to be forcing himself into a mode that had grown alien to him; he repeats himself, and debases in the process his own best coinage. To see the difference between his earlier true coin and his later Wood's ha'pence one need only compare the verbose and sentimental *Neuer Frühling* 36 with the concise and mysterious treatment of a similar theme in 'Der Tod das ist die kühle Nacht' (*Die Heimkehr* 87). All Heine's faults appear in *Neuer Frühling* in exaggerated profusion. The cycle exhibits everywhere his coquettish enjoyment of real or imagined sufferings, coupled with vulgar insistence on his nobility of soul:

> Ich such ein Herz so schön wie das meine,
> So schön bewegt.... (*Neuer Frühling* 4)

> Mein Herz ist so klug und witzig,
> Und verblutet in meiner Brust.
> (*Neuer Frühling* 40)

Nobility of soul is apt to disappear when it is talked about. Disturbing, too, is the liking Heine shows for what in the England of his day would have been called 'cockney metaphors'—a sure sign that inspiration is being forced.

> Wie ein Greisenantlitz droben
> Ist der Himmel anzuschauen,
> Roteinäugig und umwoben
> Von dem Wolkenhaar, dem grauen....
> (*Neuer Frühling* 41)

The human feelings expressed in many of these lyrics appear as false as the natural scenes within which the poet choses to exhibit them; scenes which include, in *Neuer Frühling* 8, a German forest inhabited by—storks and lapwings!

Even here, of course, there are some fine things. The patient reader finds himself rewarded by poems like *Neuer Frühling* 6 ('Leise zieht durch mein Gemüt...'), with its delicate effect of 'song within song' and its subtle use of deliberately 'impure' rhymes; or *Neuer Frühling* 29 ('Es war ein alter König...'), rhythmically one of the most striking things Heine was ever to write, a poem of love and death in high places that almost gives the lie to the poet's own apologetic statement about works of this kind:

> It is...impossible to produce in this genre anything better than has already been provided by the older masters, notably Ludwig Uhland.
> (Preface to the second edition of *Reisebilder II*)[1]

and finally *Neuer Frühling* 32 ('Durch den Wald im Mondenscheine...'), that delicate poem about the elf-queen and her train

[1] *SW*, III, 521.

which Heine was to use again in *Elementargeister* and which was soon to find so congenial an interpreter in Felix Mendelssohn. After the appearance of the full cycle, Mendelssohn wrote to Karl Immermann:

(Heine) has recently published 60 songs of spring; only a few of these seem to be alive and truly felt, but these few are splendid.

(Letter dated 11 January 1832)

These few 'splendid' lyrics cannot, however, conceal a certain hollowness at the centre of the whole cycle of which Mendelssohn shows himself well aware—a deliberate untruthfulness, a deliberate forcing of the imagination, which points the irony of the title *Neuer Frühling*.

How much Heine was forcing his imagination becomes immediately apparent if one looks at the manuscript of a poem like *Neuer Frühling* 5 ('Gekommen ist der Maie...'). The poem as we now have it is weak, mawkish and empty, a cento of folk-song reminiscences and reminiscences of images, words and phrases from the *Buch der Lieder*—yet the manuscript shows that Heine took infinite trouble over its composition, rewriting every line—every word almost—over and over again. This was of course his usual practice; but never has the final effect been as incommensurate with the effort to achieve it as it is in the weaker poems of *Neuer Frühling*.

There is, indeed, one poem in this cycle in which Heine unmistakably lifts the veil; in which he questions the pathetic fallacy that links nature to the human heart and comes down at the end—long before Ibsen!—on the side of the life-lie.

Die Rose duftet — doch ob sie empfindet
Das was sie duftet, ob die Nachtigall
Selbst fühlt, was sich durch unsre Seele windet
Bei ihres Liedes süßem Widerhall; —

Ich weiß es nicht. Doch macht uns gar verdrießlich
Die Wahrheit oft! Und Ros und Nachtigall,
Erlögen sie auch das Gefühl, ersprießlich
Ist solche Lüge, wie in manchem Fall —

(*Neuer Frühling* 20)

Here the poem breaks off, leaving the voice in mid-air, as though afraid to speak all its thought or even think out its implications to the end; and the cycle continues in the bitter-sweet manner familiar from the *Buch der Lieder*.

The problem raised by this poem is ultimately that of Heine's whole life as a poet in those years—the problem of the relation of beauty to truth, art to reality. Is the poetry of *Neuer Frühling* a salutary lie? Or perhaps a lie that is not salutary at all? When Heine writes lines like

> Ein Meer von blauen Gedanken
> Ergießt sich über mein Herz (*Neuer Frühling* 18)

or

> Horchend stehn die stummen Wälder,
> Jedes Blatt ein grünes Ohr (*Neuer Frühling* 37)

—is he not deliberately and cynically writing what he knows to be nonsense but what he also knows his public will eagerly accept?

When Heine came to reprint *Neuer Frühling* in the second edition of *Reisebilder II*, he felt impelled to broach this question of their truth to experience. He now felt his creations wanting because they were too much under the sway of late romantic poets like Ludwig Uhland; poets whose songs had—so Heine now felt—no living relation to the real problems of the time, whose medievalising lyrics

> are now lost in the noise of the latest battles for liberty, in the hubbub of a common European brotherhood of peoples, and in the sharply mingled pain and jubilation of those modern songs that refuse to pretend to a Catholic harmony of feeling but rather dissect all feelings in the cause of truth.[1]

The 'modern' songs of which Heine here speaks are of course his own less harmonious productions—poems like *Seegespenst* (in the first *Nordsee* cycle) spring at once to mind; and with a glance at *Neuer Frühling* he adds:

> It is interesting to observe how one of these lyric modes sometimes borrows its outward form from the other. It is even more interesting when the two kinds mingle in one poet's heart.[1]

[1] *SW*, III, 521.

That tells us how Heine wished his cycle to be read. We are to see in it, on the one hand, a deliberate attempt to write in a mode recognised as out-of-date and inapplicable to the poet's actual situation—and in that sense at least fundamentally untruthful. Yet paradoxically the poet of *Neuer Frühling* can pretend to a truthfulness greater than that of more simple-minded imitators of Uhland: for he is aware of his own artificiality, plays with it, parodies it even, in lyrics like *Neuer Frühling* 17 ('Was treibt dich umher in der Frühlingsnacht?...'), which are so *outré* that they compel laughter rather than sympathy.

It would be wrong to think that Heine chose to write in the Uhland manner only because he wished to parody it. On the contrary: he felt strongly drawn to a kind of poetry which presents, in a style adapted from that of folk-song, an image of medieval Germany that owes more to the ideals of the liberal *Bürgertum* of 1814 than to historical reality. If only he too could so identify himself with a group, a class, a political ideal! He succumbed also to the attraction of poems that were born out of an unequivocal delight in nature—a world of forests and hills that did not bore the singer as it so often bored Heine; and to the attraction of poems, like Uhland's justly famous *Frühlingsglaube*, that expressed a genuine confidence and hope beyond the reach of the author of *Neuer Frühling*. Above all, Heine never ceased to feel—despite some wry comments in *Die romantische Schule*—the spell of lyrics like Uhland's *Der Schäfer*, whose luxuriously melancholy refrain haunted him even in his dreams.[1] *Neuer Frühling* 29 represents a genuine homage to Uhland and contains no hint of parody.

At the same time, however, Heine felt drawn in a different direction. The oppressiveness of governments and the consequent stagnation of German political and social life made the medieval world of Uhland seem remote and irrelevant and escape to it positively harmful. The time for such poetry appeared to have passed—it was incumbent on all Germans, as G. G. Gervinus proclaimed at the end of his *Geschichte der deutschen National-*

[1] *SW*, v, 344ff.

literatur, to turn from literature to politics. Heine too, as the *Reisebilder* serves to show, had thought it worth while to serve the immediate political needs of the time. Yet he continued to feel out of place in the political sphere. In *Ludwig Börne* he was to look back on this dilemma and to sum up what he felt in 1830:

What irony of fate that I, who am so fond of bedding down on the quiet and contemplative pillow of ease, should have been marked out to scourge my poor fellow-Germans from their complacency and stir them into activity! I who love nothing better than to occupy myself with watching trailing clouds, with contriving metrical magic, with overhearing the secrets of elemental spirits, with losing myself in the wonderland of old tales—I have to edit political annals, further the interests of the time, excite revolutionary desires, stir up passions, always tweak the poor honest German by the nose and rouse him from his giant sleep....[1]

In *Die romantische Schule* Heine then seeks to show that Uhland himself felt this same dilemma and that he took the obvious and dignified course: he ceased to publish poetry which had become incompatible with his political ideals.

Just because he wanted to do so well by the new era he could no longer continue singing the old song of times past with his pristine enthusiasm; and since his Pegasus was a knightly steed that trotted gaily enough back to the past, but became obdurate when urged forward into modern life, the gallant Uhland dismounted with a smile and had the obstinate horse unsaddled and put into the stable. There it stands to the present day, and like its colleague Bayard it has every virtue under the sun and only one defect—it is dead.[2]

This simple course did not, however, commend itself to Heine. Editing the *Politische Annalen* for Cotta he looked back longingly to the wish-dream world of romantic poetry; but when he came to re-enter it, in *Neuer Frühling*, he found that here too only a part of himself—and not even, perhaps, the most important part—was engaged.

This conflict is well depicted in a poem which held at first only a subordinate place in *Neuer Frühling* but which Heine soon

[1] *SW*, VII, 42. [2] *SW*, V, 347.

recognised to be of such programmatic importance that it deserved to be prefixed, as prologue and motto, to the whole cycle.

In Gemälde-Galerieen
Siehst du oft das Bild des Manns,
Der zum Kampfe wollte ziehen,
Wohlbewehrt mit Schild und Lanz.

Doch ihn necken Amoretten,
Rauben Lanze ihm und Schwert,
Binden ihn mit Blumenketten,
Wie er auch sich mürrisch wehrt.

So, in holden Hindernissen,
Wind ich mich in Lust und Leid,
Während andre kämpfen müssen
In dem großen Kampf der Zeit.

'Während andre kämpfen *müssen*...'—the element of vile compulsion, stressed in the passage from *Ludwig Börne*, is still there; the lover still feels reluctant to allow himself to be drawn into the 'great battle' in which others are engaged. But the other world too, the world of love and the poetry associated with it, is now seen as coercive, though its chains are made of flowers. It is entered unwillingly by one whose loyalties lie—and should lie—elsewhere.

There are no overtly political poems in *Neuer Frühling*. The *amoretti*, it would seem, have here been successful in restraining their prisoner. Yet more than once the reader will feel him struggling in his chain of flowers—more than once he will feel that while speaking of love and of nature, while endeavouring (vainly!) to create his wish-dream world, the poet is straining away to other fields of thought, interest and activity. Why else should a simple love-poem like *Neuer Frühling* 11 ('Es drängt die Not, es läuten die Glocken...') begin and end with images of conspiracy and revolution; or why should *Neuer Frühling* 24 open with the startling lines:

Es haben unsre Herzen
Geschlossen *die heilge Allianz*?

This last poem tells, ostensibly, of the embrace of two lovers—but it speaks no less, for those who have ears to hear, of the fate of the smaller nations of Europe when their interests conflicted with those of the giants of the Holy Alliance:

Ach, nur die junge Rose,
Die deine Brust geschmückt,
Die arme *Bundesgenossin*
Sie wurde fast zerdrückt.

Neuer Frühling, absurd and often infuriating as it is, looks not only backwards to the *Buch der Lieder* but forwards too, to the real 'new spring-time' of Heine's poetry: to the period when private passion and public affairs were to blend in satiric poetry.

2. EXALTATION OF THE SENSES

Parcourir à loisir ses magnifiques formes;
Romper sur le versant de ses genoux énormes,
* * *
Dormir nonchalamment à l'ombre de ses seins,
Comme un hameau paisible au pied d'une montagne.

BAUDELAIRE

If *Neuer Frühling* occasionally reminded its readers of Uhland or even—as at the opening of the thirty-first poem—of Tieck, there was no mistaking the distinctive Heine atmosphere of it all. This atmosphere is created by a peculiar air of *knowingness* reminiscent of *Die Heimkehr*:

Ach! ich weiß wie sich verändern
Diese allzuholden Träume...;

(*Neuer Frühling* 27)

and by a pervasive sensuality that is Heine's own.

Wie die Nelken duftig atmen!
Wie die Sterne, ein Gewimmel
Goldner Bienen, ängstlich schimmern
An dem veilchenblauen Himmel!

Aus dem Dunkel der Kastanien
Glänzt das Landhaus, weiß und lüstern,
Und ich hör die Glastür klirren
Und die liebe Stimme flüstern.

Holdes Zittern, süßes Beben,
Furchtsam zärtliches Umschlingen —
Und die jungen Rosen lauschen,
Und die Nachtigallen singen. (*Neuer Frühling* 26)

All nature is transformed into sensually exciting images: the 'fragrantly breathing' pinks no less than the stars that 'timidly' shine in the sky. Their timidity is a virgin timidity linked with the 'trembling' of the last stanza; the timidity of a bride, suggested again by the adjective 'veilchenblau', which for Heine's contemporaries was inextricably linked with the bridal chorus from Weber's *Freischütz*.[1] And who but Heine would have so transformed a white country house half seen in the darkness into a titillating image ('lüstern' is the key-word here), reminiscent of those bathing nymphs that peep voluptuously out of the forest darkness in other poems?

Dorten an dem Bach alleine,
Badet sich die schöne Elfe;
Arm und Nacken, weiß und lieblich,
Schimmern in dem Mondenscheine.
(*Die Heimkehr* 85)

The non-human world is now more than ever reduced to a convenient medium for the expression of human—all too human—desires.

Weißt du was die hübschen Blumen
Dir Verblümtes sagen möchten?
Treu sein sollst du mir am Tage
Und mich lieben in den Nächten.
(*Neuer Frühling* 33)

The poems of *Neuer Frühling* were the last that Heine wrote in Germany. In May 1831 he arrived in Paris, which was from now on to be his home. His heart was heavy at first, full of longing for the Germany in which he had been unable to make a career for

[1] *SW*, VII, 176–7.

himself and which he yet considered his fatherland. Sorrowfully he parodied Danton in a letter to Varnhagen von Ense:

It would be easy to escape if one did *not* carry one's fatherland with one on the soles of one's shoes....It is painful to walk in the Jardin de Luxembourg and drag along everywhere a piece of Hamburg or Prussia or Bavaria....I am oppressed by dismal forebodings.

(27 June 1831)

But very soon this home-sickness grew less, until we find Heine writing to Ferdinand Hiller on 24 October 1832:

If anyone asks you how I feel here, tell him: like a fish in the sea. Or rather, tell people that if one fish asks the other how he feels in the sea, he answers: I feel like Heine in Paris.

Paris offered Heine a political, intellectual and cultural life more invigorating than anything he had known in Hamburg or Munich or Berlin. It offered him a society that welcomed him as a 'spirituel allemand' and did not despise him as a Jew and a pauper or fear him as an unwelcome critic and potential revolutionary. It offered him, as he was often to stress in later years, a new mission: the mission of informing Germany about the cultural life of contemporary France and interpreting German philosophy and literature to the French. It offered him, above all, Saint-Simonism, a new creed which seemed, for a few years, to answer his need for a community of shared belief. What attracted him to the creed of Saint-Simon and Prosper Enfantin was its stress on equality of opportunity and its opposition to hereditary privilege; but these social ideals, which merged the ideas of the eighteenth-century enlightenment (Saint-Simon was a pupil of d'Alembert) with the *laisser faire* doctrines of nineteenth-century liberalism, attracted him less powerfully than its pantheistic insistence on the divinity of man. In his account of the Paris *salon* of 1831 Heine described a painting by Leopold Robert in terms that clearly derive from Saint-Simonism:

'The earth is heaven and mankind is sacred, filled with divine spirit'—that is the great revelation which shines out of this picture with its beatific colours.'[1]

[1] *SW*, IV, 52.

The painting which seemed to reflect that dignity of the human body and of human industry proclaimed by Saint-Simon in *Le Nouveau Christianisme* was Robert's *The Reapers*; and twenty-four years later, when Heine had long been disillusioned with Saint-Simonism and all it stood for, Elise Krinitz saw a reproduction of it hanging on the wall of Heine's sick-room in the Avenue Matignon.[1]

It was some time before Heine returned to lyric poetry. The interpreter of French and German cultural life found himself more at ease in prose. In January 1833, however, the readers of *Der Freimütige*, a *Conversationsblatt* edited in Berlin by Willibald Alexis, were confronted with a new cycle of poems which seemed to most of them more 'shocking' than anything in the *Buch der Lieder* or in *Neuer Frühling*. These poems—the first Heine had written on French soil—were reprinted in the first volume of *Der Salon* (1834) and formed at last, with further revisions and augmentations, the section of *Neue Gedichte* which the poet entitled *Verschiedene*.

However much these poems differ from those of *Neuer Frühling*, there is one thing they all have in common: they are love-poems. Lyric poetry remains for Heine, even in his Saint-Simonist period, distinctly non-social; its proper subject is the love of a man for a woman; it sings, to use the image with which the *Buch der Lieder* had ended, the flowers of the cornfield rather than the sheaves.[2] Yet these new love-poems differ significantly from the old. They presuppose readers who have had some experience of the ways of a great city, and they are more frankly sensual than anything Heine had written so far. Many Germans were profoundly shocked, and Karl Gutzkow, the frosty sexuality of whose novel *Wally die Zweiflerin* had earned its author a prison-sentence some years before, wrote to Heine as late as 1838 advising against a republication of these poems because of their 'gross immorality'.[3]

[1] H. H. Houben (ed.), *Gespräche mit Heine* (Frankfurt, 1926), p. 915. This work is henceforth cited as *Gespräche*.

[2] *SW*, I, 193–4.

[3] *Heinrich Heines Briefwechsel*, ed. F. Hirth (München and Berlin, 1914–20), II, 237–41.

Heine thanked Gutzkow for pointing out the mote in his eye and went on:

> Few Germans can pronounce judgment on these poems, for they know nothing of their subject, the abnormal *amours* of a world-madhouse like Paris. (Letter to Gutzkow, 23 August 1838)

Verschiedene is Heine's attempt to break with his *Buch der Lieder* mode without abandoning his *Buch der Lieder* themes. It is an attempt to deal frankly with love of a kind that had hitherto escaped German poets: the kind of casual affair which dwellers in large cities know and which foreigners associate in particular with Paris.

When these poems first appeared in *Der Freimütige*,[1] they were preceded by a prologue which stated what was then their main theme and intention.

Nun der Gott mir günstig nicket,
Soll ich schweigen wie ein Stummer,
Ich, der, als ich unbeglücket,
So viel sang von meinem Kummer.

Ich dem tausend arme Jungen
So verzweifelt nachgedichtet,
Daß das Leid, das ich besungen,
Noch viel Schlimmres angerichtet!

O, ihr Nachtigallen-Chöre,
Die ich trage in der Seele,
Daß man eure Wonne höre,
Jubelt auf mit voller Kehle!

The new poetry is to be an expression of happy and unfettered love; it is to contrast sharply with the woes of the *Buch der Lieder* whose baleful influence on German literature the second stanza caricatures. The opening lines anticipate the objections that will inevitably be made to this new poetry of sexual fulfilment—but it insists on utterance as imperiously as the pangs of despised love had done in *Lyrisches Intermezzo*. The choirs of nightingales which had made such sweet moan in the *Buch der Lieder* and again

[1] The textual history of *Verschiedene* is well set out in *SW*, I, 533–4. Earlier readings are quoted *SW*, I, 539–42.

in *Neuer Frühling* are now to be impressed into a different kind of service. 'Daß man eure *Wonne* höre / Jubelt auf mit voller Kehle!'

The short cycles that followed this prologue in successive issues of *Der Freimütige* attempted to implement its promise by leading the reader lower and lower down the social scale into an enjoyment more and more purely of the senses. First came *Seraphine*, consisting in 1833 of the second, fourth, sixth and twelfth poems of the cycle which now bears this name in *Neue Gedichte*. *Seraphine* forms a bridge between the old poetry and the new. It opens with lyrics that would not seem out of place in *Neuer Frühling* or even *Die Heimkehr*—tearful raptures in a forest landscape, melancholy joy by a moon-lit sea. From these it moves to suggestions of physical fulfilment:

> Ich und die Sonne liegen dir
> Glückselig in den Armen;

and it ends with accusations of faithlessness.

Seraphine was followed, in 1833, by *Clarisse*, a cycle about a luscious goose with whom any serious emotional entanglement is quite unthinkable:

> Willst du meiner sicher los sein,
> Mußt du dich in mich verlieben.

The problem here is merely how to outwit Clarisse's grossly bourgeois parents:

> Hol der Kuckuck deine Mutter,
> Hol der Kuckuck deinen Vater,
> Die so grausam mich verhindert,
> Dich zu sehen im Theater.
>
> Denn sie saßen vorn und gaben,
> Breitgeputzt, nur seltne Lücken,
> Dich im Hintergrund der Loge,
> Süßes Liebchen, zu erblicken....

These stanzas show the vigour of this new poetry and its power of caricature—the adjective 'breitgeputzt', for instance, through its position in the verse as well as through its bold combination of disparate words, suggests in masterly fashion both bulk and ostentation.

From *Clarisse* the readers of *Der Freimütige* passed to *Hortense*. That cycle too was shorter in 1833 than it is now, and it contained several poems which later found their way into other sections. The *Hortense* affair begins at a street-corner under the aegis of the goddess of opportunity; it stales rapidly—the middle poems (now *Seraphine* 10 and 13) show how it turns into a parody of earlier entanglements as the vulgar light o' love becomes sentimental—and it is ended quickly and without regrets.

> Der Morgen kam, die Sonne schien,
> Der Nebel ist zerronnen;
> Geendigt hatten wir schon längst,
> Eh wir noch kaum begonnen.

Next came the ironically named *Angelique*, which contained, in *Der Freimütige*, several poems later deleted from the cycle. This openly proclaims the superiority of its heroine's body over her soul and shows how a love-relationship can be entered, conducted and concluded on a purely physical basis. Only one poem remains common to all versions of this section—but this with its revealing food-metaphor, deliberately dissonant rhyme and jaunty ending, is characteristic of its spirit and tone.

> Schaff mich nicht ab, wenn auch den Durst
> Gelöscht der holde Trunk;
> Behalt mich noch ein Vierteljahr,
> Dann hab auch ich genung.
>
> Kannst du nicht mehr Geliebte sein,
> Sei Freundin mir sodann;
> Hat man die Liebe durchgeliebt,
> Fängt man die Freundschaft an.

The 'friendship' that may be at least ironically offered to Angelique is inconceivable with the heroine of the section which concluded the cycle in 1833. *Diana* (the name is as deliberately incongruous as that of her predecessor) is nothing more than a mercenary mountain of flesh and offers enjoyment in its crudest form. With her, we reach the bottom of the scale and are ready for the 'epilogue' which points what must be reluctantly called the 'moral' of it all:

> Ehmals glaubt ich, alle Küsse,
> Die ein Weib uns gibt und nimmt,
> Seien uns, durch Schicksalsschlüsse,
> Schon urzeitlich vorbestimmt.
>
> Küsse nahm ich und ich küßte
> Also ernst in jener Zeit,
> Als ob ich erfüllen müßte
> Taten der Notwendigkeit.
>
> Jetzo weiß ich, überflüssig
> Wie so manches, ist der Kuß
> Und mit leichtern Sinnen küß ich,
> Glaubenlos im Überfluß.

That is the natural complement of the original prologue quoted on page 26; it is another farewell to the *Buch der Lieder* mode that had treated love as so awesome and serious; it is a proclamation of a new order in which love can be taken lightly, gaily and without pangs of conscience. The old faith in the solemnity of love has gone, and with it have gone the old, torturing scruples.

So, at least, we are to believe. Heine's constant parody of faith, however, and his voluble insistence on a new and happier period free from the ancient fears and allegiances, cannot fail to arouse suspicion. He is clearly protesting too much. It was not, after all, quite so easy to cast the German slough and turn into what foreigners at that time—and all too often even today—thought a Parisian was like; and while it was all very well to say that Germans could not judge such poems because they had had no experience of Parisian life, it was less easy to explain away the dislike educated and sympathetic Parisians felt for them. Saint-René Taillandier, for instance, one of Heine's sincerest admirers and translator of his poetry, contrasted the 'coarseness' of this group of poems with the finesse of Alfred de Musset's occasional exercises in the same genre.[1] The subsequent history of these

[1] *Revue des Deux Mondes*, Nouvelle Série (1845), IX, 306.

poems was to show Heine's own growing awareness of the hollowness of the professions he had made in his original prologue and epilogue.

When the poems were republished in the first volume of *Der Salon* (1834) Heine relegated this prologue and epilogue to less conspicuous positions within the cycle and added, to several of the sections, new poems that radically changed their character. The most telling of these additions were those made to *Seraphine*, which was given in 1834 the form it has retained in all subsequent editions of Heine's works.

From 1834 onwards *Seraphine* contained a poem which was to become one of Heine's most celebrated and most frequently quoted—quoted by the poet himself no less than his admirers and detractors.

> Auf diesem Felsen bauen wir
> Die Kirche von dem dritten,
> Dem dritten neuen Testament;
> Das Leid ist ausgelitten.... (*Seraphine* 7)

For the happy unbelief proclaimed in the original epilogue Heine here substitutes a new faith. The parody of the New Testament with which the poem begins warns us that this is to be a faith whose tenets stand in opposition to those of Christianity—and it is not hard to see that Heine is in fact proclaiming the *Nouveau Christianisme* of Saint-Simon. In 'Auf diesem Felsen bauen wir' he takes up the Saint-Simonist call for the 'emancipation of the flesh', which he continued to echo long after the social and political ideals of Enfantin and his followers had become unacceptable to him. God is immanent, the poem proclaims, and Paradise, if anywhere, is here on earth.

> L'humanité entière n'est-elle pas le peuple de Dieu, et le globe n'est-ce pas la terre promise?
>
> (E. Rodrigues, *Lettres sur la réligion et la politique*, Paris, 1831, p. 132).[1]

[1] Cf. M. Clarke, *Heine et la Monarchie de Juillet* (Paris, 1927), pp. 251–6, where interesting parallels are drawn between Heine's journalistic reports and Saint-Simonist writings.

There has been no Fall, matter has never been corrupted and the senses are our best guide:

Tant que les hommes crurent au principe du mal, à qui Dieu avait abandonné la matière, ils durent se représenter leur vie comme...un combat de la *chair* contre *l'esprit*...mais aujourd'hui la vie est une œuvre joyeuse. (*Ibid.* p. 131)

The Saint-Simonists therefore mocked the old poetry of renunciation:

Se séparer du monde par des pleurs, des regrets et de monotones soupirs, s'envelopper dans un individualisme souffrant, et puis s'endormir du dernier sommeil en disant: Mon Dieu! j'ai beaucoup souffert! ...ces poètes sans croyance, sans foi, sans espérance...ces bardes gémissants...ces chanteurs malades...;

(*Le Globe*, 3 September 1831)

and they claimed for the poet a new mission:

Venez faire retentir dans une société désolée une parole de foi, d'amour et d'espérance! (*Ibid.* 30 August 1831)

With *Seraphine* 7, Heine proclaims himself a Saint-Simonist poet. He weds Lessing's old dream of a Third Testament to the gospel of Enfantin and sees himself, as he takes his pleasure with the grisettes and street-walkers of Paris, as the prophet of a new order, proclaiming faith, love and hope for modern man:

Vernichtet ist das Zweierlei,
Das uns so lang betöret;
Die dumme Leiberquälerei
Hat endlich aufgehöret.

* * *

Der heilge Gott der ist im Licht
Wie in den Finsternissen;
Und Gott ist alles was da ist;
Er ist in unsern Küssen.

'Auf diesem Felsen bauen wir' is the most complete expression of the confident new *persona* Heine wished to present to his public. There are, however, certain other additions to *Seraphine* which do not go so well with this new mission and this new faith.

What is the reader to make, for instance, of *Seraphine* 11, with its haunting refrain:

Mit schwarzen Segeln segelt mein Schiff
Wohl über das wilde Meer...;

or of *Seraphine* 14, with its dreamy longings and regrets:

Es ragt ins Meer der Runenstein,
Da sitz ich mit meinen Träumen.
Es pfeift der Wind, die Möwen schrein,
Die Wellen, die wandern und schäumen...;

or, last but by no means least, of the deceptively simple *Seraphine* 3, which tells of a 'restless, wind-driven being' (the sea-gull, one of Heine's favourite symbols) between two worlds, the menacing waters below and the alluring but inaccessible moon above?

Das ist eine weiße Möwe,
Die ich dort flattern seh
Wohl über die dunklen Fluten;
Der Mond steht hoch in der Höh.

Der Haifisch und der Roche,
Die schnappen hervor aus der See,
Es hebt sich, es senkt sich die Möwe;
Der Mond steht hoch in der Höh.

O, liebe flüchtige Seele,
Dir ist so bang und weh!
Zu nah ist dir das Wasser,
Der Mond steht hoch in der Höh.

What strikes us first about such a poem is its musicality; an interplay of vowels and consonants that seems so effortless and is yet seen to be (when one comes to examine and analyse it) the result of continual filing and careful calculation. At every point, the poem reminds the reader of the artlessness of folk-song; but there are few folk-songs that build up to their climax with such economy of means, or change the import of their refrain so subtly from stanza to stanza, or shift their emphasis so inevitably from an intense visual image at the beginning (the sea-gull as a patch of white in the darkness, with the circle or crescent of the moon above) to the personal and general application of the final stanza. There is genuine feeling here, and a genuine recurrent experience; but it is all watched by an alert and rational mind that betrays itself in the very form of the poem. An appearance of simplicity and improvisation is produced by meticulous art; folk-song directness is blended with the tortuousness of a self-divided modern. The perils of such a combination are clear, and Heine did not always escape the dangerous slopes of sentimentality on the one side and cynicism on the other—but the success of his great things is enhanced by the very precariousness of their balance.

Poems like *Seraphine* 3 belie the conscious intentions of the Saint-Simonist Heine. They speak unmistakably of his sense of exile and isolation and his equally strong sense that what did attract him was likely to be dangerous and destructive. The poet of the *Buch der Lieder* was not, after all, to be so easily transmogrified into a Saint-Simonist emancipator of the flesh.

What is happening to Heine's new optimistic *persona* may best be gauged by a comparison of the end of the whole cycle in its successive versions. In 1833, as has been seen, it ended with the proclamation of gay unbelief and happy gratification of the senses. In 1834, the ending is different:

Jugend, die mir täglich schwindet,
Wird durch raschen Mut ersetzt,
Und mein kühnrer Arm umwindet
Noch viel schlankre Hüften jetzt.

Tat auch manche sehr erschrocken,
Hat sie doch sich bald gefügt;
Holder Zorn, verschämtes Stocken
Wird von Schmeichelei besiegt.

Doch, wenn ich den Sieg genieße,
Fehlt das Beste mir dabei.
Ist es die verschwundne, süße,
Blöde Jugendeselei?

The enjoyment is still there; but it is now overshadowed by regrets for lost youth and—what is more important—for those very illusions of young men to which earlier poems had said a relieved farewell. By 1844, when this group of poems reappeared, with fresh additions and in a new arrangement, in the *Verschiedene* section of *Neue Gedichte*, the disillusion is complete. *Verschiedene* ends with a drying up of the senses and a prospect of emptiness and death:

Du wirst alt und ich noch älter,
Unser Frühling ist verblüht.
Du wirst kalt und ich noch kälter,
Wie der Winter näher zieht.

Ach, das Ende ist so trübe!
Nach der holden Liebesnot
Kommen Nöte ohne Liebe,
Nach dem Leben kommt der Tod.

'Nöte ohne Liebe', pangs without love—that is the inevitable outcome of a life devoted to sensual enjoyment. The new Saint-Simonist poetry ends with the same bleak hopelessness as the abortive attempt to revive older modes in *Neuer Frühling*.

In the light of this failure to sustain the Saint-Simonist *persona*, the fourth and fifth poems of *Hortense*, added to the cycle in 1844, assume a peculiar significance. These poems treat—lightly at first, but with growing undertones of seriousness—that greatest and truest of myths whose relevance to the human situation the Saint-Simonists had strenuously sought to deny: the myth of the Fall, which indicates the corruption of pristine innocence and hence the corruption of the material world and the fallibility of the senses. In *Hortense* 5 the reader shares a lover's dawning realisation of truths he had frivolously rejected and tastes something of the despair which comes, in the end, to every libertine.

Also wahr ist jene Sage
Von dem dunklen Sündenfluche,
Den die Schlange dir bereitet,
Wie es steht im alten Buche?

Kriechend auf dem Bauch, die Schlange,
Lauscht sie noch in allen Büschen,
Kost mit dir noch jetzt wie weiland,
Und du hörst sie gerne zischen.

Ach, es wird so kalt und dunkel!
Um die Sonne flattern Raben,
Und sie krächzen. Lust und Liebe
Ist auf lange jetzt begraben.

'Auf lange' might suggest an ultimate resurrection: but the prospect on which the poem ends—like that which ends *Verschiedene* as a whole—is now undeniably one of desolation and of death.

The 'Church of the Third Testament' proclaimed in *Seraphine* 7 had been built not on rock but on shifting sands.

3. VENUSBERG

Worse than adversity the Childe befell;
He felt the fulness of satiety. BYRON

HYPOCRITES of every persuasion will once again find cause to groan at many poems in this book—but this cannot help them any more. A new generation now growing up has realised that all that I have said and sung has sprung from one great God-intoxicated vernal idea which is at least as respectable as (and probably more respectable than) the dismal, mouldy Ash-Wednesday idea that has robbed our Europe of its flowers and has peopled it with ghosts and Tartuffes.[1]

With these words Heine sought to justify, in the preface of the first volume of *Der Salon*, his new Saint-Simonist poems. From now on he liked to divide all mankind into two opposed parties of *hommes gras* and *hommes maigres*: parties he named at various times 'sensualists' and 'spiritualists', or 'Hellenes' and 'Nazarenes', or 'Greeks' and 'Jews'. The *hommes gras* take delight in the material world because they see in it the noblest manifestation of the divine; the *hommes maigres* seek to deny and mortify the senses for the sake of the spirit. In his prose works of the 1830's and in the poems already discussed Heine sought to present himself as a champion of the Hellenic spirit against the Nazarene, just

[1] *SW*, IV, 13–14.

as he tends in his letters to exaggerate his physical *embonpoint* in order to leave his correspondents in no doubt about the party to which he belonged. But as we have seen, and as sensitive readers can hardly have missed in Heine's own day, the direction in which his poems ultimately pointed was hardly that of the 'große, gottselige Frühlingsidee' to which their author consciously subscribed. For all their swagger they were no more the work of a sensualist with a good conscience than *Aus den Memoiren des Herren von Schnabelewopski*, the story which followed them in the first volume of *Der Salon*—a work in which sexual matters are treated with a frivolity that recalls a sniggering schoolboy rather than the Goethe of *Römische Elegien* or the Byron of *Don Juan*. The poems do not, on the whole, snigger in this way; but their 'boldness' is self-conscious and never approaches the classical dignity of Goethe or Byron's matter-of-fact worldliness. Heine seems happiest, in fact, when he can return—as in *Seraphine* 3—to his *Buch der Lieder* themes.

> Neue Melodien spiel ich
> Auf der neugestimmten Zither.
> Alt ist der Text!

These lines, from *Hortense* 5, offer one statement of Heine's dilemma; another, even clearer than this, will be found in a projected preface to a new edition of *Reisebilder* which was written in 1833, the very year that saw the first appearance of the poems of *Verschiedene*:

> I wanted to write in quite a different tone. But whether it was because I felt my old manner to be still appropriate or because I could not find a new one—the fact is that the old melody and the old text continue to pervade my later works.[1]

Heine never published this preface—he may well have felt that it revealed too much.

After the poems of *Verschiedene* Heine came to rely more and more on prose rather than verse for the communication of what he thought and felt. He was now eager to win the approbation of

[1] Quoted in *Heinrich Heine: Briefe*, ed. F. Hirth (Mainz, 1950–56), v, 83. This work is henceforth cited as *Briefe*.

a French as well as a German audience; and to translate German lyric poetry into French was like attempting—to use Heine's own striking phrase—to bottle moonlight. The first three volumes of *Der Salon* are therefore given over, for the most part, to prose accounts of French and German life, thought, literature and art. The first volume, it is true, still contained a considerable section of verse. It contained most of the poems of *Verschiedene*; *Tragödie*, which framed a poem Heine believed to be a genuine folk-song between two lyrics of his own; and the three poems later called *In der Fremde*, which speak of the genuine nostalgia the poet still felt—and was increasingly to feel—for his homeland. *In der Fremde*, alas, is not free from posing and exaggeration:

> Denkst du der Freunde, die da sanken
> An deine Brust, in großer Stund?
> Im Herzen stürmten die Gedanken,
> Jedoch verschwiegen blieb der Mund....

(*In der Fremde* 2—entitled *Träumereien* 2 in *Der Salon* of 1834)

The third poem of this group—'Ich hatte einst ein schönes Vaterland'—has become the darling of Heine's German apologists; but when held against Heine's later treatments of the same theme, it will be found excessively tearful and sentimental.

The first volume of *Der Salon*, in fact, contains the poet's own characteristically veiled confession of the inferiority of his new poetry to the old. This is a cycle entitled *Der Schöpfer*, which corresponds to the first four *Schöpfungslieder* of *Neue Gedichte*. Here, in the voice of God speaking to the devil, we can hear the poet rounding on those of his critics who had charged him with repeating and caricaturing himself:

> Und der Gott sprach zu dem Teufel:
> Ich der Herr kopier mich selber,
> Nach der Sonne mach ich Sterne,
> Nach den Ochsen mach ich Kälber,
> Nach den Löwen mit den Tatzen
> Mach ich kleine liebe Katzen,
> Nach den Menschen mach ich Affen;
> Aber du kannst gar nichts schaffen.

This *argumentum ad diabolum* clearly represents the poet's own *argumentum ad hominem*, and its aggressively confident tone will deceive no one. It certainly could not silence the critic within the poet himself, the uncomfortable *alter ego* which from the first had troubled him more than all the reviewers in the world. The devil of *Schöpfungslieder* is the spokesman of that other self: and it whispers that if a poet begins to imitate himself, it is time he stopped writing poetry altogether.

The second volume of *Der Salon* was originally intended to contain no lyrics at all and only a single prose work: *Zur Geschichte der Religion und Philosophie in Deutschland.* It was found, however, that the volume would not be long enough to avoid submission to the censor, and Heine therefore decided, with some misgivings, to add a truncated version of *Neuer Frühling*. No new poems at all were included in this volume, which was published in 1835. It caused a furore and encouraged the German authorities to tighten up censorship regulations. In December 1835 the Bundestag issued its famous decree against the 'Jung Deutschland' movement:

> The penal and police regulations of their country and the existing statutes against misuse of the press will be applied with full severity against authors, publishers, printers and distributors of writings of the literary school known under the designation of 'Young Germany' or 'Young Literature', to which, specifically, Heinrich Heine, Carl Gutzkow, Heinrich Laube, Ludolf Wienbarg and Theodor Mundt belong.[1]

Had this decree been rigorously enforced, it would have deprived Heine of his German public altogether. He rightly guessed that it would not be enforced—but he decided to avoid publishing anything, for the moment, which would be in the least controversial, and determined, therefore, to keep the third volume of *Der Salon* free of social and political polemic. Heine thought of entitling it 'Das stille Buch';[2] and one might have expected that

[1] Quoted in: Hugo Bieber and Moses Hadas, *Heinrich Heine. A Biographical Anthology* (Philadelphia, 1956), p. 356.

[2] *Briefe*, II, 119 (8 March 1836).

now, if ever, he would have returned to lyric poetry. Yet when *Der Salon III* finally appeared in 1837, it was found to contain only two prose works: a 'Novelle' entitled *Florentinische Nächte*, and *Elementargeister*, a charming account of folk-beliefs. For the first time there was no section of lyric poetry at all.

At the end of *Elementargeister*, however, Heine comes to speak of the legend of Tannhäuser and the Venusberg which had exerted so powerful a spell on the imagination of German poets of the Romantic period. Arnim and Brentano had included a version of the folk-song on this subject in *Des Knaben Wunderhorn*; Tieck had written a powerful modern version of it in *Der getreue Eckart und der Tannenhäuser*; Brentano had planned an opera-libretto on the subject; Eichendorff had modified the legend in *Das Marmorbild*; and before long Richard Wagner—partly at least inspired by Heine—was to give it the form in which it reached its widest if not always its most discriminating audience. Heine reprinted the *Wunderhorn* version of the folk-song in *Elementargeister*, and confessed himself particularly impressed by two features of it: by its burning sensuality—

> Next to the Song of Songs of the great king (I mean King Solomon) I do not know any more ardent lay of tenderness than the dialogue between Dame Venus and Tannhäuser. This song is like a battle of love...—[1]

and by the nostalgia and regret with which Tannhäuser yearns away from the very delights he cherishes:

> Man is not always in a mood for laughter, sometimes he becomes very still and serious and thinks of the past; for the past is the true home of his soul, and he is seized by a yearning for feelings he has once had, even if they were feelings of sorrow.[2]

The autobiographical note can hardly be missed; and it is not therefore surprising to find Heine appending to the folk-song version of *Der Tannhäuser* a version of his own which turns out to be one of the most interesting documents of his art and sensibility.

Partly at least the key to this modern restatement of the

[1] *SW*, IV, 432. [2] *SW*, IV, 429.

Tannhäuser legend must be sought in Heine's domestic circumstances. In October 1834 the impermanent unions of which he had spoken in the poems of *Verschiedene* had been succeeded by what seemed at first another union of the same kind: by a Parisian *ménage* with a plump young shop-girl who had taken his fancy and whom he seems to have literally bought from her aunt. The year 1835 found the lovers still together and Heine in transports of sensual delight that break out in a letter to August Lewald (11 April). But even then he thought that the affair would be only a brief one—'Only wait a while', he assures Lewald, 'a change is bound to come soon'; and by June he had reached that state of cloyed satiety which had always signalled the end of these fleeting relationships. To Princess Belgiojoso, who might be expected to relish his parody of Saint-Simonist terminology, Heine wrote on 4 June 1835:

> J'ai oublié ma qualité de Dieu, j'ai compromis ma divinité, je suis descendu dans la fange des passions humaines, et j'ai de la peine à me relever.

The countess offered him a place of refuge and recuperation at her country house near Saint Germain, where Heine soon came to think that the whole disreputable affair now lay behind him.

> I believe my spirit is purified at last from all dross; my verses will become more beautiful, my books more harmonious.
>
> (Letter to Campe, 2 July 1835)

Yet Heine was not to free himself so easily from the woman who had enslaved his senses. By the end of the year he had gone back to her: and from now on 'Mathilde'—Crescence Eugénie Mirat, who spoke no German and never realised that her lover was a great poet—was to become an inseparable part of Heine's life. It was partly of this new and disturbing relationship that Heine thought when he rewrote the Tannhäuser legend in 1836.

In a note to the French edition of *Der Salon* the poet himself suggests that it would be profitable to compare in detail the folk-poem he took as his model with his own more modern version. This, he suggests, would prove an interesting exercise in the 'comparative anatomy of literature'; and he goes on to give his own opinion of what such a comparison would be likely to reveal.

En lisant en même temps ces deux versions, on voit combien chez l'ancien poète prédomine la foi antique, tandis que chez le poète moderne, né au commencement du XIXe siècle, se révèle le scepticisme de son époque; l'on voit combien ce dernier, qui n'est dompté par aucune autorité, donne un libre essor à sa fantaisie, et n'a en chantant aucun autre but que de bien exprimer dans ses vers des sentiments purement humains.[1]

Heine's note to his French readers is calculated to point the irony of his opening. The folk-poet had begun with lines intended to hush the conversation of his audience and to introduce his hero:

Nun will ich aber heben an,
Vom Tannhäuser wollen wir singen,
Und was er wunders hat getan,
Mit Frau Venussinnen.

Heine begins with an appeal to 'all good Christians':

Ihr guten Christen, laßt euch nicht
Von Satans List umgarnen!
Ich sing euch das Tannhäuserlied
Um eure Seelen zu warnen.

But the irony, as so often in Heine, is double-edged. It is true that the poem will not particularly appeal to 'good Christians'; but it is no less true that there is a warning concealed beneath its lightly rippling surface, that it speaks of dangers which are not unlike the dangers of which the Church Fathers had warned the faithful and of which Heine himself had become, of late, all too painfully aware. His Tannhäuser is not the curious enquirer of the old poem, who went to the mountain of Venus out of curiosity to see its wonders:

Der Tannhäuser war ein Ritter gut,
Er *wollt groß Wunder schauen*;
Da zog er in Frau Venus Berg....

[1] *SW*, IV, 621.

Heine's Tannhäuser knows exactly what he wants: he is a voluptuary in search of love and pleasure.

> Der edle Tannhäuser, ein Ritter gut,
> *Wollt Lieb und Lust gewinnen*,
> Da zog er in den Venusberg,
> Blieb sieben Jahre drinnen.

And where the hero of the old poem tears himself from Venus against his will because he has recognised her as a devil who has ensnared his soul even as she intoxicated his senses, the hero of the new suffers the lot of all voluptuaries: he is sated, and physical delights begin to cloy. It is not anxiety for his soul which drives Heine's Tannhäuser out of the Venusberg, but a perverse and very modern longing for bitterness after so much sweetness; the typical longing of the aesthete, analysed with so much subtlety and truth by Hugo von Hofmannsthal in his essay on Oscar Wilde.[1] There is nothing in Hofmannsthal's analysis of a *fin-de-siècle* situation which is not already implied in the words with which Heine's knight induces Venus to let him go:

> Frau Venus, meine schöne Frau,
> Von süßem Wein und Küssen
> Ist meine Seele geworden krank;
> Ich schmachte nach Bitternissen.
>
> Wir haben zu viel gescherzt und gelacht,
> Ich sehne mich nach Tränen,
> Und statt mit Rosen möcht ich mein Haupt
> Mit spitzigen Dornen krönen.

Nor is Heine's Venus the remote and mysterious devil-goddess, the Frau Holle or guardian of the realm of death, she had been in the old poem: she is clearly a *femme entretenue*, who shouts at her lover, makes soup for him and occasionally even submits to a drubbing.

These domestic details do not, however, serve in any way to make the new poem a *gemütlich* parody of the old. On the con-

[1] Hugo von Hofmannsthal, *Gesammelte Werke in Einzelausgaben*, ed. H. Steiner (Frankfurt, 1951): *Prosa*, II, pp. 133–8.

trary: they lend a special piquancy and truth to the central section of Heine's ballad, in which Tannhäuser unburdens himself to the Pope and appeals for salvation from a present rather than a future hell. This, the reader is made to feel, is indeed *Höllenqual*—this clear knowledge of what the object of love really is, this satiety after over-indulgence of the senses, and this inability to renounce delights that have become a torment. Absent in body from his Venus, Tannhäuser feels his spirit all the more enchained:

Ein armes Gespenst bin ich am Tag,
Des Nachts mein Leben erwachet,
Dann träum ich von meiner schönen Frau,
Sie sitzt bei mir und lachet....

His speech to the Pope is an uncontrolled torrent of longing and praise which has no counterpart, of course, in the old poem and only a feeble counterpart in Tieck's story, but which was to have a very powerful echo in the second act of Wagner's opera.

Ich liebe sie mit Allgewalt,
Mit Flammen, die mich verzehren, —
Ist das der Hölle Feuer schon,
Die Gluten, die ewig währen?

'I am doomed', Heine had written in a letter to Laube of September 1835 which is still the best commentary on his *Tannhäuser* poem, 'to love only the lowest and the most foolish....Can you understand how this must torture a man of pride and intellect?' His Tannhäuser cannot be saved from hell: he is in hell already. There is no need, therefore, of the flowering staff which had represented, in the old poem, the possibility of salvation; and Heine's Pope—who evidently, as Heine maliciously insinuates, had some personal experience in these matters—merely states directly what Tannhäuser's outburst had already obliquely conveyed.

Der Teufel, den man Venus nennt,
Er ist der Schlimmste von allen;
Erretten kann ich dich nimmermehr
Aus seinen schönen Krallen.

Mit deiner Seele mußt du jetzt
Des Fleisches Lust bezahlen,
Du bist verworfen, du bist verdammt
Zu ewigen Höllenqualen.

That, as we know, was in fact Heine's own recurrent experience; and the valuation of this experience conveyed by this poem is not as far from that of 'good Christians' as its ironical opening would seem to suggest. It is certainly far removed from Hellenic self-sufficiency, from the 'god-intoxicated vernal idea' of uncorrupted human goodness, which poems like 'Auf diesem Felsen bauen wir' had sought to propagate.

For alas! I myself belong to this sick old world, and the poet is right when he says: mocking at one's crutches does not make walking any easier. I am the sickest of you all, and I am the more to be pitied because I know what health is.

(*Zur Geschichte der Religion und Philosophie in Deutschland*)[1]

Heine, like Nietzsche who admired him greatly and rightly saw in him a kindred spirit, knew well how to diagnose his own sickness and that of his age; but like Nietzsche he deceived himself if he thought he knew what health was. His self-sufficient and 'emancipated' man is as inadequate an answer to the aspirations of mankind as the blonde beast or the Borgian superman. The central section of *Der Tannhäuser* is proof that deep in his soul Heine was aware of this inadequacy of his conscious ideals.

For the final section of Heine's *Der Tannhäuser* there is no equivalent either in the old poem or in any subsequent retelling of the legend. The mood suddenly changes—though one feels that this new playfulness no more detracts from the seriousness of what went before than a Greek satyr-play detracted from the preceding tragedy. What, then, is the purpose of Tannhäuser's narration to Venus, which ridicules German political apathy, petty tyranny and 'Kleinstaaterei', literary and academic figures and arid commercialism?

Its first and most obvious purpose is to 'place' Tannhäuser's private hell: the Parisian Venusberg might well seem to be

[1] *SW*, IV, 249.

preferable to a Germany so described. Another is to indicate Heine's settled conviction that no predicament is without its comic as well as its tragic side—a conviction which helped him to avoid many an all-too-solemn self-dramatisation. But above all, this final section of *Der Tannhäuser*, which treats of the knight's return to the Venusberg, paradoxically shows a way of escape. The Tannhäuser that returns is no longer the self-absorbed aesthete of the first or the hag-ridden sensualist of the second section. He has acquired a new freedom, a superiority of mind that enables him to look outwards as well as inwards, to survey the world and then to *choose* the Venusberg. He becomes akin, for a moment, to the traveller of *Die Harzreise*, who may be occupied with thoughts of love, but who remains nevertheless a keen observer of the world around him. In the version of *Der Tannhäuser* that appeared in 1837 the knight says farewell to the German scene for ever:

> Zu Hamburg in der guten Stadt,
> Soll keiner mich wiederschauen!
> Ich bleibe jetzt im Venusberg,
> Bei meiner schönen Frauen.[1]

But by 1844, when the poem was reprinted in *Neue Gedichte*, Heine had come to realise that his Parisian Venusberg was not self-enclosed and that it offered as good a vantage-point as any from which to comment on German foibles and corruptions. *Der Tannhäuser* now ends less conclusively, with a promise of further tales of further adventures; it remains 'open' at the end; it suggests that the Venusberg might serve yet again as a look-out from which to observe, or at least a sheltered spot in which to remember, the social and political scene.

No one would say, however, that *Der Tannhäuser* is a wholly successful poem. It conveys forcibly a sense of enslavement to an object all too clearly seen and a resultant longing for bitterness as a relief from cloying sweetness. It combines the image of beloved and mother with a confessional truthfulness that has few counterparts in nineteenth-century literature. It adapts theological

[1] *SW*, VI, 109.

imagery to secular purposes in a superficially jocular but fundamentally serious way; and it blends skilfully, with consistent ironic effect, folk-song formulae, consciously 'poetic' phrases and a domestic, conversational tone. The overtly satirical section at the end of the poem, however, fails to satisfy. Somehow the transition has not been managed—the section appears tacked on as an afterthought, and its jokes are, on the whole, rather feeble. Heine himself, as his preface to *Der Salon III* serves to show, felt this defect in his poem:

> I am myself the author of the poem at the conclusion of this book, and I think it will give great pleasure to my enemies; I have not been able to write a better one.[1]

Der Tannhäuser is important as a way rather than as an end. It helped Heine to strike out on new paths; to break down the inhibiting distinction he had hitherto tended to make between subjects fit for prose and subjects fit for verse; to fuse the interests of the author of *Buch der Lieder* with those of the author of *Reisebilder*. It was the first step on the road to *Atta Troll*.

4. NIXIES IN PARIS

> *Facile credo, plures esse Naturas invisibiles quam visibiles in rerum universitate. Sed horum omnium familiam quis nobis enarrabit?... Quid agunt? quae loca habitant? Harum rerum notitiam semper ambivit ingenium humanum, nunquam attigit. Juvat, interea, non diffiteor, quandoque in animo, tanquam in tabula, maioris et melioris mundi imaginem contemplari: ne mens assuefacta hodiernae vitae minutiis se contrahat nimis, et tota subsidat in pusillas cogitationes.*
>
> THOMAS BURNET

WITH *Der Tannhäuser* Heine returned to a poetic form in which he had shown himself a potential master from the first—that of the ballad. In ballads he was able to objectify his own conflicts without feeling constantly tempted to

[1] *SW*, IV, 305.

exaggeration, posturing and sentimentality; here he could occasionally merge—as *Die Grenadiere* demonstrates—private passions with public concerns. Now, in his later life, Heine felt increasingly drawn to the ballad form. It was to dominate his *Romanzero*; and it plays an important part also in the sparse record of Heine's verse writings between the time of *Tannhäuser* and that of *Atta Troll*. In *Neue Gedichte*, the ballads written between 1836 and 1841 are collected in a section headed *Romanzen*.

The first of these *Romanzen*, *Ein Weib*, was written in the same year as *Der Tannhäuser* and has an obvious connection with it. In the course of his confession to the Pope, Heine's Tannhäuser had recalled with torturing vividness the hearty laughter to which his Venus was prone:

> Sie lacht so gesund, so glücklich, so toll,
> Und mit so weißen Zähnen!
> Wenn ich an dieses Lachen denk,
> So weine ich plötzliche Tränen.

This image of the 'laughing woman' which is henceforward to recur again and again in Heine's poetry, dominates *Ein Weib*.

> Um Sechse des Morgens ward er gehenkt,
> Um Sieben ward er ins Grab gesenkt;
> Sie aber schon um Achte
> Trank roten Wein und lachte.

The 'laughing woman' of *Ein Weib* is yet another of Heine's many images of destructive heartlessness and unthinking cruelty; she stands at the head of *Romanzen* as the Lorelei had stood at the head of *Die Heimkehr*. But now, in 1836, the romantic trappings of golden hair, enticing song, sunset, mountain and river have disappeared, to be replaced by suggestions of metropolitan corruption. The archetypal Lorelei story has been transferred from the banks of the Romantic Rhine to Eugène Sue country, to those lower depths of urban society with which *Les Mystères de Paris* were soon to acquaint an eagerly listening world.[1] Nor does the

[1] *Les Mystères de Paris* first appeared 1842–3. That Heine knew Eugène Sue personally is attested by A. Weill, *Gespräche*, p. 514.

heartless woman now sit in remote and inaccessible majesty. She can be enjoyed, her favours are to be had as easily as the favours of the lights o' love celebrated in *Verschiedene*—but only by those in the full flush of fortune and of health. When these fail, the woman too will desert you. She will respond to impudent vigour, but will pay no heed—like Mr Betjeman's sports-girls—to yearning appeals.

> Er ließ ihr sagen: O komm zu mir,
> Ich sehne mich so sehr nach dir,
> Ich rufe nach dir, ich schmachte —
> Sie schüttelt' das Haupt und lachte.

But just as the heartlessness of the Lorelei detracted not a jot from her desirability but, on the contrary, made it the more piquant, so the woman whose laughter dominates the very sound of *Ein Weib* is no less alluring for her fickleness and cruelty. Her mystery is that of the Sphinx who appears in another poem written about this time: the poem 'Das ist der alte Märchenwald' which Heine prefixed to the 1839 edition of the *Buch der Lieder*.

> Die Nachtigall sang: 'O schöne Sphinx!
> O Liebe! was soll es bedeuten,
> Daß du vermischest mit Todesqual
> All deine Seligkeiten?
>
> O schöne Sphinx! O löse mir
> Das Rätsel, das wunderbare!
> Ich hab darüber nachgedacht
> Schon manche tausend Jahre.'

The question 'Was soll es bedeuten?' had been asked before, and left unanswered, in Heine's most famous poem. For all his protestations in *Französische Maler*, *Zur Geschichte der Religion und Philosophie* and in the poems of *Verschiedene* Heine could never rid himself of a curiously puritanical streak which made him distrust sexual relations and which made women at once attractive and horrifying to him. 'Woman', he once said, with another of his many oblique references to that great myth which his imagination recognised as true while his reason sought to deny it, 'is at once apple and serpent.'[1]

The dreamer of 'Das ist der alte Märchenwald' kisses the stone sphinx (a sphinx in a moonlit landscape under blossoming linden trees!) and thereby awakens her to life and to love—but he cannot control what he has himself called into life or satisfy an ardour he has himself aroused. That is Heine's characteristic variation on the theme of Goethe's *Zauberlehrling*.

> Herr, die Not ist groß:
> Die ich rief, die Geister
> Werd ich nun nicht los.

The anguished cry of the sorcerer's apprentice might stand as the motto of Heine's haunting ballad *Die Beschwörung*. In this poem, in which a monk calls up beauty from the dead and then confronts it in silence and inactivity suggests feelings which were to find their fullest expression in the poems of Heine's very last years: feelings of insufficiency before the demands of beauty, before the fulness of those sensual delights which the Saint-Simonists were raucously promising all mankind. How deep an insight this poem affords into the poet's secretly 'Nazarene' soul may be gauged by his life-long obsession with classical statues—'I have loved only the dead and statues' he once confessed[2]—and by his terrifying later restatement of the 'conjuration' theme in the motto of *Der Doktor Faust*. A monk might seem an incongruous *persona* for Heine to assume—yet it is impossible to miss the urgent personal note in the confrontation that ends *Die Beschwörung*:

> Ihr Blick ist traurig. Aus kalter Brust
> Die schmerzlichen Seufzer steigen.
> Die Tote setzt sich zu dem Mönch,
> Sie schauen sich an und schweigen.

The end of *Die Beschwörung* suggests deep-rooted human fears which the optimistic positivism of the nineteenth century was disposed to overlook. It also brushes once again the theme that

[1] *SW*, VI, 394–5.
[2] Cf. Maximilian in *Florentinische Nächte*, *SW*, IV, 337.

had attracted Heine to the Venusberg legend: the obsessiveness of love, its tendency to engross all energies and obscure all other tasks. At the back of many of the works of this great love-poet we can hear such fear of love; such fear of any vital and complete human relationship. Is it not better to love the dead, or to love statues, or to love Mathilde who could offer human warmth without soul-companionship?

The sphinx, half woman and half beast, is only one of many symbols Heine found in these years to describe the mingled attraction and repulsion he found in the love-relationship. Another is the mermaid or nixie:

> Woe to the inexperienced man who drifts into their net! But woe also to the experienced who knows perfectly well that the charming monster ends in an ugly fish-tail, but who yet cannot hold out against her enchantment, or who is perhaps overcome all the more surely by a voluptuous inner terror, by the fatal attraction of a gentle destructiveness, of a sweet abyss! (*Lutetia*, 30 April 1840)[1]

In the poem *Die Nixen*, these water-sprites perform the function which *amoretti* had performed in the prologue of *Neuer Frühling*: they restrain a knight from going out to battle by keeping him in their toils of love. The knight of *Die Nixen* is in fact content to let the nixies kiss him and play with his armour: but his complement in *König Harald Harfagar* chafes in the arms of his 'Wasserfee' and longs for the world of action he has left behind. This poem ends, significantly, with the now familiar image of the 'laughing woman':

> Der König stöhnt und schluchzt und weint
> Alsdann aus Herzensgrunde.
> Schnell beugt sich hinab die Wasserfee
> Und küßt ihn mit lachendem Munde.

Heine is restating once again the dilemma of a love-poet who feels irresistibly drawn to other fields of action.

A counter-image to these helpless and inactive prisoners of love is presented in *Ali Bey*, a ballad which seems to me to express Heine's deepest aspirations at this period of his creative life. The

[1] *SW*, VI, 158.

hero of *Ali Bey* hears the call of action in the arms of his beloved, tears himself away to lead his men into battle, but dreams of love even while he annihilates his enemies.

> Und der Held besteigt sein Schlachtroß,
> Fliegt zum Kampf, doch wie im Traume; —
> Denn ihm ist zu Sinn, als läg er
> Immer noch in Mädchenarmen.
>
> Während er die Frankenköpfe
> Dutzendweis heruntersäbelt,
> Lächelt er wie ein Verliebter,
> Ja, er lächelt sanft und zärtlich.

That combination of love and politics might have seemed an impossible wish-dream in 1839, when *Ali Bey* was first published; it might have seemed then, as Heine put it in his preface to the 1839 edition of the *Buch der Lieder*, that Apollo had to lay aside his golden lyre before he could effectively flay Marsyas.[1] Yet the dream of *Ali Bey* was to be fulfilled in the very near future by the enchanting music and deadly satire of *Atta Troll*; and it is surely no accident that *Ali Bey*, almost alone among Heine's poems of these years,[2] is written in those unrhymed trochaic stanzas whose characteristic melody we associate with *Atta Troll* and the *Romanzero*.

The dream of *Ali Bey* was to become, in some measure at least, reality: that of *Bertrand de Born* never. Bertrand de Born achieves what Heine himself had always failed to achieve: by the sweetness of his song—a sweetness made actual in superbly melodious verses—he wins over the proud and mighty as well as the fair. If only every poet could live like Bertrand de Born and die like the Byron celebrated in the ballad *Childe Harold*! Reality, alas, is otherwise, and more than one poem in the *Romanzen* section of *Neue Gedichte* presents uncompromising images of reality that help to 'place' the wish-fulfilment of *Ali Bey*, *Bertrand de Born* and *Childe Harold*. Chief among these is *Unstern*, a poem written in 1840 which uncannily anticipates the

[1] *SW*, I, 10.

[2] The only other instance is the first section of *Ritter Olaf*.

Romanzero—it ends with a stanza that takes on a terrible irony for readers who know Heine's later fate:

> O fiel ich doch in den Garten,
> Wo die Blumen meiner harrten,
> Wo ich mir oft gewünschet hab
> Ein reinliches Sterben, ein duftiges Grab!

When this vain prayer was written, Heine had already had a taste of the family squabbles that embittered his last years. He had been given more than a taste, too, of the vengefulness of the Prussian and Austrian authorities who had tried to prevent his ever publishing anything in Germany again. He had come to feel the meanness, vindictiveness and low cunning of his fellow-exiles in Paris. He had been disillusioned with the Paris of the *juste milieu* in which the tone was increasingly set by an *aristocratie bourgeoise* whom he hated more even than the old aristocracy of birth; disillusioned too with Saint-Simonism, whose 'religious' ideas had led to ridiculous excesses and whose social ideas had led to unrestrained money-making and a scramble for railway shares. Above all, however, he had had unmistakable signs of the frailty of his own body, which now gave warning of a disease that was soon to paralyse and torture him for the rest of his life. The pressure of all this is behind *Unstern*, the most terrifying statement in any of Heine's poems of a disgust with the world which becomes—as in *King Lear* and *Timon of Athens*!—a disgust with sex.

> Du fragst mich, Kind, was Liebe ist?
> Ein Stern in einem Haufen Mist.
>
> Wie'n räudiger Hund, der verrecket,
> So liegt er mit Unrat bedecket.
> Es kräht der Hahn, die Sau sie grunzt,
> Im Kote wälzt sich ihre Brunst.

The image is once again of a Fall: of something naturally pure and beautiful which has fallen from on high and become corrupted. Yet against this expression of disgust must be held the end of *Ritter Olaf*: a most eloquent affirmation of life and love even at its most tragic, even in the face of death.

Ich segne das Meer, ich segne das Land,
Und die Blumen auf der Aue.
Ich segne die Veilchen, sie sind so sanft
Wie die Augen meiner Fraue.

Ihr Veilchenaugen meiner Frau,
Durch euch verlier ich mein Leben!
Ich segne auch den Holunderbaum,
Wo du dich mir ergeben.

The puzzle of Heine was that he could be so convinced of the truth of both attitudes at the same time; that he could be at once amazed at the purity and disgusted at the prurience of life and love, and that he could feel so strongly attracted where he felt equally strongly repelled.

The poems of the late 1830's bear witness to the fact that Heine was now a Parisian. *Ein Weib* takes us into regions explored by Balzac no less than Eugène Sue; *In der Frühe* begins with an unforgettably exact evocation of early morning in the city:

Auf dem Faubourg Saint-Marceau
Lag der Nebel heute morgen,
Spätherbstnebel, dicht und schwer,
Einer weißen Nacht vergleichbar;

and the vocabulary as well as the content of two stanzas added to *Angelique* 7 belong unmistakably to Paris:

Wenn ich Billette bekommen kann
Bin ich sogar kapabel
Dich in die Oper zu führen alsdann:
Man gibt Robert le Diable.

Es ist ein großes Zauberstück
Voll Teufelslust und Liebe;
Von Meyerbeer ist die Musik,
Der schlechte Text von Scribe.

The delicate parody of mythological themes at the end of *In der Frühe* has also something Parisian about it—it faintly recalls Daumier's caricatures of the gods and heroes of Greece, Clairville's revues and, above all, Offenbach's *Orphée aux Enfers* and *La Belle Hélène*. These are more strongly recalled by the cycle

Unterwelt, with which the *Romanzen* section of *Neue Gedichte* concludes; a pure Offenbachiade that mythologises, in Pluto's laments, one aspect of Heine's domestic life with Mathilde.

> Jetzt in meiner Ehstandsqual,
> Merk ich, früher ohne Weib
> War die Hölle keine Hölle;

or again:

> Wenn sie keift, so hör ich kaum
> Meines Cerberus Gebelle;

or yet again:

> Punsch mit Lethe will ich saufen,
> Um die Gattin zu vergessen.

The fifth section of the *Unterwelt* cycle, which introduces a deeper note of regret and loss inappropriate to an Offenbachiade, did not originally belong to it. It was published separately in May 1842 under the title *Zuweilen*—to suggest that this was only a passing mood which at times assailed the exiled poet. Yet by 1844 this mood had become settled enough to warrant the appearance of this despondent poem at the end of the otherwise so high-spirited cycle:

> Du nickst so traurig! Wiedergeben
> Kann ich dir nicht die Jugendzeit —
> Unheilbar ist dein Herzeleid:
> Verfehlte Liebe, verfehltes Leben!

With these subdued and disheartened lines *Unterwelt*, and the *Romanzen* section of *Neue Gedichte*, comes to an end.

Heine was not, it would seem, ever to become a Parisian through and through. He had refused tempting offers to adopt French nationality because he felt himself first and foremost a German poet:

> With regard to what we usually call 'patriotism' I was always a free-thinker, but I could never free myself from a certain dread when I was called upon to do something which might seem even remotely like breaking loose from my native land....I would find it a horrible, a mad thought to have to say to myself that I am a German poet and at

the same time a naturalised Frenchman. I would then see myself as one of those monstrosities with two heads that are exhibited at fairs.

(*Retrospektive Aufklärung*, *Lutetia*, August 1854)[1]

His ballads of the late 1830's and early 1840's show how right he had been. His imagination continued to be haunted by the formulae of German folk-song, by old German tales and legends, by the remembered German landscape, by the poetic images of Goethe and the German Romantics. *Die Beschwörung*, *Ritter Olaf*, *Die Nixen*, *Frühling*, *Lass ab*, *Begegnung* and even the irreverent *Frau Mette* all bear witness to this same fact. Above all, Heine was haunted by the rhythms and metres of that popular German poetry under whose spell he had fallen as a young man; by a four-line stanza with three (or four) main stresses and a variable number of unstressed syllables which he had made so much his own that it is now often called 'Heinestrophe'. The passage from *Lutetia* quoted above continues with an attack on French poetry which shows how deeply Heine felt himself to belong to a German tradition.

It would disturb me dreadfully in writing poetry if I thought that one of my heads would suddenly begin to scan in French turkey-cock pathos the most unnatural alexandrines, while the other poured forth its feelings in the true, inborn natural metres of the German language. And oh! as intolerable as French metres do I find the verses of the French—that perfumed rubbish—I can hardly bear even their better poets who have no scent at all. When I regard the so-called *poésie lyrique* of the French, then only I recognise the grandeur and glory of German poetry, and then I might even pride myself that this is the field in which I have earned my laurels. We will not yield a single leaf of that laurel, and the mason who is called on to decorate our last resting-place with an inscription shall fear no protest when he there engraves the words: 'Here lies a German poet.'[2]

There have been protests enough, and Heine still has no monument in Germany: but there can be no doubt of the sincerity of this passage or of the powerful and unbreakable spell the German language and literary tradition had cast on him.

[1] *SW*, VI, 390–1.
[2] *SW*, VI, 391.

Among the *Romanzen* there are two poems which speak directly of the poet's relation to his native and his adopted country. The first of these is *Anno 1829*, which was first published in the *Zeitung für die elegante Welt* under the title: '*Sehnsucht nach der Fremde* (*Bremen 1831*).' This does not mean, of course, that it was actually written in 1831; there is no record of it before 1839, and stylistically it belongs clearly to Heine's first Paris period. It means rather that the poet here seeks to recover the mood of his last year in Germany—'Bremen' being a transparent disguise for Hamburg. The poem conveys, with startling directness, a feeling of being stifled; a feeling of constriction, of fat men jostling one another, of a stench that is at once physical and moral:

Sie handeln mit den Spezerein
Der ganzen Welt, doch in der Luft,
Trotz allen Würzen, riecht man nur
Den faulen Schellfischseelenduft.

The inimitable expressiveness of that last compound is matched by lines in which Heine uses his talent—noticed by the earliest reviewers of his poetry—for depicting the corruption of the time by using its own favourite expressions. But the expressions he uses here are not those of a pretentious society ridiculed in the *Buch der Lieder*—'aimabel', 'kapabel', 'Ma Foi!' and so on; they are rather those of the counting-house:

Nur diese satte Tugend nicht,
Und *zahlungsfähige* Moral!

The all-too-concrete adjectives invalidate the abstractions of the nouns. To use such a word as 'zahlungsfähig' in this context is to conjure up a picture of the kind of society in which it is habitually used and indict its values. A society is best characterised—Heine knew this as well as Karl Kraus!—by the language it speaks.

From this narrow huckster's world any escape is welcome; any death is preferable to that of being stifled or pressed to death.

Ihr Wolken droben, nehmt mich mit,
Gleichviel nach welchem fernen Ort!
Nach Lappland oder Afrika,
Und sei's nach Pommern — fort! nur fort!

Yet when, in the next poem, the vain appeal of *Anno 1829* is answered—when the escape that seemed so impossible is shown as accomplished—the yearning for flight at once changes direction.

> O Deutschland, meine ferne Liebe,
> Gedenk ich deiner, wein ich fast!
> Das muntre Frankreich scheint mir trübe,
> Das leichte Volk wird mir zur Last. (*Anno 1839*)

The word 'fast' in the second line assures us against the kind of sentimentality that had marred poems like *In der Fremde*. There is to be no exaggeration: the communication of feelings is to be honest and exact.

Anno 1839 presents a tourist's or visitor's Paris; the Paris of the salons and boulevards, of 'leichtes Volk', 'höfliche Männer', 'lächelnde Weiber', the only Paris to which Heine himself was ever to be admitted. There is food here for the mind, but none for the soul; and the exile longs back to his native land. The goal of longing is now Germany: but it is another Germany from that depicted in *Anno 1829*. What is presented here is not the huckster's world of the trading-port, but rather the as yet self-enclosed, sleepy, provincial world whose values the great Biedermeier writers were then beginning to exalt. This Biedermeier Germany the exile of *Anno 1839* proceeds to ridicule even while expressing his yearnings. He makes fun of its outworn political and religious creeds, its provincial scorn of good manners, the docility of its womenfolk, its immobility and backwardness—and last but not least its literature.

> Mir ist, als hört ich fern erklingen
> Nachtwächterhörner, sanft und traut;
> Nachtwächterlieder hör ich singen,
> Dazwischen Nachtigallenlaut.
>
> Dem Dichter war so wohl daheime,
> In Schildas teurem Eichenhain!
> Dort wob ich meine zarten Reime
> Aus Veilchenduft und Mondenschein.

The fun is tender, entirely without malice and more than half directed—as the final lines demonstrate beyond question—

against the kind of poet that Heine had himself been. The poem indicates Heine's awareness that he was himself indissolubly bound up with this 'backward' Germany; that if its values were false values, then they were at least preferable to those of the world that sought to supplant them.

> Dem Dichter war so wohl daheime,
> In Schildas teurem Eichenhain...

—the adjective in these lines is only half ironic. The poet who wrote them is like the water-sprite in *Begegnung*, another ballad of these years: by birth and temperament a stranger to the idyllic, pre-urban world familiar from German folk-song, he yet feels happier there than in the company of his own kind.

Begegnung, written in the autumn of 1841, may in fact stand as the epitome of Heine's ballad poetry after *Der Tannhäuser*. It shows to the full the subtlety with which he used the four-line stanza he had made his own, finding ever new and ever appropriate variations on the ancient pattern.

> Sie schweben auf, sie schweben ab,
> In seltsam fremder Weise,
> Sie lachen sich an, sie schütteln das Haupt,
> Das Fräulein flüstert leise....

Here the alternation of grammatically bisected and grammatically unbroken lines renders to perfection the sway of the dance and the absorption of the dancers now in their movements, now in their whispered conversation. In the nixie's speech similar rhythmic subtleties may be observed:

> Ihr seid der Wassermann, Ihr wollt
> Verlocken des Dorfes Schönen.
> Ich hab Euch erkannt, beim ersten Blick,
> An Euren fischgrätigen Zähnen.

No one can miss the force with which the stress is here controlled to fall on the key-word 'verlocken' (one of Heine's most constant themes!), or the mocking lilt of the final line with its extra syllable. Mockery is as much a matter of sound as of rhythm: of the half-rhyme 'Schönen'–'Zähnen' and the echoing assonance that links the strange adjective 'fischgrätig' to its noun. Heine's control of the sound of his poetry is as perfect as ever, and it is not altogether absurd to say that lines like

> Wohl unter der Linde erklingt die Musik

not only speak of music but *are* music.

With its folk-song formulae and its village setting, *Begegnung* shows Heine's continued preoccupation with German popular culture—but it shows also his constant endeavour to transform the figures of folk-lore into symbols for his own problems and state of mind. The merman in the village world is in the position of a German in Paris, or a Jewish poet writing for a German audience. He is a stranger who feels it important to preserve a disguise. To do this successfully he must keep his distance, remain in the polite world of social relations, the world of the second person plural; and the most shattering moment in *Begegnung* is that in which this world is suddenly invaded by an unwonted familiarity, by the second person singular.

> Mein schönes Fräulein, sagt mir, warum
> So eiskalt Eure Hand ist?
> Sagt mir, warum so naß der Saum
> An Eurem weißen Gewand ist?
>
> Ich hab Euch erkannt, beim ersten Blick,
> An Eurem spöttischen Knixe —
> Du bist kein irdisches Menschenkind,
> Du bist mein Mühmchen, die Nixe.

It is not good to come too close or pry too deeply—being a stranger can have its advantages. At the end of the poem polite distance is restored and the mask reassumed.

The fascination that figures from folk-lore continued to exert on Heine is not to be explained, however, merely by their convenience as symbols for his own state of mind. In them he felt the presence of a *numen* of which his conscious mind knew little. In the nixie of *Begegnung* he playfully depicted his own anima—that uncomfortable being which brings self-knowledge and, at the same time, knowledge of realms that lie deeper than the self. C. G. Jung has shown what lies behind such figures:

> The nixie is an early stage, still on the level of instinct, of a magical feminine being that I call the anima, the woman in man.... Yet, since the collective unconscious is *more* than personal, the anima is not always merely the feminine aspect of the individual man. It has an archetypal aspect—*das ewig Weibliche*—which embodies an experience of woman far older than the individual. This anima is reflected, of course, in mythology and legend. It can be siren or wood-nymph, Grace or Erlking's daughter, lamia or succubus....[1]

> With the archetype of the anima we enter the realm of the gods or of metaphysics, for everything in which the anima appears takes on the quality of the *numen*—that is, becomes unconditional, dangerous, taboo, magical.[2]

Whilst dramatising his inner conflicts and social difficulties with the lightest touch and the most charmingly mocking smile, Heine allowed deeper, unknown and unknowable forces to flow into his poetry. For all his sincere belief in the power of reason and the necessity of enlightenment, he retained always a tap-root into the unconscious, and was therefore saved from that mean and narrow rationalism he had so unforgettably depicted in the Dr Saul Ascher of *Die Harzreise*. He needed his German nixies even in Paris.

5. DREAM OF A SUMMER NIGHT

Je ne crains que ce que j'estime.

STENDHAL

I

In spite of the new possibilities glimpsed in the third part of *Der Tannhäuser*, Heine remained determined to separate his poetry (verse) from his social and political comment (prose).

[1] C. G. Jung, *The Integration of the Personality*, transl. S. M. Dell (London, 1940), p. 73.

[2] *Ibid.* p. 77.

Ja, in guter Prosa wollen
Wir das Joch der Knechtschaft brechen —
Doch in Versen, doch im Liede
Blüht uns längst die höchste Freiheit.

Hier im Reich der Poesie,
Hier bedarf es keiner Kämpfe,
Laßt uns hier den Thyrsus schwingen
Und das Haupt mit Rosen kränzen!

(Parergon of *Atta Troll*)[1]

Nor did he seem tempted to change his mind by the events of 1840. That year brought a new king to the throne of Prussia and new hopes to German liberals and enthusiasts for unification—for Frederick William IV had professed, as crown-prince, ideas which might have been mistaken for liberal. His accession therefore fostered a crop of political poetry such as had not been seen in Germany since the Wars of Liberation. The grandiloquent rhetoric of Georg Herwegh's *Gedichte eines Lebendigen*, the mild satire (so soon to recoil on its renegade author's head!) of Franz Dingelstedt's *Lieder eines kosmopolitischen Nachtwächters*, the prosings of Hoffmann von Fallersleben's *Unpolitische Lieder*—all these were calculated to arouse Heine's amusement rather than his admiration, and though he went out of his way, in a later preface to *Atta Troll*, to pay his respects to Ferdinand Freiligrath, who had renounced a Prussian pension and assumed the mantle of a paladin of freedom, there are enough *obiter dicta* to make it clear that Heine had little respect for Freiligrath's powers as a political poet. 'After or rather with Hoffmann von Fallersleben, all poetry is at an end',[2] he noted in his commonplace book; and in the *Augsburger Allgemeine Zeitung* he wrote on 20 March 1843:

Artists who choose as their subject liberty and liberation are usually men of limited, inhibited understanding, unfree at heart. The truth of this remark is exemplified especially by the German poetry of today, where we see with dismay how the boldest, the most unbridled singers of liberty for the most part turn out to be, on closer inspection, nothing but narrow-minded Philistines whose pigtails peep out from beneath

[1] *SW*, II, 526. [2] *SW*, VII, 418.

their red caps.... Truly great poets have always interpreted the great issues of the time otherwise than in rhymed newspaper articles.[1]

The year of Frederick William IV's accession had also brought a scare of war: Thiers' ministry had threatened to extend the frontiers of France to the Rhine and aroused a justifiable upsurge of national sentiment in Germany which found literary expression in Max Schneckenburger's *Die Wacht am Rhein* and in Niklas Becker's instantly popular *Rheinlied*:

Sie sollen ihn nicht haben,
Den freien deutschen Rhein....

Heine himself wrote a poem, in this summer of 1840, in which he compared the German people to Siegfried the dragon-slayer and warned Germany's neighbours against a conflict in which they were bound to be overcome.[2]

Heine's main contribution, however, to the year 1840 was a prose work, *Ludwig Börne*, which brought howls of execration about his head. The men of the political Right loathed the book because of its attacks on the priesthood and the Church; liberals because of its anti-egalitarianism and its vilification of Börne; and respectable burghers everywhere because certain passages were libellous and scatological. Throughout Germany judgments on Heine echoed—though with rather less sympathy and respect—the lines with which the *Gentleman's Magazine* had chastised Byron in 1818:

Yes, hapless bard! Thine errors I deplore—
Rich were thy talents, but thy morals poor!

Never had Heine's stock been so low in Germany. Never had he stood as alone as he did in 1840.

Heine's answer was the mock-epic *Atta Troll*, which first appeared in Laube's *Zeitung für die elegante Welt* in 1843. In this early version it was slightly shorter—it did not contain, for instance, Caput VII, with its excursions on the human smile, or Caput VIII, with its delightful evocations of a bear's view of heaven. These and other sections were not written until Heine

[1] *SW*, VI, 348–9.

[2] *SW*, II, 167–8.

prepared the work for separate publication in 1847. In some cases, however, omissions and alterations were due to the editorship of Laube, who could not risk the suppression of his journal: he left out, for instance, Atta Troll's famous epitaph in Caput XXIV, because it parodied too perfectly the lapidary participial style of King Ludwig I of Bavaria. This early version also contained one long section (then Caput XIX) which Heine himself later decided to omit—its satire on German 'Lumpen' and excursus on the language of birds and the Queen of Sheba, he may well have felt, added nothing essential to the poem. For the book version of 1847 Heine went back to his original draft manuscript, restoring many readings Laube had rejected and making many changes of detail; but he did not tamper with the original conception, so that the later version only brought out more clearly and with greater artistry what had been implicitly there from the beginning. In my analysis of the work, I shall quote for the most part the text of 1847, though I shall refer occasionally to that of 1843 and to the several manuscripts that have been preserved.[1]

The main fable of *Atta Troll* was not of Heine's own invention. It is the old fable of the dancing bear who escapes into the forest, which had attracted more than one of the writers of the German *Aufklärung*. Gellert, for instance, had used it in *Der Tanzbär*, which describes the jealousy of the forest bears when they see how much more skilfully than they the returned captive can dance; the moral being that you should not boast of your accomplishments.

Sei nicht geschickt, man wird dich wenig hassen,
Weil dir dann jeder ähnlich ist;
Doch je geschickter du vor vielen andern bist,
Je mehr nimm dich in acht, dich prahlend sehn zu lassen....[2]

The bear, in Gellert's fable, stands for the accomplished man who neglects to consider that society cannot brook any too obvious

[1] The textual history of *Atta Troll* is recounted by Ernst Elster in *Die Heine-Sammlung Strauß* (1929), p. 37. The MS. I have inspected is that in the Landes- und Stadtbibliothek Düsseldorf; it contains passages rejected before *Atta Troll* was printed in the *Zeitung für die elegante Welt* in 1843, as well as subsequent alterations made for the new edition in book form in 1847.

[2] C. F. Gellert, *Werke*, ed. F. Berend (Goldene Klassiker Bibliothek), I, 56.

deviation from the norm of mediocrity. Lessing had used this fable too: but in his poem, also called *Der Tanzbär*, the forest bears are not impressed by the skilful display of dancing.

> Geh, brummt ein alter Bär,
> Dergleichen Kunst, sie sei so schwer,
> Sie sei so rar sie sei,
> Zeigt deinen niedern Geist und Sklaverei.[1]

The moral, explicitly drawn, is a condemnation of the arts and wiles of the courtier ('ein Mann, dem Schmeichelei und List / Statt Witz und Tugend ist') on the part of the less worldly but more honest and dignified burgher.

In the second volume of *Reisebilder* (1827) Heine had taken this typical *Aufklärung* fable and given it a characteristic twist. His dancing bear is now no longer a personification of skill and grace. He represents a German nobleman who has been trained—not very successfully—by Parisian dancing-masters and who now returns to impress other German nobles with tales of the difficulties encountered by all those who would learn to dance and with protestations of his own skill. 'And indeed', Heine comments, 'the poor beasts could not withhold admiration from the samples of his art which he proceeded to display.'[2]

The shift of meaning and emphasis is unmistakable here. Lessing had confronted agile servility with dignity and solid worth and had invoked the good sense of society to resist fraudulent or ill-formed claims. Gellert had been less unequivocally on the side of society—he had seen its weaknesses and had counselled moderation in face of its envy of unusual accomplishments; but Gellert clearly appealed to men of sense and reason, to a group whose standards and interests, he felt, coincided with his own. For both there had been no doubt of the dancing-bear's skill and grace, though they had judged it differently. Heine, however, sees clumsiness and stupidity on both sides. He asks his reader, in *Reisebilder* as in *Atta Troll*, to feel superior to the dancing bear *and* to those before whom he performs. His standard of judgment

[1] Lessing, *Werke*, ed. F. Muncker (Stuttgart, 1890), I, 168.
[2] *SW*, III, 110.

is not society or a group of men of good sense: his standard is embodied in the hunter, the gay outsider who appears as the 'lyric I' of *Atta Troll*.

II

Nothing could be further off the mark than to take this debonair hunter, the 'I' of *Atta Troll*, as a simple representation of Heine himself. The early 1840's were years of worry and anxiety for the poet: years in which he found himself attacked by literary and personal antagonists, in which his financial resources were dangerously strained as his income from royalties diminished and his expenditure increased, in which the sickness that was soon to cripple him for ever frighteningly announced itself in temporary paralysis and blindness. *Atta Troll* was conceived during a stay at Cauterets in the Spanish Pyrenees, where Heine had gone in a vain attempt to mend his shattered health. An early draft of Caput II has been preserved[1] in which the poet tries to introduce himself into the poem as the sick man he really was. Atta Troll has just broken away from his keeper:

> Dies geschah den zweiten Juli
> Achtzehnhunderteinundvierzig
> Und ein kranker deutscher Dichter
> Der vom sicheren Balkone
>
> Diesem großen....

At this point Heine broke off, crossed out the last two and a half lines and substituted:

> Und ein großer deutscher Dichter
> Der dem großen Schauspiel zusah
>
> (Von dem sicheren Balkone)
> Seufzte tief: O Vaterland....

The adverted reader is, however, reminded of Heine's real situation by a telling image towards the end of *Atta Troll*. The bear has been tracked down and killed; strapped to a chair he is borne

[1] MS. in Landes- und Stadtbibliothek Düsseldorf.

in triumph through the streets of a Pyrenean village. The scene deliberately echoes Herder's *Der Cid*, from which Heine borrowed the trochaic stanzas that lend themselves so perfectly to his unbuttoned style and whose 'four-footed' tread recalls that of his hero.

Vier gewaltge Männer trugen
Im Triumph den toten Bären;
Aufrecht saß er in dem Sattel
Wie ein kranker Badegast. (Caput XXI)

That last line clearly recalls what Heine himself was in Cauterets and Barèges—in fact, after a sudden seizure Heine had to be borne into Barèges in just this way. But the image has been transferred to the bear, while the 'I' of the poem knows nothing of such weakness of the body. In physical and mental agility as in imaginative depth the hunter is the perfect foil of Atta Troll himself, of his fellow-bears and of the animals encountered in Uraka's hut. He is not, of course, a *persona* in the way Swift's Gulliver is. Heine was never capable of that sort of objectivity; he can seldom resist—and this is a weakness in his work—the temptations of autobiography. In *Atta Troll*, the 'I' is yet another embodiment of Heine's own deepest aspiration: to be, like the hero of *Ali Bey*, lover and hero at once, to annihilate enemies while still dreaming of love.

At the centre of *Atta Troll* we find, therefore, once again a dream of fair women. The hunter, in the thick of his pursuit of the bear, has a vision of a different kind of chase: of the 'Wilde Jagd' of German legend, the procession of the damned and doomed across the sky. Goethe is part of it, for the orthodox theologian Hengstenberg had condemned him as immoral and un-Christian; so is Shakespeare, who traverses the sky on a wild charger, closely followed by a poor frightened German commentator clutching the saddle of an ass.

Ganz ohnmächtig, fest sich krampend
An den Sattelknopf des Grauchens,
Doch im Tode, wie im Leben,
Seinem Autor treulich folgend. (Caput XVIII)

One does not have to read far in German Shakespeare commentaries of the nineteenth century to appreciate the force and justice of Heine's satire here. But all these arabesques only decorate and frame the clearest vision Heine was ever to vouchsafe his readers of La Belle Dame sans Merci, of the archetypal Lorelei, of that 'White Goddess' whose figure Robert Graves has seen at the root of so many of the world's great myths:

> There is one story and one story only
> That will prove worth your telling,
> Whether as learned bard or gifted child;
> To it all lines and lesser gauds belong
> That startle with their shining
> Such common stories as they stray into.
>
> (Robert Graves: *To Juan at the Winter Solstice*)

Heine was never to tell as fully that 'one story' which obsessed him as in Caput XVIII, XIX and XX of *Atta Troll.*

The merciless and alluring goddess appears here in threefold form; and Freud has taught us, in his famous analysis of the 'three women' motif, to see the force behind such triplication, with its memories of the three Fates and of mother, beloved and 'Mother Earth'.[1] She appears first as Diana, though not as the chaste goddess of classical legend. The oppressed senses have exacted vengeance and turned chastity into devouring lust. This fallen Diana is accompanied by the Celtic fairy Abunde: another presentation of that 'laughing woman' whose image we meet so often in Heine's poetry after his union with Mathilde.

> Ach! Sie hätte nur gelacht,
> Wenn ich unten in dem Abgrund
> Blutend fiel zu ihren Füßen —
> Ach! ich kenne solches Lachen! (Caput XIX)

The third guise the 'White Goddess' assumes in this vision of a Wild Hunt is that of Herodias, who here plays a part which the Bible assigns to Salome. In the passage about Herodias, Heine comes closest to the spirit of the *décadents* and the aesthetes of the

[1] 'The Theme of the Three Caskets', in *Collected Papers* (London, 1925), IV, 244 f.

later nineteenth century: the spirit of Gustave Moreau's painting of Salome, of Baudelaire, J. K. Huysmans and Oscar Wilde.

Auf dem glutenkranken Antlitz
Lag des Morgenlandes Zauber,
Auch die Kleider mahnten kostbar
An Scheherezadens Märchen. (*Ibid.*)

In this figure Heine concentrates all that longing for strange *frissons* and dangerous indulgences, for a love that is death, for cruelty and suffering, with which the aesthetes of the nineteenth century anticipated the realities of the twentieth. At the same time he plays here with a Jewish nostalgia that was to become ever stronger in the course of his life. Originally this nostalgia had rung out unmistakably in three stanzas in which the hunter sees himself as a Wandering Jew, as a reincarnation of a courtier of Herod's, and quotes that 137th Psalm which was later to serve as the *Leitmotiv* of *Jehuda ben Halevi*:

Ihre Flammenblitze trafen
Mich wie Blitze der Erinnrung:
Sind das nicht dieselben Augen
Die vor achtzehnhundert Jahren

In mein junges Herz geleuchtet
Als ich Mundschenk war am Hofe
Unsres großen Viertelsfürsten
In der Stadt Jeruscholayim?

Heilge Stadt Jeruscholayim!
Wenn ich deiner je vergesse
So verwelke meine Rechte
So vertrockne meine Zunge![1]

Heine never published these lines; but in the published versions of *Atta Troll* this note is by no means absent, though it is played on more muted instruments.

Ja, am Tage sitz ich weinend
Auf dem Schutt der Königsgrüfte,
Auf dem Grabe der Geliebten,
Bei der Stadt Jeruscholayim.

[1] MS. Düsseldorf.

Alte Juden, die vorbeigehn,
Glauben dann gewiß, ich traure
Ob dem Untergang des Tempels
Und der Stadt Jeruscholayim. (Caput XX)

In rhythm, melody and imagery these stanzas anticipate the later *Hebräische Melodien.*

The 'Wild Hunt' chapters would seem to be, at first glance, a strange constituent of a work which is for the most part a satire on political poetry. Its function is clearly to convey to the reader something of the view of life that lies behind the satire; to allow him to look more deeply into the mind and soul of the hunter, who has earlier been seen as the lover of the light-hearted Parisian Juliette and as the man who, when kissing a country girl, finds proofs of his existence more cogent than those of Descartes:

Ja, ich küsse, also leb ich! (Caput XIV)

The Wild Hunt is a more subtle and complicated image of love than any of these; and it is also a fuller image than any Heine had found before of art and of life. It brings before the reader a vision of the three worlds of art from which Heine himself had drawn his inspiration: the Greek, the Nordic-Celtic and the Jewish. At the same time it presents a vision of life: life as the dream of a wild procession, with the dreamer himself as onlooker and outsider—full of beauty and danger, luring towards strange sensations that will leave the sense high sorrowful and cloyed, will leave it with a sense of emptiness and desolation after ecstatic pleasures. There is a suggestion, too, that all these pleasures do not belong to the prosaic world of the nineteenth-century present; that they are spectres of the past, too overpowering in the end for those who summon them up. It is entirely fitting, therefore, that Caput XX of *Atta Troll* should include Heine's first poetic evocation of that land of the imagination and of poetry which he then called 'Avalon' but which he was later to call 'Bimini':

Dieses Eiland liegt verborgen
Ferne, in dem stillen Meere
Der Romantik, nur erreichbar
Auf des Fabelrosses Flügeln.

Niemals ankert dort die Sorge,
Niemals landet dort ein Dampfschiff
Mit neugierigen Philistern,
Tabakspfeifen in den Mäulern.

* * *

Dort, in ungestörtem Frohsinn,
Und in ewger Jugend blühend,
Residiert die heitre Dame,
Unsre blonde Frau Abunde. (Caput XX)

'You know Avalon', Heine had told his French readers in *Elementargeister*, 'but the Persians know it too, and they call it Ginnistan. It is the land of Poetry.'[1] But as *Atta Troll* makes quite clear, Avalon is not only the land of poetry. It is also the land of love and, like Bimini, the land of death.

With their nostalgia, their strange blend of exoticism and elements from German folk-lore, their search for ineffable sensations beyond the reach of ordinary existence, their mingling of love and death, the 'Wild Hunt' chapters of *Atta Troll* present most compellingly a *Romantic* view of life. They, more than anything else in this work, justify Heine's contention that he had here written 'the last free forest-song of Romanticism'. They leave no doubt of the tradition to which Heine belongs.

Yet though the German Romantics had known how to mingle irony and satire with their ecstasies, Heine shows even in these 'Wild Hunt' sections a detachment that goes beyond 'romantic irony'. Genuine Romantic music—

Warum hast du mich so zärtlich
Angesehn, Herodias? (Caput XIX)

—is followed by passages of self-parody and parody of the very gratifications that seem to be so eagerly sought.

Liebe mich und sei mein Liebchen,
Schönes Weib, Herodias!

Liebe mich und sei mein Liebchen!
Schleudre fort den blutgen Dummkopf
Samt der Schüssel, und genieße
Schmackhaft bessere Gerichte.

[1] *SW*, IV, 388.

Bin so recht der rechte Ritter,
Den du brauchst — Mich kümmert's wenig,
Daß du tot und gar verdammt bist —
Habe keine Vorurteile —

Hapert's doch mit meiner eignen
Seligkeit.... (Caput xx)

Romanticism had helped the poet to see deeper into the nature of life than the shallow optimists of the political Left. On him as on Baudelaire had fallen the shadow of the Divine Marquis. Like Novalis he had felt the unity of love and death and like Brentano the lure and threat of natural forces that could invade and destroy the conscious self. But here too he stands outside, saved from ultimate dangers and debarred from ultimate ecstasies by his ever-lively, ever-mocking intellect.

And was it not right to resist the Romantic lure? Was there not much in the tendencies and attitudes especially of the German Romantics that was pernicious and destructive? The French, Heine said in the third volume of *Der Salon*, might safely toy with Romantic attitudes and admire the medieval past; but in Germany the trappings of Romanticism were worn by dangerous men and the Romantic mystique was shading over dangerously into politics.

Vous pouvez, vous autres Français, admirer et aimer la chevalerie. Il ne vous en est rien resté que de jolies chroniques et des armures de fer. Vous ne risquez rien à amuser ainsi votre imagination, à satisfaire votre curiosité. Mais chez nous, Allemands, la chronique du moyen-âge n'est pas encore close; les pages les plus récentes sont encore humides du sang de nos parents et de nos amis, et ces harnois étincellants protègent encore les corps vivants de nos bourreaux.[1]

The weapon of ridicule is therefore turned against Romantic medievalism no less than against modern political poetry: Sir Ogier the Dane, riding in the Wild Hunt, is likened to a frog:

Und Herr Ogier, der Däne,
Trug er nicht den schillernd grünen
Ringenpanzer, daß er aussah
Wie ein großer Wetterfrosch? (Caput xviii)

[1] *SW*, iv, 616.

But the Romantics, at least, had known how to write; they had not used their poetry as a cart-horse of political ideologies; and their vision of human life, however inadequate, had at least taken in more of the truth than that of the liberal enthusiasts of 1840. Novalis, Brentano, Eichendorff, Hoffmann, Chamisso—they had a *stature* to which the Herweghs and Hoffmanns von Fallersleben could never pretend.

Welch ein Sumsen, welterschütternd!
Das sind ja des Völkerfrühlings
Kolossale Maienkäfer,
Von Berserkerwut ergriffen!

Andre Zeiten, andre Vögel!
Andre Vögel, andre Lieder!
Sie gefielen mir vielleicht,
Wenn ich andre Ohren hätte! (Caput XXVII)

Romantic poets might not always have had the best character—but they did have talent; while those who opposed and those who succeeded them were all too often, in Brentano's immortal phrase, 'gute Leute und schlechte Musikanten'.

III

The opposition of character and talent had become, by the 1840's, all too familiar to Heine. Since 1831, when a reviewer of *Reisebilder* had spoken in the Tübingen *Literaturblatt* edited by Menzel, of 'Blößen des Charakters... die kein Talent je zudeckt',[1] critics had never tired of ringing the changes on this theme—Börne especially, in private and published utterances, had taken it up. *Atta Troll* seeks to turn the tables on such critics by presenting an eponymous hero who is everything the poet himself was not; a hero who could therefore, despite his liberal tendencies, find a niche in the 'Valhalla of Fame' recently erected by King Ludwig of Bavaria.

Atta Troll, Tendenzbär; sittlich
Religiös; als Gatte brünstig;
Durch Verführtsein von dem Zeitgeist,
Waldursprünglich Sanscülotte;

[1] *SW*, III, 374.

Sehr schlecht tanzend, doch Gesinnung
Tragend in der zottgen Hochbrust;
Manchmal auch gestunken habend;
Kein Talent, doch ein Charakter! (Caput XXIV)

It has been objected that the qualities united in Atta Troll are incompatible. He is at once religious, nationalistic and communist—a combination unusual even in the 1840's. But this objection misses the very point of the poem. Heine is here satirising German political poetry and through it the German opposition *as a whole*; he shows precisely that there is nothing to choose between the various opposition parties, that they are all equally respectable, equally devoid of talent and therefore ultimately equally ineffective. In speaking at one time like a 'Burschenschaftler' and Teutomaniac, at another like a communist, at yet another like a defender of religious orthodoxy, Atta Troll comes to represent what all the parties had in common: that heaviness and clumsiness which has always been the bane of German life and literature and which was to be castigated by Nietzsche as 'der Geist der Schwere'. What better symbol could be found for this than a dancing bear?

Atta Troll is Heine's most delightful creation. His speeches, though apparently a farrago of nonsense, have an inner logic and consistency that make them highly effective parodies of human attitudes.

Menschen, seid ihr etwa besser,
Weil ihr Wissenschaft und Künste
Mit Erfolg betreibt? Wir andre
Sind nicht auf den Kopf gefallen.

Gibt es nicht gelehrte Hunde?
Und auch Pferde, welche rechnen
Wie Kommerzienräte? Trommeln
Nicht die Hasen ganz vorzüglich?

Schreiben Esel nicht Kritiken?
Spielen Affen nicht Komödie? (Caput V)

Without commenting in his own person, Heine has here managed to hit off, not only the foibles of nationalists and egalitarians of his own day (with startling side-swipes at professors, *Kommerzienräte*, literary critics, actors and others), but also the kind of argumentation common to all men at all times when they feel that the merits of their own group are being underrated. It is the same argumentation as that of the Ishmaelite orator at Hyde Park Corner in Evelyn Waugh's *Scoop*:

Who built the Pyramids?...A Negro. Who invented the circulation of the blood? A Negro. Ladies and gentlemen, I ask you as impartial members of the great British public, who discovered America?

In *Atta Troll*, Heine keeps the reader conscious at once of human traits he wishes to satirise and of his bears *as* bears: he presents a bear's eye view of life which is at once a parody of the human world and delightfully consistent in itself. In sovereign play, he translates human types into bear types. Here, for instance, is the communist orator:

Grundgesetz sei volle Gleichheit
Aller Gotteskreaturen,
Ohne Unterschied des Glaubens
Und des Fells und des Geruches.

Strenge Gleichheit! Jeder Esel
Sei befugt zum höchsten Staatsamt,
Und der Löwe soll dagegen
Mit dem Sack zur Mühle traben. (Caput VI)

This is the popular theologian:

Droben in dem Sternenzelte,
Auf dem goldnen Herrscherstuhle,
Weltregierend, majestätisch,
Sitzt ein kolossaler Eisbär.

* * *

Ihm zu Füßen sitzen fromm
Bärenheilge, die auf Erden
Still geduldet, in den Tatzen
Ihres Martyrtumes Palmen.

Manchmal springt der eine auf,
Auch der andre, wie vom heilgen
Geist geweckt, und sieh! da tanzen
Sie den feierlichsten Hochtanz —

Hochtanz, wo der Strahl der Gnade
Das Talent entbehrlich machte.... (Caput VIII)

And here, finally, is the sentimental love-poet Heine had himself once been:

Werd ich nie dich wiedersehen,
Oder nur jenseits des Grabes,
Wo von Erdenzotteln frei
Sich verkläret deine Seele?

Ach! vorher möcht ich noch einmal
Lecken an der holden Schnauze
Meiner Mumma, die so süße,
Wie mit Honigseim bestrichen! (Caput V)

There is Swiftian power and precision in these caricatures, but little of Swift's venom. The reader cannot but become fond of Atta Troll, despite his clumsiness and stupidity; and it is not surprising to find Heine, in later years, actually claiming kinship with his own butt. 'Ma belle Lutèce', he assures his Parisian audience, 'n'oublie pas ma nationalité; bien que je sois un des mieux léchés d'entre mes compatriotes, je ne saurais pourtant pas tout à fait renier ma nature: c'est ainsi que les caresses de mes pattes tudesques ont pu te blesser parfois....'[1] In Atta Troll he portrayed some of the temptations that beset poets who venture into politics, and some of the feeling of every German writer who measures his own achievement against the elegance of the French.

Connected with this sympathy is a striking ambivalence of tone. When we read a passage like that about the bear-heaven in Caput VIII, we are aware as much of the poetry of the conception as of its absurdity; but when we read passages like the following, assent and dissent mingle in a different way:

Ja, sogar die Juden sollen
Volles Bürgerrecht genießen
Und gesetzlich gleichgestellt sein
Allen andern Säugetieren.

[1] *SW*, VI, 569.

Nur das Tanzen auf den Märkten
Sei den Juden nicht gestattet;
Dies Amendement, ich mach es
Im Intresse meiner Kunst. (Caput VI)

So far, the drift is clear enough. Heine is satirising those curious pockets of prejudice and illiberality in advocates of enlightenment which appear most clearly when their livelihood or their vanity is threatened. As the poet himself told Fanny Lewald in 1848:

I did not invent this...I copied this trait from a very reasonable and liberal man, a chemist with whom I had some dealings in Göttingen. He was of the opinion that the Jews must be emancipated and must be allowed to enter any profession—except that they should not be permitted to become chemists.[1]

But when Heine now goes on to write, in Caput VI of *Atta Troll*:

Denn der Sinn für Stil, für strenge
Plastik der Bewegung, fehlt
Jener Rasse, sie verdürben
Den Geschmack des Publikums,

then the reader cannot but feel that he is laughing, not only at his liberal bear, but also at some of the Jews he has known. It was this kind of ambiguity which had most infuriated Börne. 'Even if a crown were at stake', Börne had said in *Briefe aus Paris*,[2] 'Heine could not suppress a smile, a mock or a joke.' Such satire, as Börne rightly felt and Heine admitted, is ill adapted to advance the cause of any particular party:

Ist kein nützlich tugendhafter
Karrengaul des Bürgertums,
Noch ein Schlachtpferd der Parteiwut...,
(Caput III)

for it ridicules the general imperfections of men, whatever their party or whatever their creed. Ultimately, it smiles at the poet himself too, who had after all clear affinities with the Germans, the Jews, the liberals whom he mocked; and it thus bears out

[1] *Gespräche*, p. 608.

[2] *Gesammelte Schriften von Ludwig Börne* (Hamburg and Frankfurt, 1862), XII, 130.

Kenneth Burke's contention that satirists tend to attack in others the weaknesses and temptations they feel within themselves.

IV

The high spirits of the first part of *Atta Troll*, which chronicles for the most part the doings and sayings of the eponymous bear, are clouded over in the second half, which follows more closely the activities of the hunters. Here we come again on that 'dark foundation' of his wit of which Heine had spoken to Moses Moser: 'Wit in its isolation is worth nothing at all; I find it bearable only when it rests on a foundation of seriousness' (Letter of 1 July 1825). Heine's favourite image for wit was that of the streak of lightning:

> Durch die schwarze Wolkenwand
> Zuckt der zackige Wetterstrahl,
> Rasch aufleuchtend und rasch verschwindend,
> Wie ein Witz aus dem Haupte Kronions;
>
> (*Die Nordsee*, II, 2)

an appropriate simile which points not only to the surprising flashes that wit seeks to achieve but also to the prevailing gloom it lightens for a moment.

Caput XI, for instance, speaks of the comic indignity of the traveller in remote parts whose bed is infested with unwelcome insects, and leads the reader to draw a parallel with similar 'battles' that men of talent have to fight in the modern world.

> Schlimmer als der Zorn von tausend
> Elefanten ist die Feindschaft
> Einer einzgen kleinen Wanze,
> Die auf deinem Lager kriecht.
>
> Mußt dich ruhig beißen lassen —
> Das ist schlimm — Noch schlimmer ist es,
> Wenn du sie zerdrückst: der Mißduft
> Quält dich dann die ganze Nacht.
>
> Ja, das Schrecklichste auf Erden
> Ist der Kampf mit Ungeziefer,
> Dem Gestank als Waffe dient —
> Das Duell mit einer Wanze!

The passage speaks for itself; but it takes on additional point if the reader remembers the kind of attack to which Heine was constantly subjected in German newspapers, and the kind of whispering campaign that was conducted against him at the court of his millionaire uncle. The startling paradox of the last line—a *duel* with a bed-bug!—will be fully understood by those who remember the farcical duel Heine had been forced to fight with Salomon Strauss in 1841.

In the chapters that follow Heine recreates, within the world of *Atta Troll*, the wish-dream world of simple contentment and innocent sensuality he had summoned up once before in the *Bergidylle* section of *Die Harzreise*. In the evocation of that world, folk-tales and folk-songs play an important part. The ferryman on Lake Gobe tells a tale of the supersession of giants by men (the foolish giants fled at the advent of man, reached the sea and threw themselves into it, under the delusion that they were throwing themselves into heaven) and speaks of dwarves waiting, in their turn, to supersede men:

> . . . die winzig klugen Leutchen,
> Die im Schoß der Berge hausen,
> In des Reichtums goldnen Schachten,
> Emsig klaubend, emsig sammelnd.
>
> Wie sie lauern aus den Löchern,
> Mit den pfiffig kleinen Köpfchen,
> Sah ich selber oft im Mondschein,
> Und mir graute vor der Zukunft!
>
> Vor der Geldmacht jener Knirpse!
> Ach, ich fürchte, unsre Enkel
> Werden sich wie dumme Riesen
> In den Wasserhimmel flüchten!'

The word 'Geldmacht' in this passage from Caput XII fulfils the same function as the word 'Duell' in that from Caput XI. It startles the reader sufficiently to make him think of other applications without breaking out of the fantasy-world of *Atta Troll*. The tale of dwarves and men becomes transparent; the reader remembers Heine's own apprehensions, so often and earnestly voiced in the reports for the *Augsburger Allgemeine Zeitung*, of the commercialisation of all values and the increasing tyranny of money.

The fears for the future voiced by the ferryman in Caput XII are followed by thoughts of death in Caput XIII. The hunter is accompanied by Lascaro, thought by some to be a dead man resuscitated by his mother, Uraka the witch: a symbol, perhaps, for political reaction (the dead 'ancien régime' revived by Metternich and the Holy Alliance), for it is to be Lascaro who slays that incarnation of clumsy liberalism, Atta Troll. Looking at Lascaro, the hunter thinks for a moment that he too is among the dead; but he is reassured by a glance at the Rubensian daughters of the ferryman:

> Nein, ich bin noch nicht gestorben
> Und erloschen — in der Seele
> Glüht mir noch und jauchzt und lodert
> Die lebendge Lebensflamme.

Is this affirmation not a little too frenzied? The dark fears that opened Caput XIII can be no more forgotten than the ferryman's ominous exclamation:

> Und mir graute vor der Zukunft!

Nor is Caput XV calculated to make the reader forget such apprehensions. The very landscape mirrors them; and a 'Doppelgänger' image introduces—as so often in Heine—an atmosphere of oppressive fear:

> Seltsam! Graue Wolken schweben
> Drüber hin, wie Doppelgänger....

This is the setting for the hunter's encounter with outcast 'Cagoten'; a strange episode that reflects a characteristic ambiguity of feeling within Heine himself. The shades of superstition, the reader is told, are lifting; those who were outcasts in the Middle Ages are granted equal rights, are justly regarded as *brothers* towards whom we have a responsibility.

Stehn blieb draußen der Lascaro,
Während ich in des Cagoten
Niedre Hütte trat. Ich reichte
Freundlich meine Hand dem Bruder.

Und ich küßte auch sein Kind,
Das, am Busen seines Weibes
Angeklammert, gierig saugte;
Einer kranken Spinne glich es.

The complexity of feeling is unmistakable here. Like the hunter of his poem, Heine is aware of his kinship with the rejected and oppressed—his own ancestors, he once said, belonged to the quarry rather than the chase; but at the same time he feels physical and spiritual revulsion at the sight of the objects of his sympathy, a revulsion which reveals itself in the image of the final line. Caput XV of *Atta Troll*, which speaks of modern enlightenment—

Aber die geweihten Kerzen
Des Jahrhunderts flackern lustig,
Und das Licht verscheucht die bösen
Mittelalterlichen Schatten —

hints at the reality of a curse:

Eine häßlich wüste Gegend.
Liegt darauf ein Fluch?

The question remains unanswered; but there is a shudder in the line that ends this section which hardly suggests an enlightened, optimistic negative.

The 'Cagoten' episode of *Atta Troll* is followed by another of deepest disillusion. The royal gold and purple with which distance had invested the mountain-tops disappear as the hunter approaches them.

Aber in der Nähe schwindet
Diese Pracht, und *wie bei andern*
Irdischen Erhabenheiten
Täuschten dich die Lichteffekte.

Was dir Gold und Purpur dünkte,
Ach, das ist nur eitel Schnee... [my italics].

With this snow the hunter now engages in colloquy. It complains of being bored on its lonely eminence and speaks of its longing to reach the world below, to fall into the valley, be taken up by the river and carried out to sea, where it might find itself, one day, transformed into a pearl. The mood of *Anno 1839* is clearly recalled here; but the hunter's answer is in the darker vein of *Unstern.* 'Be comforted', he assures the snow,

> Tröste dich. Nur wen'ge unten
> Werden Perlen, und du fielest
> Dort vielleicht in eine Pfütze,
> Und ein Dreck wärst du geworden!

The reader cannot but remember here the fear of the *dirt* of the world, the fear of being spiritually soiled, which breaks out so frighteningly in many of Heine's poems and is to culminate in *Nächtliche Fahrt*, where only death can save the soul from 'der Welt Unfläterei'. Caput XVI of *Atta Troll* therefore ends with a frightening visual image. Lascaro has suddenly shot down a bird and now moves on with his prey, his shadow lengthened by the setting sun. In the manuscript version[1] of this passage the key-word is clearly 'grauenhaft'.

> Grauenhaft unheimlich war es
> Wenn sein langer dunkler Schatten...

—these lines emerge after many trials, to be themselves crossed out to make way for:

> Wie sein langer dunkler Schatten
> Mit dem Spitzhut und der Feder
> Auf dem weiten, weißen Schnee
> Grauenhaft sich hinbewegte!

In the final version 'grauenhaft' is rejected as too melodramatic; but the terror is there all the more strongly for being presented in a precise image rather than talked about.

> Schier unheimlich war der Anblick,
> Wie sein Schatten mit der Feder
> Auf dem weißen Schnee der Koppen,
> Schwarz und lang, sich hinbewegte.

[1] MS. Düsseldorf.

The limiting and valuing 'schier'[1] that now opens the stanza ensures the reader against melodrama and sentimentality.

The lower, darker notes that have invaded the work are heard at their clearest in the 'Wild Hunt' episode which follows—a dream within a dream that allows the reader a glimpse of fears and desires such as would seem to have no place in this predominantly light-hearted poem. But then comes the modulation back: with the vision of the dance of bears and ghosts in Caput XXI (a wonderful evocation of the mixture of clumsiness and spirituality that fascinated Heine in the Germany of his day); the ridicule of Swabian poets in the pug-dog episode of Caput XXII; and Atta Troll's vision of bear-angels in Caput XXIII. This vision is clearly a parody of a famous episode at the opening of E. T. A. Hoffmann's *Der goldne Topf* and it introduces a riot of parody in which the poem culminates. Lessing's *Emilia Galotti*, Herder's *Cid*, Schiller's *Götter Griechenlands*, King Ludwig's *Walhallas Genossen* are all pressed into the service of the poet's high spirits, which now triumphantly reassert themselves. With parody the poem had begun: it had mocked Freiligrath's *Der Mohrenfürst*, one of those 'exotic' ballads in which Freiligrath had sought to present to his sleepy contemporaries images of a more colourful and more heroic existence.

Finster schaut er wie ein schwarzer
Freiligräthscher Mohrenfürst,
Und wie dieser schlecht getrommelt,
Also tanzt er schlecht vor Ingrimm. (Caput I)

Behind the forced imagery of *Der Mohrenfürst* Heine detected the pigtail of the Philistine lost in dreams of the colourful desert.

Aus dem schimmernden weißen Zelte hervor
Tritt der schlachtgerüstete fürstliche Mohr;
So tritt aus schimmernder Wolken Tor
Der Mond, der verfinsterte, dunkle, hervor.[2]

[1] The word 'schier' is already present in an early draft (MS. Düsseldorf) but was subsequently deleted. Heine went back in the end to the early reading.

[2] Freiligrath, *Werke*, ed. P. Zaunert (Meyers Klassiker), I, 44; cf. Heine's criticism of Freiligrath's Orient, *SW*, VII, 424–5.

This passage from *Der Mohrenfürst*, which, with its all-too-insistent rhymes and its image of a black moon aroused Heine's special mirth, is parodied in the penultimate section of *Atta Troll*. Freiligrath's heroic figure is there transposed into the contented Philistine who loved to read about him: he has become a zoo-keeper in the Jardin des Plantes and has married an Alsatian cook who is feeding him well.

Hab mir schon ein rundes Bäuchlein
Angemästet. Aus dem Hemde
Schaut's hervor, wie'n schwarzer Mond,
Der aus weißen Wolken tritt.

Here the hunter has truly brought down his quarry. No one could ever read Freiligrath's 'lion and desert poetry' without smiling after having read its parody in *Atta Troll*.

Even this, however, is not quite the end. Sadness and nostalgic regret enter the poem again in the final Caput XXVII, an epistle of dedication to Varnhagen von Ense which turns into a regretful farewell to German Romanticism and an expression of dismay at being left behind. Here the mask of the hunter is finally dropped, and the author steps forward in his own person to confess to a 'friend in a corner' his anxiety about his own poetry.

Ach, es ist vielleicht das letzte
Freie Waldlied der Romantik!
In des Tages Brand- und Schlachtlärm
Wird es kümmerlich verhallen.

He need not have worried. *Atta Troll* has long outlasted the political poets it satirises; and though it may sometimes be neglected by those who are dazzled or put off by the *Buch der Lieder*, it will never cease to delight that 'fit audience, though few' Heine would himself have desired.

V

The shape of *Atta Troll* is dictated partly by its well-chosen fable. The reader watches the bear break loose and escape into his native mountains; he follows him there and listens to his comic tirades;

he then turns to the hunter and shares his adventures, meditations and dreams; he sees the bear shot, follows the fate of his skin and learns—Heine could hardly have resisted this opportunity!—that his mate has consoled herself with a huge Russian bear in the Jardin des Plantes; and at last he takes leave of the author in a valedictory epistle. The framework is large and loose enough to accommodate all sorts of digressions, all sorts of visions and dreams within dreams. But as we have seen, the shape which the work assumes in the reader's mind is in the end all but independent of the fable. Its real shape lies in its changes of mood: in the high spirits with which it opens, the gradual intrusion of darker thoughts and feelings, and the return to high spirits that cannot altogether conceal a fundamental melancholy.

> Trotz des Übermutes wirst du
> Hie und dort Verzagnis spüren.... (Caput XXVII)

The true unity of *Atta Troll* must be sought in its evocation of a complex state of mind—a state of mind analogous to that of its author in the early 1840's. For all its epic trappings, the work has the confessional quality of a lyric poem.

Within this larger whole, the individual sections or 'Capita' of *Atta Troll* have a unity and shape of their own. They gain by being read in their context: but many of them are detachable and can be enjoyed as poems in their own right. This appreciation of *Atta Troll* will therefore end with a closer look at one of its lesser known sections—at Caput XIV, which tells of the hunter's encounter with a group of children in a remote mountain village.

Like most of these sections, Caput XIV opens with an impression of the natural scene. The landscape of the Pyrenees, as we learn from his letters to Cécile Heine, to Gustav Kolb and to Campe, had powerfully affected the poet. But more than ever Heine seeks in landscape the image of man; and when he does not openly anthropomorphise it, he seeks to see it (as Oscar Wilde was to do later) under the aspect of *art*. The term 'Goldgrund' subtly transforms an ostensible description of the natural scene into an imaginary painting of that scene:

Aus dem sonn'gen Goldgrund lachen
Violette Bergeshöhen,
Und am Abhang klebt ein Dörfchen,
Wie ein keckes Vogelnest.

There is no mistaking, though, the visual delight the poet takes in the scene he metamorphoses in this way, or the pleasure he finds in the human beings encountered there. Lucy Duff Gordon, Heinrich Laube and many others have described the wonderful way Heine had with children, who understood him and whom he, in his turn, understood better than their elders. Even his union with Mathilde was in the end nothing more than a liaison with an overgrown child! Something of that delight in children is communicated in Caput XIV of *Atta Troll*.

Hübsche Bübchen, kleine Mädchen,
Fast vermummt in scharlachroten
Oder weißen wollnen Kappen....

The colour, the articles of dress, are precisely seen and are presented economically, yet with all appropriate devices of word-music. Then comes a description of the games these children play; and here quite unforcedly, without any obvious break in tone, any remission of tenderness, the satirist begins to assert himself. The children's game of love and marriage unconsciously reflects the realities of the adult world.

Armer Prinz! Er wird vermählt
Mit der Schönen. Mürrisch zankt sie,
Und sie beißt ihn und sie frißt ihn;
Tote Maus, das Spiel ist aus.

Remaining a credible description of a children's game, this passage provides a commentary on love and marriage worthy of the author of *Unterwelt*. It recalls, in fact, the famous 'Mein Kind, wir waren Kinder' of *Die Heimkehr*: here as there a genuine delight in the poetry and innocence of childhood coexists with awareness, at once sorrowful and amused, of adult disillusion.

At the end of their game, the children crowd round the hunter and ply him with questions; and these provoke a mock address

('Lieben Freunde!') in which attacks on enemies of promise mingle with self-persiflage.

Lieben Freunde, — sprach ich — Deutschland
Heißt das Land, wo ich geboren;
Bären gibt es dort in Menge,
Und ich wurde Bärenjäger.

Manchem zog ich dort das Fell
Über seine Bärenohren.
Wohl mitunter ward ich selber
Stark gezaust von Bärentatzen.

Doch mit schlechtgeleckten Tölpeln
Täglich mich herumzubalgen
In der teuren Heimat, dessen
Ward ich endlich überdrüssig....

The bear-and-hunter fable is never abandoned, yet the meaning of it all is perfectly clear and the aim accurate and deadly: more accurate and deadly, it should be said, in this oblique later version than in the more directly venomous earlier one to which Laube raised justifiable objections:

Doch der schlechtgeleckten Bären
Meiner Heimat, dieser plumpen
Und zugleich perfiden Bestien
Ward ich endlich überdrüssig.[1]

What is wisely retained in both versions is the adjective 'schlechtgeleckt'. This is one of many dead metaphors which Heine miraculously resuscitates by restoring their literal and at the same time retaining their figurative meaning, as he does in this very passage with such terms as 'das Fell über die Ohren ziehen', 'gezaust werden' and 'sich herumbalgen', which have one meaning for the bears of the fable and another for the clumsy and boorish adversaries they are meant to caricature.

The charm of Caput XIV (a charm characteristic of the whole of *Atta Troll*) is not, however, felt to the full until after the hunter's long address. As he turns to go, the children crowd round him with the refrain of yet another game which is to echo

[1] *SW*, II, 529.

throughout all the stanzas that remain. There is satire still, and self-persiflage; this second game too has a meaning for the hunter and the reader that it could not possibly have for the children themselves; but the dominant impression here, as at the very beginning of this section, is once again one of delight in human life, delight in gaiety and grace, delight in the sheer beauty of sound.

> 'Girofflino, Girofflette!'
> Wiederholt das Chor, und neckend
> Wirbelte um meine Beine
> Sich der Ringeltanz und Singsang.
>
> Während ich das Tal hinabstieg,
> Scholl mir nach, verhallend lieblich,
> Immerfort, wie Vogelzwitschern:
> 'Girofflino, Girofflette!'

The echoing, constantly repeated refrain—the echo is there in the very *movement* of that final stanza!—seems one of those 'sounds of nature' which Heine had linked, in *Die Bäder von Lucca*, with the highest poetry: 'Deep sounds of nature, such as we find in folk-song, in the songs of children and in some poets.'[1]

The image of these children circling about the hunter with their gay refrain is only one of many such images that stay with the reader long after he has replaced the book on his shelf. He is not likely to forget Atta Troll leaping in the moonlight to the astonishment of his cubs:

> Stumm, mit aufgesperrten Schnauzen,
> Schauen zu die Bärenjungen,
> Wie der Vater hin und her springt
> Wunderbar im Mondenscheine; (Caput IV)

nor will he forget the three women of the Wild Hunt, the dance of bears and ghosts, Lascaro casting his shadow on the snow, or the child 'like a sick spider', clutching its mother's breast in the outcast's hut. Such images remain with us because they have a symbolic ambience that can be more easily sensed than analysed. They are signs for feelings that can be expressed by these signs only and by no other.

[1] *SW*, III, 352.

Atta Troll is not a flawless work. Like many of Heine's larger designs it is only a fragment of its original conception—'it has suffered', Heine wrote in December 1846,

> the fate of all great German works: Cologne cathedral, Schelling's God, the Prussian constitution, etc.—it has remained unfinished. In this unfinished form...I present it today to the public, obeying an urge that certainly does not come from within.[1]

The reader will wish occasionally that the 'I' of the work, the hunter, were more of an anti-self, like Swift's Gulliver, and less an idealisation of the historical Heine—though the poet has here managed surprisingly well to avoid the sentimentality and posing to which such transparent *personae* invite. He will also wish away a few of the jokes, notably those directed against Prince Lichnowsky ('Schnapphahnski') in Caput XXIII, which seem in poor taste. Yet for all that reading *Atta Troll* is sheer delight, even today when so many of its contemporary allusions have, of necessity, become incomprehensible; for this work has an ease, a grace, an urbanity unique in German literature. It achieves, apparently without effort, what Grillparzer had proclaimed in 1841 as at once the most urgent and the most difficult task of contemporary poetry:

> Es gibt nun bald kein Tiefstes mehr,
> Das Jeder nicht erreichte,
> Und in der Welt ist Nichts mehr schwer
> Als Eines nur: das Leichte.[2]

Nor are these qualities of grace, ease and urbanity mere accidental qualities of style, mere 'réjouissances' in the sense in which Heine explains this term in his *Romanzero* postscript.[3] They are also the ultimate standard of judgment, the yardstick with which the deficiencies satirised are to be measured. The clumsiness of Freiligrath, Prutz, Hoffmann von Fallersleben and the rest appears the more leaden because of Heine's own lightness of touch—just as the brightness of Pope's wit in the *Dunciad* had

[1] *SW*, II, 351.

[2] Grillparzer, *Sämtliche Werke*, ed. A. Sauer and R. Backmann (Wien, 1932), *Erste Abteilung*, X, 254.

[3] *SW*, I, 486.

thrown into blacker shadows the dulness of Cibber, Welsted and Ambrose Philips. How heavy even the Goethe–Schiller *Xenien* appear when compared with *Atta Troll*! How pedantic, how dead beside this work seems Platen's *Der romantische Oedipus*, or Prutz's *Die politische Wochenstube*, or any sustained attempt at literary satire in German before Karl Kraus! If Heine had never written anything except this 'dream of a summer night', he would still deserve to be remembered as one of the masters of his country's literature.

6. THE CALL OF THE AGE

O navis, referent in mare te novi
fluctus! O quid agis? Fortiter occupa
portum! HORACE

'IT is well known', wrote Robert Prutz in his *Literarhistorisches Taschenbuch* for 1843, 'that we Germans tend to regard poetry and politics as irreconcilable opposites, and that therefore political poetry is usually thought of as something which is either impossible and therefore does not exist, or else is unjustifiable and therefore should not exist.'[1] In this view, Prutz explains, two opposed parties concurred: a party which believed that only men actually engaged in the business of governing had any right to concern themselves with politics; and another which objected to political poetry on aesthetic grounds, believing that poetry was too exalted an art to concern itself with the political questions of the day. It was the government party which weakened first, encouraging and furthering political poetry if it seemed to champion a safe course. Patriotic songs and national anthems like 'Heil dir im Siegerkranz' prepared the way for a new attitude; Becker's *Rheinlied* and similar verse manifestoes received official encouragement, and gave the signal for a host of political poems by Dingelstedt, Herwegh, Hoffmann von Fallersleben and others

[1] *Op. cit.* (Leipzig, 1843), p. 251.

whose tenor was rather less 'loyal'. Since then, Prutz concluded, the German public relished political verse more wholeheartedly than any other.

Atta Troll was a manifesto against this new poetry of political commitment; and constantly, in the early 1840's, we find Heine insisting on 'freedom of art' and 'autonomy of the spirit'.[1] Yet it is clear that *Atta Troll* represents a step towards political poetry. Again and again satire on bad literature shows a tendency to slide towards satire on bad politics. Freiligrath's *Mohrenfürst* suggests to Heine the image of a German prince, Frederick William IV of Prussia, whose avidity for liquor and for fame is celebrated in a clever pun:

Aus den weißen Wolkenschleiern
Tritt der Mond, nicht Freiligräthisch
Pechschwarz wie ein Mohrenkönig
Sondern purpur, daß er aussieht

Wie'n germanisch christlich zahmer
Potentat, der *rhumestrunken* [*sic*]
Roten Angesichts hervortritt
Aus dem Herbstmanöverzelt[2] [my italics].

These stanzas did not survive the manuscript stage; but the rain-drenched hunter's parody of *Richard III*—

'Einen Regenschirm! Ich gebe
Sechsunddreißig Könige
Jetzt für einen Regenschirm!'
Rief ich, und das Wasser troff. (Caput XXI)

—had political overtones which could be heard even in the carefully muted version of the *Zeitung für die elegante Welt*:

Sechs und dreißig Kronen gäb ich
Jetzt für einen Regenschirm!

The author of *Ludwig Börne*, whom Arnold Ruge, Ferdinand Lassalle, Friedrich Engels and most other opponents of the

[1] *SW*, II, 352f.; *SW*, VI, 348f.

[2] MS. Düsseldorf. In contemporary cartoons Frederick William IV is constantly depicted with (or even *as*) a bottle of champagne.

established order in Germany regarded as an apostate from the cause of freedom, would soon be hailed as a powerful ally by the men of the extreme left.

> Wunderbare Nacht! Ich wage
> Kaum die Dinge zu erzählen
> Die ich sah. Das Publikum
> Glaubt am End ich sei ein Schwachkopf
>
> Wo nicht gar ein arger Schelm
> Der das Mittelalter aufwärmt
> Statt gesunde Wassersuppen
> Zeitgemäß dem Volk zu kochen!
>
> Sagen gar zuletzt, ich spiele
> Mit der Propaganda heimlich
> Unter einer Decke, fördernd
> Romas dumpfe Geisterherrschaft.
>
> Ach! Ich ward in jüngsten Tagen
> Öfters schon, mit barschen Lauten
> Angeschnauzt, ob retrograder
> Antiliberaler Richtung.[1]

This deleted passage from the 'Wilde Jagd' section of *Atta Troll* shows how much Heine was hurt by charges of apostasy —charges which were stilled, for a few years at least, by the appearance of his new volume of poetry in 1844.

Neue Gedichte, about which Heine had conducted negotiations with Campe since 1837, was intended to form a sequel to the *Buch der Lieder*. Like the earlier collection, *Neue Gedichte* was to offer a 'lyrical self-portrait': to exhibit, through careful arrangement of the poems it contained, the development of its author's mind and art since 1830. This new volume therefore opened with *Neuer Frühling*, an attempt—as we have seen—to recapture old modes and enchantments; and this was followed by *Verschiedene*, a new kind of love-poetry born of the experience of a metropolis and a shallow Saint-Simonist faith in the raptures of the flesh. Then came *Der Tannhäuser*, singing of a new kind of torturing obsession of the senses and ending with a glimpse of the politico-

[1] MS. Düsseldorf.

satirical turn Heine's lyric poetry was soon to take. The poems which immediately followed *Der Tannhäuser*, however, in this volume of 1844, suggest the poet's desire to reverse this trend and to keep his love-poetry divorced from a social and political satire whose 'natural' medium was prose. The *Schöpfungslieder* resolve themselves into a defence against charges of repetitiousness and self-parody; the poems of *Friedrike* (a cycle written in 1823!) belong to the world of the *Buch der Lieder*, and those of *Katharine* to the worlds of *Neuer Frühling* and *Verschiedene*; while *In der Fremde* and *Tragödie* exhibit that kind of limpid melancholy which had first endeared Heine's poetry to its more sentimental public.

Tragödie is followed, in *Neue Gedichte*, by the section of *Romanzen* that has already been analysed: a section which exhibits clearly the struggle between the old Heine and the new. Poems like *Childe Harold* or *Die Nixen* or *Frühling* might well have been written in Germany twenty years before; but *Ein Weib* is a poem of modern Paris, and so are *In der Frühe* and *Unterwelt*, while a simple comparison of *Anno 1839* with *In der Fremde* will show the extent to which the social and political commentator has already invaded the world of Heine's lyric poetry. It is quite natural, therefore, that in the 1844 edition of *Neue Gedichte* the *Romanzen* should be followed by two sections of political poetry proper—first by a section of *Zeitgedichte*, and then by the work which was to make the book such a *succès de scandale*: by *Deutschland. Ein Wintermärchen*.

The artificial division Heine had made between his verse and his prose had at last broken down. Henceforward the whole of him, *zoon politicon* as well as *zoon eroticon*, was to find expression in his lyric poetry.

Zeitgedichte—the very title is a programme. 'Die Zeit ist die Madonna der Poeten', Herwegh had said, and Gutzkow: 'Ich glaube an die Zeit.'[1] 'Zeit' meant the immediate present, the religious, social and political actuality of the day, which for the liberal writers of the 1830's and 1840's supplanted—as Fritz

[1] Quoted in: Fritz Strich, *Deutsche Klassik und Romantik* (München, 1922), p. 344.

Strich has shown—the timelessness of German classicism and the Romantic search for infinity.

Ich sang nach alter Sitt und Brauch
Von Mond und Sternen und Sonne,
Von Wein und Nachtigallen auch,
Von Liebeslust und Wonne.

Da rief zu mir das Vaterland:
Du sollst das Alte lassen,
Den alten verbrauchten Leiertand.
Du sollst die Zeit erfassen.[1]

The call that Hoffmann von Fallersleben has described in these lines was heard and answered by Heine too.

The first of these *Zeitgedichte* is a poem, written in 1844 and first published in Heinrich Börnstein's Paris journal *Vorwärts*, in which Heine seeks to revise an earlier and somewhat premature attempt to define his own place in the history of German liberalism. 'I do not know', he had written in the 1829 volume of *Reisebilder*,

> whether I deserve that my coffin should one day be adorned with a laurel-wreath. Poetry, however much I loved it, was never more to me than a sacred toy, a consecrated means to divine ends. I never attached great importance to my fame as a poet, and whether my songs are praised or blamed concerns me little. But a sword should be placed on my coffin; for I was ever a worthy soldier in the war of liberation of mankind.[2]

That description of himself is hardly just. All readers of Heine's letters know how much importance he did attach to his reputation as a poet; and most readers of his prose comments on social and political life will agree that he was more at home with a pin or a stiletto than with a sword. As for being a 'worthy soldier' (*ein braver Soldat*)—it is significant that Heine shows himself increasingly unable, after 1829, to use the adjective *brav* without parody and ridicule:

Wir sind Germanen, gemütlich und brav,
Wir schlafen gesunden Pflanzenschlaf....

(*Zur Beruhigung*)

[1] Quoted in: E. Ermatinger, *Deutsche Dichter, 1700–1900* (Bonn, 1949), II, 412.

[2] *SW*, III, 281.

The word constantly attracts to itself such rhymes as *Schlaf* and *Schaf*, with their associations of sleepy backwardness and docile stupidity. In *Doktrin*, the opening poem of *Zeitgedichte*, Heine finds a better image for himself; that of a disturber of sleep, one who rouses from sloth and calls to battle—a military drummer beating his drum.

Schlage die Trommel und fürchte dich nicht,
Und küsse die Marketenderin!
Das ist die ganze Wissenschaft,
Das ist der Bücher tiefster Sinn.

The amorous suggestions of the second line are well in character; they go some way towards explaining the presence, in this section of *Zeitgedichte*, of the poem *Geheimnis*, whose natural place would seem to be its original one in *Verschiedene*. The drummer is a reincarnation of Ali Bey; or more precisely perhaps, he is a reincarnation of the eponymous hero of *Das Buch LeGrand* whose image is revived in *Zeitgedichte*:

Wenn er mit Trommelwirbelschall
Einzog in Städten und Städtchen,
Da schlug das Herz im Widerhall
Den Weibern und den Mädchen.

Er kam und sah und siegte leicht
Wohl über alle Schönen;
Sein schwarzer Schnurrbart wurde feucht
Von deutschen Frauentränen.

Wir mußten es dulden! In jedem Land,
Wo die fremden Eroberer kamen,
Der Kaiser die Herren überwand,
Der Tambourmajor die Damen.

(*Der Tambourmajor*)

The subsequent fate of this Napoleonic drum-major, conquered by European reaction, poverty and old age, may well be felt to throw a shadow over the drummer of *Doktrin* who so boldly seeks to draw revolutionary consequences from Hegelian philosophy.

There are other poems of self-assertion and self-interpretation in *Zeitgedichte*: poems like *Wartet Nur!*, for instance, or *Adam der Erste*, in which Goethe's rebellious Prometheus merges with the Biblical Adam to defy tyrannical authority in whatever shape it comes—as Jove or Jehovah, as duodecimo king or university rector.

Du kannst nicht ändern, daß ich weiß
Wie sehr du klein und nichtig,
Und machst du dich auch noch so sehr
Durch Tod und Donnern wichtig.

O Gott! wie erbärmlich ist doch dies
Consilium abeundi!
Das nenne ich einen Magnificus
Der Welt, ein Lumen Mundi!

The scorn here lies not only in what the words say, but also in the superbly controlled rhythm—the second of the stanzas just quoted spits out its insults in an inimitable way. Yet it is not these poems of self-interpretation which linger most in the mind. The reader is much more likely to remember verses in which the poet assumes—with deadly effect—the very voice and accent of his victims or in which he pretends to a solidarity the reader knows he must not share. *Der Tambourmajor* feigns assent to the spirit of 1813:

Wir haben lange getragen das Leid,
Geduldig wie deutsche Eichen,
Bis endlich die hohe Obrigkeit
Uns gab das Befreiungszeichen.

Wie in der Kampfbahn der Auerochs
Erhuben wir unsere Hörner,
Entledigten uns des fränkischen Jochs
Und sangen die Lieder von Körner.

Entsetzliche Verse! Sie klangen ins Ohr
Gar schauderhaft den Tyrannen!
Der Kaiser und der Tambourmajor,
Sie flohen erschrocken von dannen.

Bei des Nachtwächters Ankunft in Paris speaks with the voice of Dingelstedt's 'Cosmopolitan Nightwatchman' (the natural antithesis of the drummer who rouses from sleep!) to expose a proud 'inwardness' which masks laziness and time-serving and servility. *Georg Herwegh* hilariously exposes the 'literary' and unpractical nature of German liberalism in Herwegh's lament—invented for him by Heine—of the ill-success of his famous interview with Frederick William IV of Prussia; while Frederick William himself, in his guise as the liquor-tippling Emperor of China, is made to reveal the fantasies on which his repressive rule was based.

Die große Pagode, Symbol und Hort
Des Glaubens, ist fertig geworden;
Die letzten Juden taufen sich dort
Und kriegen den Drachenorden.

Es schwindet der Geist der Revolution
Und es rufen die edelsten Mandschu:
Wir wollen keine Konstitution,
Wir wollen den Stock, den Kantschu!

(*Der Kaiser von China*)

The fun in this last poem lies in the recognition of German affairs under their Chinese disguise: in seeing China—'das Reich der Mitte'!—as Prussia, the 'great pagoda' as Cologne Cathedral, the 'order of the dragon' as the newly founded 'Schwanenorden', 'Konfusius' as Schelling, and so on. Its purpose, like that of so many others of Heine's political poems, is to destroy respect for authority and to discredit the sort of submissive quietism which is most successfully ridiculed in *Zur Beruhigung*. Here Frederick William's subjects complacently contrast themselves with the freedom-loving Romans of Brutus' day; and nothing that has ever been said about the 'paternalism' and submissive servility of Biedermeier Germany can equal Heine's witty and profound play, in *Zur Beruhigung*, on the words 'Vater', 'Vaterland' and 'Kinderstube'. This is worthy of taking its place with the 'surprising tropes, felicitously odd images and profoundly imaginative puns' that F. R. Leavis has analysed in the work of Alexander Pope.[1]

[1] F. R. Leavis, *The Common Pursuit* (London, 1952), p. 94.

In *Zur Beruhigung*, *Der Kaiser von China*, *Bei des Nachtwächters Ankunft in Paris*, *Georg Herwegh* and the rest Heine enriches German literature with the kind of satire which Friedrich Theodor Vischer had sadly missed in the poetry of Herwegh, Prutz and the other political poets of the 1840's—a satire free from hollow *Pathos* and rhetoric, free from humourless self-dramatisation, which was calculated to dissipate all fear of the enemy by holding him up to ridicule. This is the sort of satire, too, which the Hegelian Left—notably Arnold Ruge and the young Karl Marx—were ready to welcome. Ruge, in fact, tried in later years to claim credit for Heine's conversion to the cause of political verse satire. 'This turn', Ruge writes to a friend on 18 February 1870, 'he owed to Marx and myself. We said to him: "Stop this continual moaning about love and show the [political] poets how things should really be done: with a whip."'[1]

Ruge's statement, as has often been pointed out, is not quite accurate. Heine did not meet Marx until after his return from Germany in December 1843; and by then many of his most incisive political poems had already been written. Even the *Lobgesänge auf König Ludwig*, which appeared in the same issue of *Deutsch-Französische Jahrbücher* as Marx's *Kritik der Hegelschen Rechtsphilosophie* and which Heine himself called 'das Sanglanteste' among his satiric writings, were written before Heine had had any personal contact with the young Karl Marx. 'Marx's doctrine', William Rose rightly sums up, 'which was still in process of formulation, had no influence whatsoever on Heine's thought either then or later'; to which Ludwig Marcuse adds: 'If Marx did play a role in Heine's production of the year 1844, it was perhaps in the sense that he established contact between Heine and certain periodicals (*Deutsch-Französische Jahrbücher*, *Vorwärts*), in which the poet could write with a venom which would previously have consigned such poems to his desk drawer. Marx did not influence him with his temperament or his theory, but with his connections—and only in the

[1] *Gespräche*, p. 467 (October 1844).

intensity of his formulations.'[1] In the sole number of *Deutsch-Französische Jahrbücher* (1844) Heine published nothing but the *Lobgesänge auf König Ludwig*; *Vorwärts* printed Heine's most powerful protest against the oppression of the poor, *Die armen Weber*,[2] which soon found its way into Germany in clandestine leaflets, as well as *Der neue Alexander* and many of the poems of the *Zeitgedichte* section of *Neue Gedichte*; Püttmann's *Album* of 1847 brought a revised version of *Die armen Weber* and the *Pariser Horen* of the same year the scurrilous *Schloßlegende*. All these publications were closely associated with the extreme political Left, and in 1844 Friedrich Engels could report to *The New Moral World* with some appearance of justice: 'Henry Heine, the most eminent of all living German poets, has joined our ranks.'[3]

When Heine had been asked, some fifteen years earlier, whether he really esteemed Immermann as highly as he claimed, the poet had answered: 'It is so dreadful to be quite alone.'[4] Again and again he tried to escape his inevitable loneliness—and where in the thirties he had sought to ally himself with the Saint-Simonists in a common faith, he now sought to join Ruge and Marx in a common hatred. 'Dear friend', he writes to Heinrich Laube on 7 November 1842,

> we must not play at being Prussian doctrinaires, but must harmonise with the *Hallische Jahrbücher* and the *Rheinische Zeitung*, we must never conceal our political sympathies and social antipathies, we must call evil by its right name and must defend the good without considering what the world will say....

The *Hallische Jahrbücher* were then being edited by Arnold Ruge; the *Rheinische Zeitung* by Karl Marx. 'If we do not harmonise

[1] W. Rose, *Heinrich Heine. Two Studies of his Thought and Feeling* (Oxford, 1956), p. 71; and L. Marcuse, 'Heine und Marx', *Germanic Review*, XXX (1955), p. 118.

[2] This is the original title of the poem subsequently known as *Die schlesischen Weber* or simply *Die Weber*. An analysis of this poem is attempted in my book on *German Lyric Poetry* (London, 1952), pp. 143 f.

[3] Quoted Marcuse, 'Heine und Marx', p. 116.

[4] To Ludolf Wienbarg, *Gespräche*, p. 178 (1830).

with these', Heine concludes this passage of his letter to Laube, 'we will fare even worse than we do at the moment—fare badly we will in any case.'

This caustic conclusion suggests how uncomfortable Heine felt at any prospect of alliance with political radicalism. He was at one with the *Rheinische Zeitung* in hatred of Prussia; but he shrank far too much from contact with the 'great unwashed' to be more than temporarily attracted by 'radical democracy' or revolution from below. Of the horrors of such a revolution he spoke frequently and earnestly in his reports from Paris for the *Allgemeine Zeitung*. Recognising his kinship and community of interest with the poor and underprivileged, he yet disliked—as Caput XV of *Atta Troll* obliquely conveyed—personal contact with them. The shroud which his Weavers were justly preparing for Old Germany would envelop, he could not help feeling, all that he himself held dear.

This ambivalent attitude to the associates he wooed in the 1840's appears most clearly in a poem which Heine first wrote into Hans Christian Andersen's autograph album; which was then reprinted, inappropriately, in Kobbe's *Humoristische Blätter* (1 June 1843) and again in Laube's *Zeitung für die elegante Welt* (9 August 1843); and which at last found its way, virtually unchanged, into the *Zeitgedichte* section of *Neue Gedichte*.

The poem is entitled *Lebensfahrt* and uses a 'boat' image which Heine, like Goethe and Brentano before him, had found convenient on more than one occasion to depict the course of his life: in *Junge Leiden* (*Lieder* 7) in *Die Heimkehr* 16, in *Die Nordsee* I, 10, in *Verschiedene* (*Seraphine* 11) as well as, most recently, in Caput XIII of *Atta Troll*. *Lebensfahrt* begins gaily enough, with suggestions of laughter, singing, bright sunshine and gay companionship—but all this is soon shattered by a shipwreck that sends the mariner clambering, now friendless and alone, on a foreign shore. The line

Mich warf der Sturm an den *Seine*strand

leaves no doubt of the autobiographical background of this poem. When, therefore, a new voyage with new companions is announced in the third stanza, the reader cannot but think of the new associations Heine himself was even then forming: associations with radicals with whose views he felt he ought to harmonise and whose journals he was soon to use for his own more outspoken satires. What is so striking, however, about this second voyage is that it lacks all the exhilaration of the first. The voyager no longer joins in the laughter and singing of his fellow-mariners, but is conscious only of his strangeness, loneliness and heaviness of heart. The poem which had begun with evocations of bright sunlight and carefree fellowship therefore ends with a storm, with darkness and the melancholy of exile—ends, indeed, with the prospect of yet another and more disastrous shipwreck.

> Und das ist wieder ein Singen und Lachen —
> Es pfeift der Wind, die Planken krachen —
> Am Himmel erlischt der letzte Stern —
> Wie schwer mein Herz! Die Heimat wie fern!

Heine could join with the editors of the *Rheinische Zeitung* and later of the *Deutsch-Französische Jahrbücher* in attacking common enemies in Prussia and Bavaria; he could help them contrast German aspirations with German reality and make fun of outmoded political and social attitudes; he could write, in harmony with them, stirring poems like *Die armen Weber* which joined consciousness of wrongs suffered with threats of imminent revolt; but when he contemplated their actual aims and ideals, when he contemplated the age whose expression they were, his heart sank within him. 'A man is very little', he said of Marx in later years, after he had made his personal acquaintance, 'if he is nothing but a razor',[1] and in Lassalle, whom he had at first (in 1845) hailed as the 'Messiah of the century', he came to see 'one of the most terrible villains, capable of anything, murder, forgery and theft' (Letter to Gustav Heine, 21 January 1851).

Distrust of the new associations he was forming by the very act of writing political *Zeitgedichte* is undoubtedly responsible for some of the melancholy and anxiety which belie, in *Lebensfahrt*,

[1] Heine said this to Moritz Carrière in 1851 (*Gespräche*, p. 830).

the gay drumming of *Doktrin.* Such melancholy and anxiety are present, too, in the disturbing *Entartung*:

> Hat die Natur sich auch verschlechtert,
> Und nimmt sie Menschenfehler an?

The brisk rhythms and witty formulations of this poem throw into relief a fundamental misanthropy and despair. As always, when Heine talks about nature he means man—and his picture of man is darker, in this eighth of his *Zeitgedichte*, than it had ever been; it is nearly as dark as it was soon to show itself in the *Romanzero.*

> Die Wahrheit schwindet von der Erde,
> Auch mit der Treu ist es vorbei.
> Die Hunde wedeln noch und stinken
> Wie sonst, doch sind sie nicht mehr treu.

This too has its bearing on Heine's political satire. *Entartung* presents the picture of a society that has lost the feudal virtues without acquiring new ones: the society depicted by Balzac, with its motto *Enrichissez-vous.* There seems little prospect of improving a society so constituted (the cure advocated by the extreme Left seemed as bad as or worse than the disease); and Heine's satire is therefore gradually permeated by a misanthropy which is quite foreign to his admired model Aristophanes, but which is anything but foreign to the creator of the Struldbrugs and the Yahoos.

It would of course be absurd to resolve *Lebensfahrt* into an allegory of Heine's actual or projected political allegiances, though the position of this poem among the *Zeitgedichte* might tempt one to do so. It presents powerfully a feeling of *exile*, of sailing foreign seas while longing for home—and it is therefore clearly linked with *Nachtgedanken*, the moving poem which ends *Zeitgedichte* and which now concludes *Neue Gedichte* as a whole. *Nachtgedanken* expresses longings not so much for Germany itself—as *In der Fremde* and *Anno 1839* had both done in their different ways—as for the dear ones left behind there. It uses deliberately the vocabulary and imagery of the *Buch der Lieder*:

> Ich kann nicht mehr die Augen schließen,
> Und *meine heißen Tränen fließen*,

Zwölf Jahre sind schon hingegangen;
Es wächst *mein Sehnen und Verlangen.*
Mein Sehnen und Verlangen wächst . . . [my italics];

and it culminates in a dream-picture. Longing turns to nightmare as the dreamer passes in review those who have died in his absence:

Seit ich das Land verlassen hab,
So viele sanken dort ins Grab,
Die ich geliebt — wenn ich sie zähle,
So will verbluten meine Seele.

Und zählen muß ich — mit der Zahl
Schwillt immer höher meine Qual,
Mir ist, als wälzten sich die Leichen
Auf meine Brust . . . .

This is a *Traumbild* more horrible because less meretricious than any in *Junge Leiden*; a nightmare made actual by obsessive repetition and the meaningful *enjambement* of the last-quoted lines, which seem to re-enact the 'wälzen' of which they speak. The dream, it is true, is dispelled by the morning light and its human embodiment:

Gottlob! durch meine Fenster bricht
Französisch heitres Tageslicht;
Es kommt mein Weib, schön wie der Morgen,
Und lächelt fort die deutschen Sorgen.

Yet memories of the dream and of the longing that preceded it linger on; and poem and section end with the words 'die deutschen Sorgen', which form a natural bridge between *Zeitgedichte* and the poem which followed them in the *Neue Gedichte* of 1844. They lead into *Deutschland. Ein Wintermärchen.*

7. GERMANY REVISITED

Die wahrhafte Widerlegung muß in die Kraft des Gegners eingehen, und sich in den Umkreis seiner Stärke stellen: ihn außerhalb seiner selbst angreifen und da Recht zu behalten, fördert die Sache nicht. HEGEL

I

In October 1843, after an absence of over twelve years, Heine revisited Germany. He was impelled to do so by a variety of motives: by longings to see his family again; by the wish to conduct negotiations with Campe face to face; and, last but by no means least, by the urgent need to refresh his memory of German conditions and to regain lost strength through contact with his native land. In a poem which was originally intended to form an introduction to *Deutschland. Ein Wintermärchen* but which Heine later deleted—feeling that its place had been adequately taken by *Nachtgedanken*—he speaks of this need in his own ambivalent way.

Ade, du heitres Franzosenvolk,
Ihr meine lustigen Brüder,
Gar närrische Sehnsucht treibt mich fort,
Doch komm ich in Kurzem wieder.

Denkt euch, mit Schmerzen sehne ich mich
Nach Torfgeruch, nach den lieben
Heidschnucken der Lüneburger Heid,
Nach Sauerkraut und Rüben.

Ich sehne mich nach Tabaksqualm,
Hofräten und Nachtwächtern,
Nach Plattdeutsch, Schwarzbrot, Grobheit sogar,
Nach blonden Predigerstöchtern.

Auch nach der Mutter sehne ich mich,
Ich will es offen gestehen,
Seit dreizehn Jahren hab ich nicht
Die alte Frau gesehen.

Ade, mein Weib, mein schönes Weib,
Du kannst meine Qual nicht fassen,
Ich drücke dich so fest an mein Herz,
Und muß dich doch verlassen.

Die lechzende Qual, sie treibt mich fort
Von meinem süßesten Glücke —
Muß wieder atmen deutsche Luft,
Damit ich nicht ersticke. (*Abschied von Paris*)[1]

German air at once stimulated the poet in Heine; soon after his return in December 1843, he reported to Campe: 'I have written many verses in the course of my journey, which come with greater ease when I breathe German air' (Letter of 29 December 1843). The verses here referred to became part of the new series of 'versified travel-pictures' on which Heine began to work immediately after his return to Paris: a cycle of satires on German themes, held together by a fictitious itinerary, which the poet entitled *Deutschland. Ein Wintermärchen.* This was completed in April 1844; and in July 1844 Heine returned once more to Germany to see through the press the volume which contained *Neue Gedichte* and the *Wintermärchen.* Later in the same year a slightly toned-down version of the *Wintermärchen* was published as a separate book, with a preface in which Heine passionately defended himself against charges of immorality and lack of patriotism.

What I foresee with even greater apprehension is the outcry of those Pharisees of nationalism who now share the antipathies of the government, enjoy the affection and high esteem of the censorship, and are able to set the tone in the daily press, where it is possible for them to attack their opponents who are at the same time opponents of their lords and masters. Our hearts are fortified against the displeasure of these heroic lackeys in their black, red and gold liveries. I can already hear their beery voices: 'You even blaspheme our colours, you contemner of the fatherland and friend of the French, to whom you would yield our free Rhine!' Calm yourself. I will regard and respect your colours when they deserve it, when they are no longer merely an idle or servile pastime. Plant the black, red and gold banner on the heights

[1] *SW*, II, 540–1.

of German thought. Make it the standard of free humanity and I will offer up my best heart's blood for it.... The people of Alsace-Lorraine will once more attach themselves to Germany if we complete what the French have begun, if we outstrip them in action as we already have in thought, if we soar up to the ultimate consequences of this thought, if we destroy servitude everywhere, even in its last place of refuge, in heaven, if we redeem the God who dwells on earth within man, if we become God's redeemers, if we restore to pristine dignity the poor people that has been deprived of its heritage of happiness, and genius that has been derided and beauty that has been outraged; as our great masters have said and sung and as we, their disciples, wish it.—Yes, then not merely Alsace and Lorraine, but the whole of Germany will become ours, the whole of Europe, the whole world—the whole world will become German. Of this mission and universal sovereignty of Germany I often dream when walking under oak-trees. That is *my* patriotism.[1]

That such a book, and such a preface, could pass the censorship at all is proof of the amazing loopholes in Metternich's net and the diplomatic skill of Heine's publisher Campe, who delighted in outwitting authority. He submitted the *Wintermärchen* to the Hamburg censor at a moment when there was some disagreement between the censorship offices of Hamburg and Berlin; at a moment when Hamburg was not unwilling to allow satire on Prussian conditions to slip by. And once a book was printed and distributed, no amount of confiscation and chicanery could keep it out of the hands of those who wanted to read it. This state of affairs had been pointed out by Herwegh in the letter to Frederick William IV which so offended the king:

Forbidden books fly through the air and what the people wants to read it will read despite all government decrees. Your Majesty's ministers forbade my poems fifteen months ago, and I am now in the happy position of seeing a fifth edition of them through the press. Your Majesty's ministers have ordered the confiscation of books that appeared dangerous, and on my journey through Germany I have been able to see for myself that they are in everyone's hands.[2]

[1] *SW*, II, 429–30.

[2] Georg Herwegh, *Briefwechsel mit seiner Braut*, ed. M. Herwegh (1906), p. 267.

'Even censorship', Herwegh concludes in this same letter of December 1842, 'has ceased to be a reality; as is proved by daily confiscation of books that have already passed the censor.' The history of Heine's *Wintermärchen* fully bears out what Herwegh here told the Prussian king.

This is not to say, of course, that censorship and confiscations were not deterrents for authors and publishers alike; for they could have crippling effects on the official distribution of books and on the profits to be derived from them. Heine always tried, therefore, to 'censor' his works in his head: to put his satiric observations in such a way that they could *just* slip by a benevolent or inattentive or—more usually—imperceptive censor. Again and again his manuscripts will show versions very much stronger than those he ultimately chose to print. Ernst August of Hanover, for instance, was originally to have been described, in Caput XIX of *Wintermärchen*, as an

Englischer Tory, jagdjunkerlich stolz,
Ein hagerer Volksverächter.[1]

But this direct description would never have been passed: and Heine therefore found himself forced into irony. An official guide who conducts the traveller through the town of Hanover speaks of his sovereign with respect:

Hier wohnt
Der Ernst Augustus, ein alter,
Hochtoryscher Lord, ein Edelmann,
Sehr rüstig für sein Alter;

yet in the description of the king and his activities that follows the reader can perceive a figure that deserves little respect. In this particular case, Heine's self-censorship did not do him much good: the Hamburg censor deleted most of Caput XIX even in its mild later form—but in most cases ironic statements stood a better chance of being passed than direct ones. As Heine himself had said in *Die romantische Schule*:

Writers who pine under censorship and spiritual oppression of every kind and yet cannot suppress the truth they feel in their hearts are par-

[1] *SW*, II, 545.

ticularly dependent on irony and humour. It is the only expedient left to their honesty....[1]

Official censorship actually *benefited* Heine's satire by transforming direct abuse into ironic presentation.

Even after all the toning-down, all the transformation and excision dictated by self-censorship, by Campe's wishes and by the 'higher criticism' of the Hamburg censor, *Deutschland. Ein Wintermärchen* remains Heine's most controversial work. To Prussian apologists, German nationalists and conservatives of all shades it proved, of course, a red rag from the first; but even such liberal admirers of Heine as Strodtmann, Karpeles, Elster and Wolff seem embarrassed by it and inclined to explain it away. Its most unequivocal and whole-hearted admirers have always been Social Democrats and Communists, from Marx himself, August Bebel and Franz Mehring to Georg Lukács and Hans Kaufmann in our own day. In East Germany, it has even become prescribed reading in schools, where it is enlisted in a cause that Heine regarded with a dropping rather than an auspicious eye. The poet himself would no doubt have been amused by this development, and would have speculated what these school-children made of the final 'Hammonia' sections of his work; but he would have been flattered too. For with *Deutschland. Ein Wintermärchen* he hoped to affect the political scene; he hoped, by ridiculing Prussia and all it stood for, to undermine the hegemony which that vigorous state was even then assuming in Germany. In *Deutschland. Ein Wintermärchen* he abandoned most decisively that doctrine of art for art's sake which he had lately preached to Gutzkow:

My motto is always: art is the purpose of art, as love is the purpose of love and life the purpose of life. (Letter of 23 August 1838)

Here he made no distinction between the poet, the critic of society and—*horribile dictu*!—the political journalist. Here he ranged himself more unequivocally than ever before on the side of the political Left.

[1] *SW*, v, 290.

II

The framework of the poem, not surprisingly, is a journey. As in the *Reisebilder* of Heine's earlier years, as in Anastasius Grün's *Spaziergänge eines Wiener Poeten* and Dingelstedt's *Nachtwächters Weltgang*, a peregrinatory hero looks about him and comments satirically on German conditions and personalities. The traveller of *Deutschland. Ein Wintermärchen* is clearly related to the hunter of *Atta Troll*: here as there Heine presents us with the vigorous, optimistic *persona* he found so useful for his satiric works and so difficult to sustain in real life. But as in the central sections of *Atta Troll*, so in certain sections of the *Wintermärchen* Heine allows us a glimpse behind the façade—allows us to guess at conflicts and troubles of the mind that are not immediately related to the satiric purpose and may even conflict with it. It is such elements as these which make the poem a more complex organism than most of its admirers and detractors realise and give it a life and truth that transcend its avowed political purpose.

The opening section establishes at once a vigorous and confident tone. Crossing the frontier from France into Germany, the traveller hears a little girl singing of renunciation of earthly and expectation of heavenly joys—a romantic figure which serves as a 'title-page' of Germany much as the beggar on the Pont d'Espagne had served, in Caput XI of *Atta Troll*, as the frontispiece of Spain. The romantic appeal of this song of renunciation, conveyed by the very music of Heine's verse, is soon deflated by a sly reference to the disproportion between character and talent—

> Sie sang mit wahrem Gefühle
> Und falscher Stimme

—and to the reactionary purposes for which such sentiments have been exploited. To this lullaby composed by those who preach water and drink wine the traveller then opposes his new and better song.

> Ein neues Lied, ein besseres Lied,
> O Freunde, will ich euch dichten!
> Wir wollen hier auf Erden schon
> Das Himmelreich errichten.

Wir wollen auf Erden glücklich sein,
Und wollen nicht mehr darben;
Verschlemmen soll nicht der faule Bauch
Was fleißige Hände erwarben.

Es wächst hienieden Brot genug
Für alle Menschenkinder,
Auch Rosen und Myrten, Schönheit und Lust,
Und Zuckererbsen nicht minder.

Ja, Zuckererbsen für jedermann,
Sobald die Schoten platzen!
Den Himmel überlassen wir
Den Engeln und den Spatzen.

These are famous lines which have been quoted by socialist and communist orators on many occasions—most memorably by August Bebel in a speech to the Reichstag in which he outlined the programme and presented the demands of German Social Democracy. It is lines like these which caused the *Spartakusbund* to issue the works of Heine in 1918 with the accompanying declaration:

Members of the Revolution of 1918! Take this and read! Here you will find words so brilliant and so fresh that they might have been written yesterday—or even today in our own times of rebellion.[1]

In these lines from Caput I of *Deutschland. Ein Wintermärchen* we see the traveller, and Heine himself, abandoning his isolation and attempting to range himself with an oppositional group, the 'friends' that are being addressed:

Ein neues Lied, ein besseres Lied,
O Freunde, will *ich euch* dichten!
Wir wollen....

Here, as Hans Kaufmann has pointed out,[2] we can see the transition actually taking place, can see the traveller seeking to identify himself with the group he harangues. Tersely and brilliantly,

[1] Quoted Marcuse, 'Heine und Marx', p. 113.

[2] Hans Kaufmann, *Politisches Gedicht und klassische Dichtung* (Berlin, 1958), p. 132. Cf. my review of this work in *German Life and Letters*, N.S. XII (1958/9), p. 76.

Heine here conveys hatred of injustice, and irreverence in face of authority human or divine; but he does so without abandoning one jot of his hedonism. Who but Heine would have thought of offering the underprivileged not only bread but 'Zuckererbsen'?

Auch Rosen und Myrten, Schönheit und Lust...[1]

—it is as though Karl Marx and Oscar Wilde had combined to produce a programme of social reform.

'Programme' is not, perhaps, the right word here. These lines —and *Deutschland. Ein Wintermärchen* as a whole—do not propound a political or social *programme*, nor (in spite of clear echoes of Saint-Simonist slogans) liberal or socialistic *ideas*. Their strength lies rather in their forcible expression of *sentiments* or *attitudes of mind* behind many such programmes and many such ideas in the nineteenth century. It is this which gave them their power at the time and has enabled them to be relished today when more overtly programmatic poetry has been rightly forgotten; and it is this also which has made them liable to be impressed into causes they were never intended to serve.

The unbiased reader, however impressed by the concreteness and terseness and wit of Heine's lines, will not be able to stifle certain doubts. He will admire the way in which Heine, by using Livy's image of the body politic and the interdependence of its members, removes all abstraction from his enunciation of the principle of social justice:

Verschlemmen soll nicht der faule Bauch,
Was fleißige Hände erwarben.

But—he will ask—does not this image invalidate the very principle it is meant to announce? Has not the 'lazy belly' a perfect answer to the charge?

Note me this, good friend;
Your most grave belly was deliberate,

[1] Cf. *SW*, IV, 223: 'We do not wish to be *sansculottes*, frugal citizens or cheap presidents....You demand simple costumes, austere manners and unseasoned pleasures; we, on the contrary, demand nectar and ambrosia, purple garments, costly perfumes, luxury and splendour, dances of laughing nymphs, music and comedies.'

Not rash like his accusers, and thus answered:
'True is it, my incorporate friends', quoth he,
'That I receive the general food at first,
Which you do live upon; and fit it is,
Because I am the storehouse and the shop
Of the whole body: but, if you do remember,
I send it through the rivers of your blood,
Even to the court, the heart,—to the seat o' the brain;
And, through the cranks and offices of man,
The strongest nerves and small inferior veins
From me receive the natural competency
Whereby they live: and though that all at once,
You, my good friends'—this says the belly, mark me,—
'Though all at once can not
See what I do deliver out to each,
Yet can I make my audit up, that all
From me do back receive the flour of all,
And leave me but the bran.'

(Shakespeare, *Coriolanus*, I, i)

In Heine's context, unlike that of Livy and Shakespeare, the image will not work. The correspondence of the body politic and the human body could be exploited only by generations with a firm and settled world-order—it embodies a conservative and aristocratic principle that goes counter to all the beliefs Heine's *Wintermärchen* sought, on the surface, to implant in its readers. Yet the use of this image in such a context is significant: for it illuminates the dilemma of a poet whose sense of justice was outraged by social and political privilege and who was yet, by temperament, an aristocrat rather than an egalitarian and a hedonist rather than a reformer.

Heine himself was almost certainly unconscious of the conflict between the symbolism of Caput I and the meaning it was intended to convey; but in a later section he shows himself fully aware of another clash of the same kind. In Caput XIV the traveller passes through a dreary tract of country between Paderborn and Minden and instead of looking outwards he listens to voices in his own heart and mind. Childhood reminiscences crowd in on him, folk-songs and folk-tales he heard from his old nurse: a ballad of a girl murdered in a forest, whose death was discovered and betrayed by the sun; the story of the princess degraded into a goose-girl, familiar from Grimm; and last but not least, the tale of Barbarossa waiting in his mountain-hall to reassume his empire. All these stories are made to serve a liberal, anti-feudal *Tendenz*: Barbarossa will return to avenge the German people on its privileged oppressors.

> Der Kaiser hält ein strenges Gericht,
> Er will die Mörder bestrafen —
>
> Die Mörder, die gemeuchelt einst
> Die teure, wundersame
> Goldlockigte Jungfrau Germania —
> Sonne, du klagende Flamme!
>
> Wohl mancher, der sich geborgen geglaubt,
> Und lachend auf seinem Schloß saß,
> Er wird nicht entgehen dem rächenden Strang,
> Dem Zorne Barbarossas! —
>
> Wie klingen sie lieblich, wie klingen sie süß,
> Die Märchen der alten Amme!
> Mein abergläubisches Herze jauchzt:
> Sonne, du klagende Flamme!

The word 'abergläubisch' prepares already for the change that is to come in the next section. Caput XIV had interpreted the Barbarossa story in the same way as the French version of *Elementargeister*—as a symbol of a coming revolution of the people against their oppressors:

> Peut-être le dieu de la révolution ne peut-il remuer par la raison le peuple allemand, peut-être est-ce la tâche de la folie d'accomplir ce difficile ouvrage? Quand le sang lui montera une fois, en bouillonnant, à la tête, quand il sentira de nouveau battre son cœur, le peuple n'écoutera plus le pieux ramage des cafards bavarois, ni le murmure mystique des radoteurs souabes; son oreille ne pourra plus entendre que la grande voix de l'homme.
>
> Quel est cet homme?
>
> C'est l'homme qu'attend le peuple allemand, l'homme qui lui rendra enfin la vie et le bonheur, le bonheur et la vie après lesquels il a si longtemps aspiré dans ses songes. Combien tardes-tu, toi que les

vieillards ont annoncé avec un si brûlant désir, toi que la jeunesse attend avec tant d'impatience, toi qui portes le sceptre divinatoire de la liberté, et la couronne impériale sans croix?[1]

But Barbarossa—so Caput xv of the *Wintermärchen* would seem to suggest—is hardly the right symbol for such revolutionary desires. How can *his* sceptre be that of liberty, *his* crown be a crown without a cross? Does he not belong to the very feudalism which is oppressing Germany, is he not an embodiment of those Christian Middle Ages that Novalis had exalted in *Die Christenheit oder Europa*? The Barbarossa symbol might suit the old 'Burschenschaftler' Ernst Moritz Arndt:

Kaiserschein, du höchster Schein,
Bleibst du denn im Staub begraben?
Schrein umsonst Prophetenraben
Um den Barbarossastein?

Nein! Und nein! Und aber nein!
Nein! Kyffhäusers Fels wird springen,
Durch die Lande wird es klingen:
Frankfurt holt den Kaiser ein;[2]

(E. M. Arndt, *Die Ausfahrt zur Heimholung des deutschen Kaisers, 17. Mai 1849*)

it suited even better the conservative and religious Emanuel Geibel:

Laut in seinen Angeln dröhnend
Springet auf das ehrne Tor;
Barbarossa mit den Seinen
Steigt im Waffenschmuck empor.

Auf dem Helm trägt er die Krone
Und den Sieg in seiner Hand;
Schwerter blitzen, Harfen klingen,
Wo er schreitet durch das Land.

Und dem alten Kaiser beugen
Sich die Völker allzugleich,
Und aufs neu zu Aachen gründet
Er das heilge deutsche Reich,[3]

(Geibel, *Friedrich Rotbart*)

[1] *SW*, v, 617.

[2] Quoted by Benno v. Wiese in *Politische Dichtung Deutschlands* (1931), p. 69.

[3] *Gedichte von Emanuel Geibel* (Berlin, 1851), p. 166.

—for Heine it smacked too much of the idyllic feudalism whose end he proclaimed in his *Wintermärchen*. Barbarossa therefore turns, in Caput XV, into a Philistine antiquarian, into a champion of the divine right of kings, into a tattered spectre whose reappearance would make the new Germany the laughing-stock of Europe:

Die Republikaner lachen uns aus,
Sehn sie an unserer Spitze
So ein Gespenst mit Zepter und Kron;
Sie rissen schlechte Witze.

Auch deine Fahne gefällt mir nicht mehr,
Die altdeutschen Narren verdarben
Mir schon in der Burschenschaft die Lust
An den schwarz-rot-goldnen Farben.

Das Beste wäre, du bliebest zu Haus,
Hier in dem alten Kyffhäuser —
Bedenk ich die Sache ganz genau,
So brauchen wir gar keinen Kaiser. (Caput XVI)

A song of Barbarossa, Heine realised, would have sounded well in the mouth of the *Harfenmädchen* of Caput I; it was a romantic dream inappropriate to a traveller who bore with him 'the crown jewels of the future'.

But however equivocal the Barbarossa figure might be; however much longing for Barbarossa's return might smack of the Romantic desire to remodel the future in the image of the past—there is no doubt in the traveller's mind that the *genuine* past, the genuine Middle Ages with all their oppression and class-distinction, was preferable to the *parody* of that past in which Frederick William IV was then indulging. Caput XVII therefore ends with a renewed appeal to Barbarossa:

Das alte heilige römische Reich,
Stell's wieder her, das ganze,
Gib uns den modrigsten Plunder zurück
Mit allem Firlefanze.

Das Mittelalter, immerhin,
Das wahre, wie es gewesen,
Ich will es ertragen — erlöse uns nur
Von jenem Zwitterwesen,

Von jenem Kamaschenrittertum,
Das ekelhaft ein Gemisch ist
Von gotischem Wahn und modernem Lug,
Das weder Fleisch noch Fisch ist.

Jag fort das Komödiantenpack,
Und schließe die Schauspielhäuser,
Wo man die Vorzeit parodiert —
Komme du bald, O Kaiser!

The genuinely talented Frederick William IV, in whom dreams of the divine right and the divine inspiration of kings mingled with progressive thoughts, who maintained the military traditions of his house while being himself weak, pensive, totally unmilitary, who spoke with feeling of liberty while prosecuting those who took him at his word—he, it seemed to Heine, had no style, no stature, no greatness of any kind. A *gemütlich* tyrant, a kindly obscurantist with dreams of progress, he was the ideal representative of the Germany which had been mocked in the comic fantasies of Caput XI: a Germany whose Horace was Ferdinand Freiligrath, whose Cicero was the coarse and ugly Massmann, and whose Nero was—a triple dozen of *Landesväter*.

Wir hätten einen Nero jetzt
Statt Landesväter drei Dutzend.
Wir schnitten uns die Adern auf,
Den Schergen der Knechtschaft trutzend.

In this lament of the passing of greatness, of genuineness, of *style* Heine has more affinities with Nietzsche—the Nietzsche of *Unzeitgemäße Betrachtungen* and *Jenseits von Gut und Böse*—than with the republicans he had evoked at the end of Caput XIV.

III

Deutschland. Ein Wintermärchen is Heine's wittiest poem. It is full of the most telling jokes. In Caput II, for instance, a simple patriot is made to link the *Zollverein* with the censorship as the supreme unifying forces of Germany:

'Der Zollverein' — bemerkte er —
Wird unser Volkstum begründen,
Er wird das zersplitterte Vaterland
Zu einem Ganzen verbinden.

Er gibt die äußere Einheit uns,
Die sogenannte materielle;
Die geistige Einheit gibt die Zensur,
Die wahrhaft ideelle —

Sie gibt die innere Einheit uns,
Die Einheit im Denken und Sinnen;
Ein einiges Deutschland tut uns not,
Einig nach außen und innen.'

The argument has a mock-logic that is irresistible, and through its surprising juxtaposition of customs union and censorship it invalidates—as Heine liked to do—the fine slogan of the final lines. The tone, too, is just right: we can almost see the patriot's uplifted forefinger in the line: 'Die sogenannte materielle.' Heine is happiest when he can ridicule Prussia and Prussianism, which repelled and amused him as they repel and amuse so many Rhinelanders. Caput III is full of deflating comments on Prussian militarism, of which contemporaries relished particularly the stanza that comments on the recent abolition of the pigtail in the Prussian army:

Der lange Schnurrbart ist eigentlich nur
Des Zopftums neuere Phase:
Der Zopf, der ehmals hinten hing,
Der hängt jetzt unter der Nase.

And then, of course, there is the irreverent Caput XI, which details what would have happened if Arminius had lost the battle of the Teutoburg forest and the Germans had become Roman: a mock-lament which enables Heine to contrast the *style* of Roman tyranny with that of the German princes and to introduce a whole gallery of his favourite butts: the Swabian poets, Freiligrath, Massmann,

Schelling, Charlotte Birch-Pfeiffer. Caput XI contains the feeling lines:

> Die Wahrheitsfreunde würden jetzt
> Mit Löwen, Hyänen, Schakalen
> Sich raufen in der Arena, anstatt
> Mit Hunden in kleinen Journalen.

It is the verse form which gives such jokes their thrust, their ultimate point. In the stanza just quoted Heine controls his rhythms towards his anticlimax with superb accuracy—he could not have hoped to achieve in prose anything like the effect he gains here by the pause before the word 'anstatt', followed by the sudden flow of the final *enjambement*. Not only rhythm but rhyme too becomes a component of Heine's wit. The association of 'Schakalen' and 'Journalen' startles into laughter as surely as the absurd combinations used elsewhere in this poem: 'Rheinfluß'–'Einfluß', 'Strohwisch'–'Philosophisch', 'Punsch ein'–'Mondschein', 'Mittag'–'Respittag' and (most notorious of all, though Heine did not invent this rhyme) 'Romantik'–'Uhland Tieck'.

Compared with the unrhymed trochees of *Atta Troll*, the rhymed folk-song stanza Heine has chosen to employ for *Deutschland. Ein Wintermärchen* is taut and terse. Within it, the poet achieves epigrammatic effects that are utterly foreign to folk-song; effects which give many of the stanzas an elegance and a point that makes them resemble—as nearly as any German verse ever could resemble—the satires of seventeenth-century France and eighteenth-century England. It is Heine the Parisian who characterises the boredom of a sleepy German city in Caput III:

> Zu Aachen langweilen sich auf der Straß
> Die Hunde, sie flehn untertänig:
> Gib uns einen Fußtritt, O Fremdling, das wird
> Vielleicht uns zerstreuen ein wenig;

or who, in the ambivalent Caput IX, comments on German food and German people at once:

> Es stand auf dem Tische eine Gans,
> Ein stilles, gemütliches Wesen.
> Sie hat vielleicht mich einst geliebt,
> Als wir beide noch jung gewesen.

Sie blickte mich an so bedeutungsvoll,
So innig, so treu, so wehe!
Besaß eine schöne Seele gewiß,
Doch war das Fleisch sehr zähe.

Auch einen Schweinskopf trug man auf
In einer zinnernen Schüssel;
Noch immer schmückt man den Schweinen bei uns
Mit Lorbeerblättern den Rüssel.

That has a sophistication which stands in most piquant contrast to the popular folk-song stanza—the rhymed *Vagantenpaar*—in which *Deutschland. Ein Wintermärchen* is written.

Nevertheless there is some truth in Treitschke's complaint that this poem seems to be the work of a carnival-fool or a street-urchin. A few comparisons will help to establish this. Here is a passage from Robert Prutz's *Die politische Wochenstube*, in which a doctor, refusing to give a donation for a monument to Arminius, comments on the new Prussian helmet, the pointed *Pickelhaube*:

Auch nicht den Nachttopf, diesen selbst am wenigsten!
Denn in der Nähe bleiben muß mir der,
Weil ich mitunter etwas lesen muß von Mundt —
Ja, lieber setzt' ich einen Knopf mir unten dran
Und trüg als Helm ihn, nach dem preußischen Staatsmodell,
Dem bronceprahlerischkindischmittelaltrigen![1]

And here, by contrast, is the traveller of Heine's *Wintermärchen* on the same subject:

Das ist so rittertümlich und mahnt
An der Vorzeit holde Romantik,
An die Burgfrau Johanna von Montfaucon,
An den Freiherrn Fouqué, Uhland, Tieck.

Das mahnt an das Mittelalter so schön,
An Edelknechte und Knappen,
Die in dem Herzen getragen die Treu
Und auf dem Hintern ein Wappen.... (Caput III)

Hoffmann von Fallersleben, in *Rheinlied und Rheinleid*, contrasts the sentiments of Becker's *Rheinlied* with the actions of the Hes-

[1] *Die politische Wochenstube* (Zürich and Winterthur, 1845), pp. 26–7.

sians in damming up the course of the Rhine at Bibrich in order to impede the development of that port at the expense of Mainz:

Du magst nun ruhen, gehen, traben,
Du hörst in tausend Melodei'n:
'Sie sollen, sollen ihn nicht haben'
Von Tilsit bis nach Wesel schrei'n.

Ganz Deutschland singt — und unterdessen:
'Der liebe, freie deutsche Rhein!'
Da schmeißen unsre blinden Hessen
Ihm Quaderstein' ins Bett hinein![1]

In *Deutschland, ein Wintermärchen* the Rhine is himself introduced and made to speak of this same incident:

Zu Biberich hab ich Steine verschluckt,
Wahrhaftig, sie schmeckten nicht lecker!
Doch schwerer liegen im Magen mir
Die Verse von Niklas Becker. (Caput v)

Here is Georg Herwegh, in *Quid Novi ex Africa*, asking ironic questions about conditions in contemporary Prussia:

Seit sich der Fürsten Romantiker jüngst mit dem Fürst der Romantik
Enge verbunden, wie ist's um das Theater bestellt?
Liest er noch immer so hübsch, der Tieck? Was machen die Alten?
Welche Komödie wird eben bei Hofe studiert?[2]

Caput XXVII of Heine's *Wintermärchen* also comments on the Prussian king's passion for the theatre, especially for Aristophanes' *Frogs* which Tieck produced for him in Berlin:

Der König liebt das Stück. Das zeugt
Von gutem antikem Geschmacke;
Den Alten amüsierte weit mehr
Modernes Froschgequacke.

Der König liebt das Stück. Jedoch
Wär noch der Autor am Leben,
Ich riete ihm nicht sich in Person
Nach Preußen zu begeben.

[1] *Unpolitische Lieder von Hoffmann von Fallersleben* (Hamburg, 1840), p. 40.
[2] *Herweghs Werke*, ed. H. Tardel (Goldene Klassiker Bibliothek), I, 144.

Dem wirklichen Aristophanes,
Dem ginge es schlecht, dem Armen;
Wir würden ihn bald begleitet sehn
Mit Chören von Gendarmen.

And as a last contrast, here is Ferdinand Freiligrath, after his day of Damascus, ridiculing the contradiction in the policy of Frederick William IV by referring to the Prussian king's early education at the hands of the theologian Ancillon, author of a two-volume work entitled *Zur Vermittlung der Extreme in den Meinungen* (1828–31):

Der Schüler Ancillons

Im Jahre Vierzig stellt' ich auf den Satz;
Jetzt geb' ich euch den Gegensatz!
Und dabei bleibt's, trotz Murren und trotz Rütteln:—
Sucht die Extreme zu vermitteln![1]

Heine, in a poem which belongs, in metre and in spirit, to *Deutschland. Ein Wintermärchen*, also makes the Prussian king refer to the mentor of his earlier years:

Mein Lehrer, mein Aristoteles,
Der war zuerst ein Pfäffchen
Von der französischen Kolonie,
Und trug ein weißes Bäffchen.

Er hat nachher, als Philosoph
Vermittelt die Extreme,
Und leider Gottes hat er mich
Erzogen nach seinem Systeme.

Ich ward ein Zwitter, ein Mittelding,
Das weder Fleisch noch Fisch ist,
Das von den Extremen unsrer Zeit
Ein närrisches Gemisch ist.

Ich bin nicht schlecht, ich bin nicht gut,
Nicht dumm und nicht gescheute,
Und wenn ich gestern vorwärts ging,
So geh ich rückwärts heute;

[1] *Freiligraths Werke*, ed. cit. I, 342.

Ein aufgeklärter Obskurant,
Und weder Hengst noch Stute!
Ja, ich begeistre mich zugleich
Für Sophokles und die Knute....

(*Der neue Alexander*)

In every case, Heine's poem has a vigour and incisiveness which is lacking in the satire of his contemporaries and which is connected with his use of the rhythms and vocabulary of popular speech. In fact, the nearest counterpart to the tone of *Deutschland. Ein Wintermärchen* will be found in the popular songs and pamphlets that circulated at the time of the 1848 revolution—songs like *Uf die neue Mode* which describes recent events in Berlin:

Dortens lebt ein jroßer König,
Der bis jetzt in Taten wenig
Für sein Volk hervorjebracht,
Doch viel Worte hat jemacht
Uf die neue Mode.

Als das Volk von ihm bejehret,
Daß er nun nicht länger wehret,
Was der Papa einst versprach,
Rümpft er seine Nas und sprach
Uf die neue Mode:

'Daß ich mich nich ärjern werde,
Es bringt keene Macht der Erde
Zwischen meine Leut und mir
Ein beschriebnes Blatt Papier
Uf die neue Mode....[1]

The anonymous popular poet who wrote these verses had little of Heine's elegant sophistication; but he did have his urban, urchin mockery, his disrespectful vigour, and his ear for the rhythms of everyday speech which make the satires of Prutz, Hoffmann, Herwegh and Freiligrath appear, by comparison, so hopelessly 'literary'.

[1] Quoted by C. Petzet in *Die Blütezeit der politischen Lyrik von 1840 bis 1850* (München, 1903), p. 494.

IV

In *Deutschland. Ein Wintermärchen* Heine attempted to assume in earnest the role he had selected for himself in *Doktrin*: the role of the drummer whose task it was to rouse Germany from its sleep. Prussian ambitions, aggressive nationalism, the muzzling of literature and economic backwardness are all vigorously castigated; and literary figures too are satirised once again, for Heine felt that they reflected their readers, that their works reeked of the cultural and social atmosphere within which they flourished. Above all, the poem seeks to combat the very Romanticism to which *Atta Troll* had been such a glowing tribute; a Romanticism which leads to parodies of the past instead of regeneration of the present. It is in this spirit that the *Wintermärchen* protests against the completion of Cologne cathedral, though only two years before Heine had himself signed an appeal for its completion and subscribed to the parish branch of the *Domverein*.[1]

Er ward nicht vollendet — und das ist gut,
Denn eben die Nichtvollendung
Macht ihn zum Denkmal von Deutschlands Kraft
Und protestantischer Sendung. (Caput IV)

In the same anti-Romantic spirit the *Wintermärchen* follows every flight of enthusiasm with a deliberately sober reflection, and in its treatment of Father Rhine (Caput V) and Barbarossa (Capita XV and XVI) employs a disillusioning technique which is clearly directed against the tendency of contemporary poets to endow such figures as these with unwarranted glamour.

Heine's target in this satire is not, however, merely the oppressiveness of governments and the Romanticism of German princes and poets. He attacks no less the inactivity of those who have pledged themselves to change existing conditions. Caput XIX, for instance, reflects on the palace of the king of Hanover:

Idyllisch sicher haust er hier,
Denn besser als alle Gewehre

[1] Cf. E. Galley, 'Heine und der Kölner Dom', *Deutsche Vierteljahrsschrift*, XXXII, 1958.

Beschützet ihn der manglende Mut
Der deutschen Revoluzionäre.[1]

So, at least, Heine had written originally; for publication, he thought it wiser to tone the passage down:

Idyllisch sicher haust er hier,
Denn besser als alle Trabanten
Beschützet ihn der mangelnde Mut
Von unseren lieben Bekannten.

As usual, Heine is fighting a battle on two fronts; but he wants to avoid, as this alteration shows, arousing the hostility of the German Left. For the moment, he has cast in his lot with those German revolutionaries whom he cannot whole-heartedly respect. In *Deutschland. Ein Wintermärchen* the revolutionaries, beyond the pale of the law, appear most clearly in Caput XII—as a pack of wolves with whom the traveller claims an equivocal kinship.

Mitwölfe! Ihr zweifeltet nie an mir,
Ihr ließet euch nicht fangen
Von Schelmen, die euch gesagt, ich sei
Zu den Hunden übergegangen.

Ich sei abtrünnig und würde bald
Hofrat in der Lämmerhürde —
Dergleichen zu widersprechen war
Ganz unter meiner Würde.

* * *

Ich bin ein Wolf und werde stets
Auch heulen mit den Wölfen —
Ja, zählt auf mich und helft euch selbst,
So wird auch Gott euch helfen!

In one way, that is clear enough: it is a dig at Dingelstedt and other ex-revolutionaries who had made their peace with the government, as well as a rebuttal of those charges of apostasy, of sympathy with reaction, which had been brought against Heine by Börne and many others. But in another way, the passage is profoundly equivocal: it is pervaded by self-parody, filled with the clichés of any bread and butter speech, and culminates in that

[1] *SW*, II, 545.

phrase *heulen mit den Wölfen* which has such ominous opportunist associations. Clearly the traveller does not belong with the sheep —but he does not really belong with the wolves either. He cannot escape his destiny of loneliness. No political group can ever hold him; and in a later section we find in fact a veiled yet unmistakable statement of this refusal ever to become politically 'committed'. In Caput XX the traveller has arrived in Hamburg where he sees his mother again after long separation; and she, as mothers will, makes him first sit down to eat. In the course of serving him with food she asks certain questions which the traveller seeks to evade by praising the dishes before him; yet all these ostensible comments on food have, for the reader, a direct relevance to the question that preceded them. The last stanzas of this section read:

'Mein liebes Kind! Wie denkst du jetzt?
Treibst du noch immer mit Neigung
Die Politik? Zu welcher Partei
Gehörst du mit Überzeugung?'

'Die Apfelsinen, lieb Mütterlein,
Sind gut, und mit wahrem Vergnügen
Verschlucke ich den süßen Saft
Und ich lasse die Schalen liegen.'

The most memorable section of *Deutschland, ein Wintermärchen* is one in which satire is only incidental: Capita VI and VII, which recount the traveller's nocturnal adventure in the streets of Cologne. Here Heine revives that figure which had haunted him from the first: the 'Doppelgänger' of *Die Heimkehr* 20. But where the spectre of *Die Heimkehr* had been a phantom of the past, that of *Deutschland. Ein Wintermärchen* is an anticipation of the future.

Ich bin von praktischer Natur,
Und immer schweigsam und ruhig.
Doch wisse: was du ersonnen im Geist,
Das führ ich aus, das tu ich. (Caput VI)

Half lictor and half executioner, the 'Doppelgänger' here becomes a symbol of that power of *ideas* over the shape of human history which Heine had emphatically proclaimed in *Zur Geschichte der Religion und Philosophie in Deutschland*:

Remember this, you proud men of action! You are nothing but the unconscious agents of the men of thought, who often, in their humble silence, have prescribed exactly the course your actions can but follow. Maximilien Robespierre was nothing but the hand of Jean Jacques Rousseau....[1]

But where Shelley had been glad to see in poets the 'unacknowledged legislators of the world', Heine did so with misgivings:

The flickering fear which marred Jean Jacques' life—was it perhaps due to his knowledge of what sort of a midwife would be needed to help his ideas bodily into the world?[1]

The spectre of the future is no less terrible than that of the past.

In Caput VII of *Deutschland. Ein Wintermärchen* Heine now evokes, powerfully, a dream-image of nocturnal desolation in which the traveller and his 'Doppelgänger' walk the deserted streets of Cologne. The traveller dreams of a wound in his breast and of marking certain houses he passes with blood from this wound—and as he does so, a death-knell sounds in the distance. At length he reaches the deserted shell of the still unfinished cathedral and enters the chapel that houses the bones of the Three Magi. These Magi, skeletons symbolic (as we know from Caput IV) of outmoded tyranny and absolutism, are sitting up in their coffins; and one of them demands, in the name of all three, the respect due to kings, to saints and to the dead.

Ich gab ihm zur Antwort lachenden Muts:
'Vergebens ist deine Bemühung!
Ich sehe, daß du der Vergangenheit
Gehörst in jeder Beziehung.

Fort! Fort von hier! im tiefen Grab
Ist eure natürliche Stelle.
Das Leben nimmt jetzt in Beschlag
Die Schätze dieser Kapelle.'

The gay *persona* of the *Wintermärchen* seems here to be once again in control, even in this eerie dream: the claims of life are once more

[1] *SW*, IV, 248.

asserted against those of the past. This becomes even clearer in the following stanza, with its parody of Goethe and its irreverent colloquialism:

> Und weicht ihr nicht willig, so brauch ich Gewalt
> Und laß euch mit Kolben lausen!

The quotation from *Erlkönig* points the contrast: for while in Goethe's ballad the spectre had seized on life and destroyed it, here, in Caput VII of *Deutschland. Ein Wintermärchen*, life seeks to assert its rights against the spectres of the past. But significantly, it is not the dreamer himself who accomplishes the work of destruction: he beckons rather his ghostly lictor, his 'Doppelgänger', the spectre of the future; and as this lictor approaches to perform his horrible task, the tone of the poem once again changes radically.

> Er nahte sich, und mit dem Beil
> Zerschmetterte er die armen
> Skelette des Aberglaubens, er schlug
> Sie nieder ohn Erbarmen.
>
> Es dröhnte der Hiebe Widerhall
> Aus allen Gewölben, entsetzlich! —
> Blutströme schossen aus meiner Brust,
> Und ich erwachte plötzlich.

Could the dilemma have been more clearly presented? The future is even more frightening than the past. The changes that are recognised as right and necessary bring with them terrors worse than those they sought to overcome.

> Blutströme schossen aus *meiner* Brust —

the dreamer is involved, in the most intimate way, with the very things he has pledged himself to destroy. Through all the irreverent satire that is to come the reader will hear that note; and he cannot fail to remember it when he is brought up against the distasteful vision with which the traveller ends the account of his journey through the Germany of the 1840's.

V

There can be little doubt that the final sections of the poem, describing the traveller's stay in Hamburg, fail to sustain the brilliance of its opening. After the nocturnal visions of Capita VI and VII, the tongue-in-cheek characterisation of the German character (under pretence of characterising the German *cuisine*) of Caput XI, the image of a 'Roman' Germany in Caput XI, the address to the wolves in Caput XII, the masterly contrapuntal use of three German legends in Caput XIV, the encounter with Barbarossa in Capita XI–XVII, the Promethean dream of the Prussian eagle in Caput XVIII, the ironic reflections on Hanover in Caput XIX and the tender yet unsentimental encounter with the mother in Caput XX—after all this the Hamburg chapters are something of an anticlimax. For a while the poem degenerates into amusing but not very relevant gossip about various unimportant personalities and then declines still further into scabrous and gratuitous indecency. Hamburg, it would seem, held too many personal associations for Heine; he could not achieve the necessary artistic distance, and he could not speak—for fear of offending his wealthy relatives!—his full mind. That he should see Hamburg's patron goddess Hammonia as a woman of the streets was perhaps to be expected, in view of the company he had so often kept there in earlier days; but he fails to develop this vision in the telling way in which he develops elsewhere his vision of Frederick William IV as an emperor of China. The parodies, too, in which the *Hammonia* chapters of the *Wintermärchen* indulge so freely, have none of the point of, say, the *Erlkönig* quotation in Caput VII; these references to *Emilia Galotti*, *Wallenstein*, *Faust*, *Hamlet* and so on are more like knowing winks at readers who feel flattered because they recognise the originals. And some of the jokes, it must be admitted, smack more of the commercial traveller than the great poet.

But whatever the taste of these final chapters, there can be no doubt of their import. Hammonia herself is *gemütlich* enough, but she foresees an end to *Gemütlichkeit*.

Es poltert heran ein Spektakelstück,
Zu Ende geht die Idylle.... (Caput XXV)

Liberation is approaching; not the 'pure ideal' of which German liberals had been dreaming, but the real thing. Germany's future is to be divined only by those who put their head in a close-stool:

Entsetzlich waren die Düfte, O Gott!
Die sich nachher erhuben;
Es war, als fegte man den Mist
Aus sechsunddreißig Gruben. (Caput XXVI)

A manuscript version of this passage is even more explicit:

Es roch nach Blut, Tabak und Schnaps
Und nach gehenkten Schuften —
Wer übelriechend im Leben war,
Wie mußt er im Tode duften!

Es roch nach Pudeln und Dachsen und auch
Nach Mopsen, die zärtlich gelecket
Den Speichel der Macht und fromm und treu
Für Thron und Altar verrecket.

Das war ein giftiger Moderdunst
Entstiegen dem Schinderpfuhle —
Drin lag die ganze Hundezunft,
Die ganze historische Schule.[1]

The past has so poisoned life that the future will be an unbearable miasma.

The reader has had a frightening glimpse of Heine's own deepest fears; but now he is to be taken back, with a kind of *salto mortale*, to the spirit of the opening of the poem. The final Caput indulges once again in confident affirmations of life, based on faith in the rightness of the liberal cause and hope for Germany's future.

Das alte Geschlecht der Heuchelei
Verschwindet, Gott sei Dank, heut,
Es sinkt allmählich ins Grab, es stirbt
An seiner Lügenkrankheit.

[1] Quoted by Hans Kaufmann, *op. cit.* pp. 157–8.

Es wächst heran ein neues Geschlecht,
Ganz ohne Schminke und Sünden,
Mit freien Gedanken, mit freier Lust —
Dem werde ich alles verkünden. (Caput XXVII)

How this is to be squared with what has just gone before, the poet does not tell us; perhaps, after the stench and blood of a revolution, a new generation will arise in Germany which will achieve what two revolutions in France had (if we are to believe Heine's *Lutetia*) so singularly failed to achieve. The appeal to a coming generation in any case relieves the traveller of the embarrassing necessity of formulating a programme of his own or of particularising further his vision of the future. *That* he will do when the new generation has come into its inheritance. In the meantime Heine can end his poem, not with an image of what is to come (which would, at best, be uncertain) but with an attack on the present—with a warning to the king of Prussia that the poets whose works he sought to outlaw had powers exceeding his own.

Kennst du die Hölle des Dante nicht,
Die schrecklichen Terzetten?
Wen da der Dichter hineingesperrt,
Den kann kein Gott mehr retten —

Kein Gott, kein Heiland erlöst ihn je
Aus diesen singenden Flammen!
Nimm dich in Acht! daß wir dich nicht
Zu solcher Hölle verdammen!

Heine knew what he was *attacking*, and could launch his offensives brilliantly, with every weapon in the satirist's arsenal; but when he envisaged what he was trying to *bring about*, his heart grew heavy and his touch faltered. Then he would long back to the past, in the best Romantic tradition:

Der Fortschrittsfahne folg ich getreu,
Und trage sie selber zuweilen,
Doch manchmal möchte mein Herz so gern
In der Vorzeit Schatten verweilen;
(Paralipomenon of *Deutschland. Ein Wintermärchen*)[1]

[1] *Ibid.* p. 189.

then he would regard with affection and respect the German present with its 'picturesque feudalism' denounced by Karl Marx:

> One thinks of Germany, of fragrant lime-trees, of Hölty's poems, of the stone statue of Roland in front of the town hall, of the old deputy headmaster, of his rosy niece, of the forester's house with the stag's antlers, of bad tobacco and good fellows, of grandmother's churchyard stories, of guileless nightwatchmen, of friendship, of first love and all such sweet fads and fancies...;
>
> (*Französische Maler: A. Scheffer*)[1]

then he would look forward with horror to a future in which his lictor, his 'Doppelgänger', would have converted 'progressive' thoughts into reality.

8. THE COMIC WORLD

> *How easy is it to call rogue and villain, and that wittily! But how hard to make a man appear a fool, a blockhead or a knave, without using any of those opprobrious terms!...There is still a vast difference betwixt the slovenly butchering of a man, and the fineness of a stroke that separates the head from the body, and leaves it standing in its place.* DRYDEN

DEUTSCHLAND. EIN WINTERMÄRCHEN shows up the dangers to which Heine the satirist was exposed. Unable to identify himself with any particular party or programme and unwilling to formulate any but the vaguest programme of his own, he lacked the positive standards, the background of firm convictions, which sustain in their several ways a Horace and Juvenal, a Sebastian Brant, a Lafontaine, a Dryden, Pope and even Swift. No wonder that he sometimes mistook his object—as in the Platen passages of *Die Bäder von Lucca* or the remarks on Börne's private life and relationships in *Ludwig Börne*. The wonder is that he did not mistake it more often and that he managed to become, in spite of all, the greatest satirist Germany

[1] *SW*, IV, 28.

ever produced. His comic juxtapositions, sudden deflations, puns and comic rhymes; his mock wishes, mock advice and mock praises; his assumption of the very voice and accent of his butts; his diminishing and mock-exalting metaphors; his sustained comic comparisons and absurd hypotheses; his ability to depict qualities of mind in physical terms and sum up a situation in a symbolic myth—all these were at the service of a genuine comic vision of the world which was not blind to the world's tragedy. Has the relation of King Louis Philippe to the subjects who put him on the throne ever been more effectively presented than in that passage from *Lutetia* which so delighted George Eliot?

I remember very well that immediately on my arrival [in Paris] I hastened to the Palais Royal to see Louis Philippe. The friend who conducted me told me that the king now appeared on the terrace only at stated hours, but that formerly he was to be seen at any time for five francs. 'For five francs!' I exclaimed, with amazement; 'does he then show himself for money?' 'No; but he is shown for money, and it happens in this way: there used to be a society of claqueurs and riff-raff who offered every foreigner that they would *show* him the king for five francs; if he would give ten francs he might see the king *raise his eyes to heaven* and lay his hand protestingly on his heart; if he would give twenty francs, the king would *sing the Marseillaise*. If the foreigner then gave five francs, they raised a loud cheering under the king's windows, and his majesty appeared on the terrace, bowed, and retired. If he gave ten francs, they shouted still louder, and gesticulated when the king appeared as if they had gone mad: then the king raised his eyes to heaven, as a sign of silent emotion, and laid his hand on his heart. English visitors, however, would sometimes spend as much as twenty francs, and then the enthusiasm mounted to the highest pitch: as soon as the king appeared on the terrace, the Marseillaise was struck up and roared out frightfully, until Louis Philippe, perhaps only for the sake of putting an end to the singing, bowed, laid his hand on his heart, and joined in the Marseillaise. Whether, as is asserted, he also beat time with his foot, I cannot say.[1]

And in verse too, if we want to see Heine at his very best, we cannot do better than go to *Atta Troll*, where all the perennial objects of his satire—from German professors to the king of Bavaria,

[1] *SW*, VI, 232–3.

from nationalists to communists, from political poets to the exotic poets of the Freiligrath school—are guyed with equal zest. Yet all this satire alternates, coexists without strain, with the most magic evocation of nature and the human moods it mirrors, and with grandiose visions of a Ghostly Chase in which Diana rides with Herodias, while Shakespeare on his charger is followed by a poor frightened German commentator precariously perched on an ass.

There are two things which Heine's satire does superbly well: it exposes the contrast between pretensions and reality, and it makes us see men and affairs afresh as for the first time. 'Sometimes', he says in *Ludwig Börne*, 'the circumstances of the time are a substitute for innate humour and a prosaically gifted, ingenious author produces truly humorous works by letting his mind mirror faithfully the comic and sad, dirty and sacred, grandiose and petty combinations of a topsy-turvy world-order.'[1] If things have come to such a pass in Prussia that even 'Willibald Alexis' (Wilhelm Häring) is driven into opposition and that Bettina von Arnim forsakes her Mignon pose to denounce social evils; if Tieck, the arch-Romantic author of *Der gestiefelte Kater*, is called to Berlin to produce the plays of Sophocles; if King Ludwig of Bavaria builds a 'Pantheon' that includes statues of Liszt and Fanny Elssler but excludes Luther; if the universities of Munich and Berlin, whose staff the younger Heine would have been glad to join, bid instead for the services of the philologist Massmann—then all the poet has to do is to chronicle such facts and he will *have* a satire.

Verkehrte Welt

Das ist ja die verkehrte Welt,
Wir gehen auf den Köpfen!
Die Jäger werden dutzendweis
Erschossen von den Schnepfen.

Die Kälber braten jetzt den Koch
Auf Menschen reiten die Gäule;
Für Lehrfreiheit und Rechte des Lichts
Kämpft die katholische Eule.

[1] *SW*, VII, 108. There is an excellent commentary on this passage in E. Eckertz, *Heine und sein Witz* (Berlin, 1908), pp. 23–4.

Der Häring wird ein Sanskülott,
Die Wahrheit sagt uns Bettine,
Und ein gestiefelter Kater bringt
Den Sophokles auf die Bühne.

Ein Affe läßt ein Pantheon
Erbauen für deutsche Helden.
Der Massmann hat sich jüngst gekämmt,
Wie deutsche Blätter melden....

But this, of course, is not mere chronicling. The idea that German newspapers think it worth while to report the unusual fact that Massmann recently combed his hair is a comic fantasy such as we often find in Heine—a fantasy which startles into laughter through its inherent absurdity, but which conveys forcibly Heine's sense at once of the triviality of contemporary news-reports (what, after all, *could* they report under censorship except trivialities?) and of the uncouthness of a certain type of old *Burschenschaftler*. In the very act of making us see the real world anew, of exposing false pretensions, Heine calls into being a fantasy-world with a delightful logic and cohesion of its own.

Above all, Heine shows himself capable of creating, with a few strokes, comic caricatures that throb with life; caricatures that can be relished long after their originals have been forgotten.[1] Massmann, whose full-length portrait is painted in *Die Reise von München nach Genua* and who is then introduced in poem after poem, is a caricature of this kind: his valuable work on Germanic philology has now been superseded and forgotten, and he lives only in Heine's image of him. King Ludwig may well lament, after his departure to Berlin—

Ich sehe die kurzen Beinchen nicht mehr,
Nicht mehr die platte Nase;
Er schlug wie ein Pudel frisch-fromm-fröhlich-frei
Die Purzelbäume im Grase...

(*Lobgesänge auf König Ludwig* 2)

[1] Chamisso said of Heine: 'He is a poet to his finger-tips. He creates living beings, and whatever he touches—be it a cat or a man—steps out of the page and stands there to be mocked or just be to looked at.' (Quoted in *Briefe*, v, 167.)

—posterity will always see Massmann not as he was, but as Heine made him. That is the 'hell' of which the poet warned the king of Prussia at the end of *Deutschland. Ein Wintermärchen*; that is the amber of poetry of which he had spoken in *Die romantische Schule*:

> Round many a tiny writer did he spin the wittiest mockery and most precious humour, and they are preserved for eternity in the works of Lessing like insects in a piece of amber. In killing his enemies he made them immortal.

Massmann, Posa-Herwegh before his Prussian King Philip, Freiligrath, Charlotte Birch-Pfeiffer have been preserved in this way by Heine's comic vision.

Heine's method of caricature has been well described by another poet of a very different kind: by Oscar Loerke. 'The individuality of his victims', Loerke explains, 'shrinks to the point of their greatest strength and their greatest weakness; then this point swells to give birth to a dwarf-like or gigantic image of the original, which is of the same material through and through, quite without the accidentals of the victim's everyday existence, although the most valuable part of this has also been melted down: physical characteristics are transformed into an ironic, humorous, stupid, proud, Philistine, clumsy but always *living* soul-image. What seems malice in Heine is mostly the joy and high spirits of creation.'[1] That is well said, and shows the links between the verbal art of Heine and the graphic art of the French—for Loerke's description could apply, word for word, to the procedure of Honoré Daumier.[2]

Loerke's comment on Heine's satiric method contains within it the answer to a charge that has been so frequently levelled against him by contemporaries and by posterity: the charge of excessive indulgence in personalities. Persons became for Heine living symbols of conditions. In pillorying them, he pilloried, in the most effective way he knew, intellectual, social and political

[1] Introduction to *Der lyrische Nachlaß von Heinrich Heine*, ed. E. Loewenthal (Hamburg and Berlin, 1925), p. xv.

[2] Charles Andler attributes to Heine 'procédés caricaturaux pris à l'art graphique français' in 'L'œuvre lyrique de Heine', *Études Germaniques*, I (1946), p. 203.

abuses. Their physical characteristics—Schlegel's impotence, Massmann's unwashed and uncouth appearance, Meyerbeer's weak bowels—he saw as symbols for mental states and artistic or social facts. In attacking specific persons, he attacked not only them, but also the intellectual, social and political conditions in which they flourished, the taste to which they appealed and the state of mind they shared with their admirers.

Nur jenen, die fern in Zeit oder Land,
Wird der Inhalt meiner Satiren bekannt.
Nachbar Meier mich einen Kleingeist nennt,
Weil er den Müller persönlich kennt.[1] (Karl Kraus)

Now that the personalities of Massmann, Freiligrath, Herwegh and the rest have faded into the distance and the nineteenth-century rulers of Prussia and Bavaria seem remote, it should be easier to do justice to Heine's comic creations.

One tiny instance, selected at random among many similar ones, will serve to show Heine in the actual process of creating his comic world.[2] At the beginning of *Deutschland. Ein Wintermärchen* he exhibits the contrast between Romantic dream and political actuality by juxtaposing the song of the little *Harfenmädchen* with the activity of Prussian customs officials.

Während die Kleine von Himmelslust
Getrillert und musizieret,
Ward von den preußischen Douaniers
Mein Koffer visitieret.

Mit schmutzigen Fingern stöberten sie....[3]

This last image of the officials' dirty fingers is crossed out in the draft manuscript of this section preserved at Düsseldorf. It is too crass, too obvious: and again and again we find Heine, in his satires, first writing down a crassly 'powerful' version only to delete it and substitute a more restrained and therefore more effective one:

[1] Karl Kraus, *Epigramme* (Wien, 1927), p. 93.
[2] A more extended example will be found in the Appendix, p. 288.
[3] MS. Düsseldorf.

Beschnüffelten alles, kramten herum
In Hemden, Hosen, Schnupftüchern;
Sie suchten nach Spitzen, Bijouterien,
Auch nach verbotenen Büchern.

But the really interesting change—which can be well observed in Friedrich Hirth's facsimile edition of the manuscript of *Deutschland. Ein Wintermärchen*[1]—comes a few stanzas later on.

Und viele Bücher trag' ich im Kopf!
darf
Ich [kann] es Euch versichern,
Mein Kopf ist ein zwitscherndes Vogelnest
lichen
Von [laut] konfiszier[baren] Büchern.

The image of forbidden books twittering in the traveller's skull like birds in a nest is delightful in itself: but it is not converted into actuality until the normal word *konfiszierbar* is transformed into *konfiszierlich*. Only then does the reader actually *hear* the birds twittering—only then do the voices which authority so vainly attempts to stifle inform the whole stanza.

. . . ein *zwitschern*des Vogelnest
Von kon*fiszierlich*en Bü*ch*ern:

that is 'zierlich' indeed, and mocks, with its gracefully gay sound, the clumsiness of the foiled searchers.

Heine's satire—this is the important point—is a matter of sound and rhythm as much as of plain literal meaning. It is the work of a man concerned with language in its physical as well as its semantic aspect. In *Die Tendenz*, for instance, he generates mounting excitement through ever shorter grammatical units and ever more martial word-music, until he deflates it all in a final stanza that is devoid of such music and in which the lines limp lamely along; and in *Unsere Marine* he causes as much amusement with consciously jaunty rhythms as with deliberate semantic incongruities. His is the satire of a poet.

Throughout his life Heine was fond of likening himself to Aristophanes, whose *Birds* he admired more than any work of

[1] *Heinrich Heine: Deutschland. Ein Wintermärchen. Faksimiledruck nach der Handschrift des Dichters*, ed. F. Hirth (Berlin, 1915), Caput II, stanza 6.

comic literature except *Don Quixote*—but the comparison draws attention to what he lacked rather than to his essential greatness. Saint-René Taillandier pointed this out most forcibly in a review of *Neue Gedichte* published in the *Revue des Deux Mondes* of 1845:

Aristophane n'est pas seulement l'esprit le plus vif et le plus gai, l'imagination la plus gracieuse et la plus bouffonne; dans ses farces immortelles on retrouve sans cesse le citoyen, on sent battre un cœur résolu et qui sait bien ce qu'il veut.[1]

Heine was not a 'citizen' in the way Aristophanes was allowed to be. He stood ever outside the nations, the classes and the creeds to which he sought at times to pay allegiance. In the thirties he had tried to be a Saint-Simonist; in the forties he sought to become the champion of an 'anonymous' Germany whose existence he had proclaimed in *Zur Geschichte der Religion und Philosophie in Deutschland.* Here he had distinguished between 'the old official Germany, that mouldy land of Philistines' and a new Germany: 'the great, mysterious and—as it were—anonymous Germany, the sleepy sovereign whose sceptre and crown have become a plaything for monkeys'.[2] *Deutschland. Ein Wintermärchen* begins and ends with an appeal to this anonymous sovereign, this 'neues Geschlecht / Ganz ohne Schminken und Sünden' to whom the message of the future can be proclaimed—but the reader cannot help feeling that this 'new race of men' has no more existence than the noble race of Houyhnhnms, and that there is no message to transmit. Heine tried, on occasions, to identify this 'sleepy sovereign' with the German people cheated of its rights—the 'deutscher Michel' who is encouraged, in *Erleuchtung*, to claim his material rights in this world rather than the next:

Michel! fürchte nichts und labe
Schon hienieden deinen Wanst,
Später liegen wir im Grabe,
Wo du still verdauen kannst.

(*Neue Gedichte*: *Zeitgedichte* 22)

[1] *Revue des Deux Mondes, loc. cit.* p. 332. In answer to this frequently repeated charge Heine told Adolf Stahr in October 1855 that he was as good an Aristophanes as the new Athenians deserved (*Gespräche*, p. 944).

[2] *SW*, IV, 155.

In *Die armen Weber* especially Heine constitutes himself—for once without satiric overtones—the champion of the poor and oppressed. Yet he always felt uneasy in this role; and he has expressed this feeling of uneasiness in a 'symbolic myth' such as only he could invent. In a powerful passage at the end of the fourth and last volume of his *Reisebilder*, he purports to recount an anecdote from the life of the emperor Charles the Fifth:

The poor Emperor had been taken prisoner by his enemies . . . ; I think it was in the Tyrol. There he sat, lonely and dejected; all his knights and courtiers had forsaken him; no one came to his help. I don't know whether he already had, at that time, the cheese-face with which Holbein has painted him for us. But I am sure that nether lip of his, with its contempt for mankind, stuck out even more than it does in his portraits. How could he help despising the tribe which had fawned on him so devotedly in the sunshine of his prosperity, and now, in his dark distress, left him alone? Then suddenly the door of his cell was opened and in came a man in disguise; and as he threw back his cloak, the Emperor recognised in him his faithful Kunz von der Rosen, the court jester. This man brought him comfort and counsel, and he was the court jester.

O German fatherland! dear German people! I am your Kunz von der Rosen. The man whose proper business was to amuse, who was to minister to your mirth in the days of your prosperity—he now makes his way into your prison in time of need. Here, under my cloak, I bring you your strong sceptre and your fair crown: do you not recognise me, my Emperor? And if I cannot liberate you, I can at least comfort you, and you will at least have someone about you who will talk with you about your worst afflictions, who will encourage and love you, and whose best joke and best blood will be at your service. For you, my people, are the true Emperor, the true master of the land! . . . Your will is the only rightful source of power. Though you are now fettered and chained, your just cause will, in the end, prevail. The day of liberation is at hand, a new era is about to begin. My Emperor, the night is past, and out there glows the dawn.

'Kunz von der Rosen, my Fool, you are mistaken; what you take for the sun is perhaps only the gleam of the executioner's axe, and the red of dawn is only blood.'

'No, my Emperor, it *is* the sun, even though it rises in the west; these six thousand years it has always risen in the east, it is time we had a change.'

'Kunz von der Rosen, my Fool, you seem to have lost the bells that hung on your old cap, and it has now such an odd look, that red cap of yours!'

'Ah, my Emperor, your distress has made me shake my head so fiercely that the Fool's bells have dropped off my cap; it is none the worse for that.'

'Kunz von der Rosen, what is that noise of breaking and cracking out there?'

'Be calm, my Emperor! it is the noise of the saw and the carpenter's axe, and soon the doors of your prison will be burst open and you will be free, my Emperor!'

'But am I really an Emperor? It is only the Fool who tells me so.'

'Don't sigh, dear master, the air of your prison makes you so despondent. When you have regained your power, you will feel once more the imperial blood running in your veins, and you will be proud like an Emperor, and bold, and gracious, and unjust, and smiling, and ungrateful, as princes are.'

'Kunz von der Rosen, my Fool, when I am free again, what will you do?'

'Then I will sew new bells on my cap.'

'And how shall I reward your faithfulness?'

'O dear master—do not have me put to death!'[1]

That expresses perfectly the characteristic apprehension behind Heine's political poetry, animated though it is by a genuine love of freedom and a genuine sympathy with the oppressed; the apprehension he has conveyed in symbolic form in Caput XV of *Atta Troll*.

Heine attacked with unparalleled zest and effectiveness the antiquated and oppressive institutions of nineteenth-century Germany. He undermined respect for ideals and authorities which he considered, for the most part rightly, to have become hollow and false. He substituted for the 'Fools' of traditional satire, whose error consists in wanting to rise above their station, the more timely picture of fools who are content with their lot in an unsatisfactory political and social system and of knaves who use a traditional moral code to keep them so. He created a genuine comic world out of the materials of contemporary life and

[1] *SW*, III, 504–5.

literature; ousting the vague rhetoric of Herwegh and his imitators and introducing into German poetry a humour such as Voltaire had described in *Lettres sur les Anglais*: 'ce vrai comique, cette gaieté, cette urbanité, ces saillies qui échappent à un homme sans qu'il s'en doute'. But he achieved all this without hope for the future; without that faith in the rightness of his cause and the goodness of the people which sustained, in their several ways, a Börne, a Freiligrath or a Karl Marx. In a later poem, *Enfant Perdu*, he summed it all up: suggesting, in the image of a dying soldier, the hopelessness of the long struggle, the ridiculous associates who fought alongside him, the fear that lay behind his most impudent jokes, the wounds he sustained as well as inflicted, wounds which in the end proved mortal.

> Ich kämpfte ohne Hoffnung, daß ich siege,
> Ich wußte, nie komm ich gesund nach Haus.

Yet if there is no hope, there is some exhilaration in the struggle itself; there is some comfort in standing up for the right as one sees it at any given moment, and in knowing that others will continue the fight against fools and against knaves; there is comfort too in knowing that one's weapons—the weapons of satire—are effective and intact though gaiety is no more.

> Ein Posten ist vakant! — Die Wunden klaffen —
> Der eine fällt, die andern rücken nach —
> Doch fall ich unbesiegt, und meine Waffen
> Sind nicht gebrochen — nur mein Herze brach.

But *Enfant Perdu* already belongs to the world of the *Romanzero*.

II

ROMANZERO

Vivas to those who have failed!
And to those whose war-vessels sank in the sea!
And to those themselves who sank in the sea!
And to all generals that lost engagements, and
all overcome heroes! WHITMAN

---

1. MERLIN'S TOMB

I must choose between despair and energy—
I choose the latter. KEATS

EVEN in his student days Heine's health had been anything but robust. To his friends he complained of headaches so persistently that most of them suspected him of malingering in order to make himself 'interesting'. During the thirties, he had seemed to grow physically stronger, and many of those who visited him in his early Paris years commented on his florid, healthy appearance and embonpoint. But even when Heine stood, as he himself said, 'in the zenith of his fatness', there were disquieting signs which included temporary paralysis of hand and eyelid. Various doctors tried various cures, with such specious success that in 1843 and 1844 Heine felt well enough to make two strenuous journeys to Hamburg. Soon after his return from the second of these journeys, however, news reached him of the death of his millionaire uncle Salomon Heine—and the disclosure of the terms of that uncle's will, followed by years of bitter wrangling and recrimination, plunged the poet into an intense excitement which brought on a kind of stroke and helped the (possibly luetic) illness that lurked in his body to break out openly.

Heine's relations with his uncle Salomon had always been uneasy. He despised him for his cultural ignorance and respected him for the strength of character and commercial acumen which had enabled him to acquire his immense wealth. He loathed being financially dependent on his uncle; yet at the same time he had the Jewish pauper's feeling that it was the *duty* of his rich co-religionist to look after him, as well as the more universal feeling for the obligations of wealthy uncles towards less fortunate members of their family. He saw Salomon Heine as a domestic tyrant, a 'Griesgram' who had to be carefully managed ('he is always tame at feeding times', he wrote in one of his letters[1]); but he never doubted the goodness of his heart, or his essential benevolence towards his 'feckless' nephew.

Auch einem gewissen Griesgram hat
Gar mancher Seufzer gegolten;
Ich dachte mit wahrer Wollust daran,
Wie oft er mich ausgescholten.[2]

This confession, by the traveller of *Deutschland, ein Wintermärchen*, was toned down for publication; but even in the final version the mingled resentment and affection are unmistakable.

Auch jenem edlen alten Herrn,
Der immer mich ausgescholten
Und immer großmütig beschützt, auch ihm
Hat mancher Seufzer gegolten.

Ich wollte wieder aus seinem Mund
Vernehmen den 'dummen Jungen',
Das hat mir immer wie Musik
Im Herzen nachgeklungen. (Caput XXIV)

Salomon Heine, it seems, had promised his nephew that the pension of 4800 francs which he drew from him—a sum which corresponded exactly to that which the poet received annually from French government funds and which therefore doubled his steady income—would be lifelong. Yet when Salomon's will was opened, it appeared that his nephew Heinrich was to receive only a single

[1] *Briefe*, II, 41 (15 July 1833). [2] *SW*, II, 547.

legacy of 8000 marks. No mention was made of the annual payments on which Heine and Mathilde had come to rely. The bulk of the fortune went to Salomon's son Karl—and Karl Heine declared himself willing to continue the poet's pension only on condition that he published nothing about the Heine family to which any member of that family could make objection.

It may well be that this plan of action had been agreed between Karl and Salomon Heine before the latter's death. There had been much talk of the poet's memoirs in the German newspapers, and there had been frightening indications, in comments on members of the Fould family which Heine published in the *Augsburger Allgemeine Zeitung*, of the sort of material these memoirs might contain. Heine himself, in fact, was fond of using his memoirs as a threat to those who displeased him: 'it seemed to me', Levin Schücking reported after an interview with him in 1846, 'that Heine purposely talked a good deal of his memoirs and that he tended to pose as a sort of Santa Claus, who brings sweets to the good children and the birch to the bad...'.[1] Karl Heine, at any rate, wished to have some control over the gifts of this Santa Claus, and he therefore refused to pay anything but a voluntary stipend which might be withdrawn if anything in the least defamatory to the Heine family appeared in the poet's publications.

Heine's rage at this knew no bounds. He felt himself betrayed by his own family; felt himself subjected to a censorship more intolerable than that of the Prussian authorities; felt himself deprived not only of money but of love. His letters of those years are full of stratagems for forcing his family to acknowledge his unrestricted right to his pension by means sometimes fair but usually foul; and they make most painful reading. His health deteriorated rapidly—Engels saw him in September 1846 and found him 'thin as a skeleton', with a paralysed face;[2] Laube and Wolfgang Müller von Königswinter, who visited him in 1847, admired the vivacity of his spirit but described him as 'a cheerless picture of human frailty'.[3] In the early summer of 1848 he went out for the last time; in July of that year Caroline Jaubert, coming

[1] *Gespräche*, p. 506. [2] *Ibid.* p. 508. [3] *Ibid.* pp. 555, 594.

to see him at Passy, found him hopelessly paralysed, lying on two mattresses placed one upon the other on the floor. He had entered that 'mattress grave' which he was himself to compare to Merlin's tomb:

My bed reminds me of the melodious grave of the magician Merlin, which is to be found in the forest Broceliand in Brittany, beneath tall oaks whose tops flare towards heaven like green flames. I envy you those trees, cousin Merlin, and the fresh wind that blows through them; for no green leaf rustles into my mattress grave in Paris....[1]

The poetry of these years—the years between 1846 and 1851—reflects the changed circumstances of Heine's life. His great satires had been the work of an outsider who could not identify himself fully with any party and creed; yet they had depended for their functioning on the poet's passionate interest in the social and political scene. Their humour had been a worldly, urbane humour, the work of a man who loves the beauty and richness of this earth, tries to snatch from it the maximum enjoyment it will yield and attacks those who, through folly or wickedness, impede that enjoyment. Behind it all had been the belief, expressed most forcibly in *Zur Geschichte der Religion und Philosophie in Deutschland*, that the old God was dead, and that Man had succeeded to his now vacant place in the universe:

We are founding a democracy of gods equally glorious, equally sacred, equally happy.[2]

Heine's faith in his own manhood had brought with it a belief that there was nothing in the universe which was necessarily opposed to human reason and goodness. Evil was there, it is true—no one had a keener sense of evil than Heine in his middle period; but it was only accidental.

Do you know what evil is in this world? The Spiritualists have always reproached us because they contended that a pantheistic world-view made no distinction between good and evil. But evil is only a vain delusion produced by their own way of looking at the world or else it is the concrete result of the way in which they have ordered the

[1] *SW*, I, 483. [2] *SW*, IV, 223 and *SW*, VI, 535.

world....Matter becomes evil only when it is forced to conspire secretly against the usurpations of the spirit....Evil, therefore, is only the result of the Spiritualist world-order.[1]

When, however, in 1848 his health finally broke down; when he was fastened to his mattress grave, paralysed, more than half blind, racked by agonies that only greater and greater quantities of opium could temporarily relieve—then Heine recognised the inadequacy of a world-view about which he had had sneaking doubts the whole time. What could social and political reorganisation do in the face of pains and evils that were inherent in the very structure of the world, in man's mental and physical organisation? 'My constitution is even worse than the constitution of Prussia', Heine punned on his bed of pain, and summed up in a quip the shift in his outlook and interests.

Paralysis of the body, as this very quip serves to show, did not mean paralysis of the intellect; most of Heine's visitors testified, on the contrary, to the unimpaired liveliness of his mind and the enhanced trenchancy of his (often self-lacerating) wit. Nor did it mean a drying up of the well-springs of poetry. In his sleepless nights, broken by opium-induced visions and dreams, Heine composed in his head lyrics and ballads which he sought in the morning to commit to paper—a painful and difficult process, since he could hardly hold a pencil and since the eyelid of his one seeing eye could not be fully raised.

Die schaurig süßen Orgia,
Das nächtlich tolle Geistertreiben,
Sucht des Poeten Leichenhand
Manchmal am Morgen aufzuschreiben.

(*Gedichte 1853 und 1854*: *Zum Lazarus* 3)

The pile of manuscripts by Heine's bed grew rapidly, and he thought on occasions of publishing yet another volume of verse; but as late as 30 November 1850 he wrote to Heinrich Laube:

The project of publishing a new book of poems recedes into the distance again, since my illness does not allow me to write out properly

[1] *SW*, IV, 222.

what I have hastily scribbled down and put it in order for publication. If the need becomes very pressing, however, I will have to come out with such a book.

The 'pressing need' to which the poet here refers was financial; for though he had outwardly made his peace with his cousin Karl, who continued to pay his pension and even supplemented it on occasions, his financial position was growing more desperate. After the 1848 revolution, the French government discontinued the pension which the government of Louis Philippe had paid him out of secret state funds; his illness became increasingly a 'money-eating beast' and Mathilde had never learned to curb her natural extravagance in financial matters. After a visit from Campe in July 1851, Heine decided that the time had come to publish his poems, even though he could not give them the final polish his fastidious conscience demanded. By the end of 1851 two new books of his were on the market, and he confessed ruefully to Georg Werth:

God knows that I do not attach great importance to these books, and that they would not have seen the light of day so soon if Campe had not put the thumb-screws on me. (5 November 1851)

Of the two books so unceremoniously dismissed in this letter of 5 November 1851 one was a ballet scenario—*Der Doktor Faust. Ein Tanzpoem*; the other was a collection of lyric poetry for which Campe had supplied the name: *Romanzero*.[1]

The *Romanzero* does undoubtedly contain weak poems—no one, for instance, would mourn if *Der Ungläubige*, *K.-Jammer* or *Zum Hausfrieden* disappeared from the canon. It contains poems —*Jehuda ben Halevi* is one—which would have benefited by revision, by a process of tightening-up in some parts and elaboration in others. It startles the reader with scatological images for which it is not always easy to find artistic justification. More than once it 'talks' its emotions instead of presenting them. And it exhibits on occasions an obtuseness in things of the spirit which is

[1] In what follows I choose to call this collection 'the *Romanzero*' rather than simply '*Romanzero*'. Heine himself, in his letters, invariably prefixes the definite article.

astonishing in so sensitive and intelligent a poet—one need only recall the wilful misunderstanding of the symbolism of bread and wine in *Vitzliputzli*.

Yet with all its weaknesses, the *Romanzero* is one of the great books of world literature: an astonishing feat of poetic architecture both in its individual poems and in its over-all arrangement, and a powerful presentation of the experience of a tormented human soul. Gone is the Hegelian or Fourierist or Saint-Simonist optimism of Heine's earlier years; gone is the belief, so fervently proclaimed in *Die Harzreise*, that Father, Son and Holy Ghost are immanent in the progression of history;[1] gone too is all faith in the divinity of man and his perfectibility. Behind the *Romanzero* lies the contempt of others and of self brought on by the quarrel over Uncle Salomon's inheritance, which Heine himself had summed up, in his letter of 13 January 1845, in a medieval chant:

> Contemnere mundum,
> contemnere se ipsum,
> contemnere se, contemni.

Behind the *Romanzero* lies the disappointment of a liberal who saw no more hope in moderate liberalism, but thought that the choice of the future lay between crass reaction and a communism which would transform the world 'into one herd all bleating and all shorn alike'; the experience of 'a poor lamed German, who cannot forget yesterday and greets tomorrow with apprehension'. (Letter to Gustav Kolb, 21 April 1851). Behind the *Romanzero*, finally, lies the disappointment of a self-confessed sensualist cut off for ever from the pleasures he had once valued so highly and forced to exercise what he himself characteristically described as 'le vilain métier de moribond'.[2]

In his earlier volumes, as I have tried to demonstrate in my study of the *Buch der Lieder*, Heine had shown his affinity with that 'Aesthete' who conducts a memorable debate with Victor Eremita in Kierkegaard's *Either/Or*. 'Life is a masquerade, you

[1] *SW*, III, 45–6. Cf. Hegel, *Sämtliche Werke*, ed. G. Lasson, 2nd edition (1923), IX, 766.

[2] *Briefe*, III, 147 (23 June 1848).

explain, and for you this is inexhaustible material for amusement; and so far, no one has succeeded in knowing you; for every revelation you make is always an illusion.... Your occupation consists in preserving your hiding-place, and that you succeed in doing, for your mask is the most enigmatical of all.' But Victor Eremita, it will be remembered, warns this imagined aesthete of a situation in which such disguises will be of no avail: 'Do you not know that there comes a midnight hour when everyone has to throw off his mask?', and continues, with uncompromising cruelty:

> One is tempted not to pity you but rather to wish that some day the circumstances of your life might tighten upon you the screws in its rack and compel you to come out with what really dwells in you; that they might begin the sharper inquisition on the rack which cannot be beguiled with nonsense and witticism.[1]

The *Romanzero* is the fruit of such 'inquisition on the rack': and the experience which it conveys with terrifying directness is analogous to that described by Schopenhauer rather than that which lies behind the philosophy of Hegel, or Bentham, or Fourier or Marx. Of Schopenhauer's *Die Welt als Wille und Vorstellung* (1819) Heine heard for the first time from Alfred Meissner shortly before the publication of the *Romanzero*,[2] and it is doubtful whether he ever read a line of it—yet his poetry reveals directly what Schopenhauer had described. It reveals the frustration of the Will in a world in which man and beast are confounded in a universal agony. It reveals human history as a succession of scenes that mutually parody each other, presents human life as a realm of chance and error in which the stupid and base prosper more easily than the worthy, and sees even tragedy robbed of its dignity by scabrous elements that tickle to laughter.

In spite of all this, however, Heine was able to write to Campe on 15 January 1849: 'I do not belong to the pessimists.' Seeing so clearly the horror of the world, rejecting all easy consolation, ruthlessly destroying the illusions he cherished most, Heine never lost his love for life and for this earth. His sufferings did not

[1] Kierkegaard, *Either/Or*, transl. W. Lowry (London, 1944), p. 135.
[2] *Gespräche*, pp. 673–4.

succeed in turning him into the kind of crabbed and soured misanthropist that stares at us from every portrait of the later Schopenhauer. Over fifty years ago R. M. Meyer drew attention to this paradox and defined for all time the greatness of the later Heine:

> In spite of all he loved this world passionately—loved it not only as a man eager for sensation and enjoyment, for those times were past; loved it rather with the never-to-be-extinguished love of the artist. The abundance of this visible world was for him, as for Nietzsche, sufficient excuse for what seemed to him the 'deception' of existence. He looked around him keenly, and found everywhere deception and illusion; but no experience could kill in him his longing for beauty. Therein lies his greatness.[1]

This complex world-view, with its alternation of acceptance and rejection, of longing and disgusted turning away, Heine conveyed with singular power in his *Romanzero.*

2. THE MASKED DANCER

> *Masques de faiblesse, masques de force, masques de misère, masques de joie, masques d'hypocrisie, tous exténués, tous empreints des signes ineffaçables d'une haletante avidité.*
>
> BALZAC

'I SCRIBBLE many verses', Heine had written to Campe on 30 April 1849, 'and there are many among them which soften my pain like magic melodies when I hum them over to myself.' Poetry, it seemed, could provide an escape—it could help to transport the mortally sick poet away from the actuality of his pain, away also from the actuality of his anger and disgust.

> Die Saiten klingen! Ein Heldenlied,
> Voll Flammen und Gluten!
> Da schmilt der Zorn, und dein Gemüt
> Wird süß verbluten.

[1] R. M. Meyer, *Gestalten und Probleme* (Berlin, 1905), p. 161.

This stanza comes from the motto of *Historien*, the opening section of the *Romanzero*; and it points to one of the ways in which poetry might sweeten what remained of life.

The *Historien* open, in fact, with what is clearly an attempt to escape. They begin with a swift stride into the past, with images of oriental wealth and glitter, with peals of laughter that are not only talked about but are presented in rhythms and sounds:

Als der König Rhampsenit
Eintrat in die goldne Halle
Seiner Tochter, lachte diese,
Lachten ihre Zofen alle.

Auch die Schwarzen, die Eunuchen
Stimmten lachend ein, es lachten
Selbst die Mumien, selbst die Sphinxe,
Daß sie schier zu bersten dachten.

From now on these peals of laughter continue to ring through *Rhampsenit*—not only in the often and prominently repeated verb 'lachen', but also in the many words that echo its vowels and consonants. For a moment, laughter merges into articulate speech, as the king's daughter tells her story; but this is drowned again, almost immediately, in laughter even more strident.

An demselben Tag ganz Memphis
Lachte....

Men and women, mummies and sphinxes, even the crocodiles laugh; and through it all is heard the voice of a town crier reading an edict in the best Prussian *Kanzleistil*.

Are we in the 'golden hall' of Herodotus? *Is* this world so far removed, in space and time, from that in which poets bleed to death to the sound of their own lyre? As in the operettas of Offenbach and as in Heine's own *Unterwelt*, the ancient world here merges with the modern. History is annihilated in light-hearted parody. But in the midst of all the fun, the slippery allusions and *double ententes*, the anachronisms and absurdities, the spectacle of laughing mummies, sphinxes and crocodiles, the reader is quick to sense a moment of horror:

Der hat aber einen toten
Arm in meiner Hand gelassen.

The line-division forces the reader to linger on an unpleasant image. He cannot help feeling that there is something strange and cruel about laughter over a severed arm.

This grain of horror sharpens also the moral taste of this poem. The world of *Rhampsenit* is one in which theft and rape are rewarded with honour, and in which the thief, once raised to the throne, is in no way distinguishable from kings 'by the grace of God':

Er regierte wie die Andern,
Schützte Handel und Talente....

But faced with this truth, the reader finds himself impelled to react like Stubb in Melville's *Moby Dick*: 'A laugh's the wisest, easiest answer to all that's queer.'[1] Laughter has drowned terror and disgust—but only, we feel, for the moment. At the end of the poem the world of Rhampsenitus, hitherto so exuberantly and directly presented, recedes into the distance of hearsay:

Wenig, *heißt es*, ward gestohlen
Unter seinem Regimente.

The flight to the old, the distant and the strange is over.

Der weiße Elefant, a leisurely amble through an Eastern fairyland, represents yet another attempt at such a flight. The reader need not know that Heine is here ridiculing a famous beauty of his day, that same Countess Nesselrode-Kalergis who had been celebrated by Gautier in his *Symphonie en Blanc Majeur*.[2] What matters is a sense of profusion and riches—

Die Edelsteine vom höchsten Wert
Die liegen wie Erbsen hier auf der Erd
Hochaufgeschüttet....

—and a sense of utter absurdity, achieved principally by a transposition of human life into the elephantine. At the end of the

[1] *Moby Dick*, Book 1, ch. 38.

[2] This is clear from Caroline Jaubert's account of Heine's meeting with Countess Nesselrode-Kalergis (*Gespräche*, pp. 816–18).

poem Heine once again distances the improbable splendour and rich absurdity of his make-believe world. Fairytale India becomes modern Paris, where a poet vainly awaits news of his own creations:

> Was er beschlossen, das kann ich erzählen
> Erst später; die indischen Mallposten fehlen....

Once again the reader is taken out of the fairytale world and prepared to face the pressure of reality.

Rhampsenit and *Der weiße Elefant* had both been informed by the carnival spirit which is common to the German Rhineland and to Paris in the days preceding Ash Wednesday: a spirit which was to find its perfect expression in Offenbach's *Orphée aux Enfers*.[1] There had been in both poems an atmosphere of merry-making and dressing up—Prussian kings dressed up as Eastern potentates, elephants as Werther—which renders the transition to actual carnival celebrations and masquerades natural and easy. Such a transition occurs in *Schelm von Bergen*, the poem which follows *Der weiße Elefant* in the *Romanzero*.

Schelm von Bergen opens with a masked ball in a Rhenish castle, at Düsseldorf, Heine's own birth-place. The gaiety, splendour and colour of this ball are caught in the dance measure of Heine's amphibrachs and dactyls:

> Da tanzen die bunten Gestalten...
>
> Grüßen mit Schnarren und Schnalzen...;

in the vowel-music of lines like

> Da flimmern die Kerzen, da rauscht die Musik...

(how the music really obtrudes in the second half of that line!); and in the more obvious onomatopoeia of

> Und die Trompeten schmettern drein,
> Der närrische Brummbaß brummet.

Into the gaily apparelled company, and apparently belonging to it, Heine introduces a dancer in a black mask. At once the reader becomes conscious of something strange and uncanny—the patch

[1] Cf. S. Krakauer, *Offenbach and the Paris of his Time* (London, 1937), p. 165.

of black in the midst of 'bunte Gestalten' is made actual in the three dark *a* vowels ('Maske von schwarzem Samt') that have no counterparts in the earlier part of the poem. The line that follows, with its key-word 'freudig' and its ascent from dark *a* to light *i*, seems concerned to counteract this feeling; but it is followed, in its turn, by an image of unmistakable menace:

Ein Auge, wie ein blanker Dolch
Halb aus der Scheide gezücket.

Yet this too is at once drowned in the jubilation of the fourth stanza, crushed out of sight in the closely packed crowd of carnival fools.

Then music and jubilation cease, and human speech is heard for the first time: the dialogue between the masked dancer and the lady of the castle. In folk-song fashion, three snatches of dialogue are given, each introduced by the same formula: 'Durchlauchtigste Frau, gebt Urlaub mir'—a formula which recalls the old *Tannhäuser* ballad of which Heine had made such striking use in 1836:

Gebt mir Urlaub, Frau Venus zart,
Durch aller Frauen Ehre.

Here, in *Schelm von Bergen*, the repetition serves to throw into relief the progressively more frightening import of the black dancer's words. At first he speaks the language of the most ordinary conversation: 'Ich muß nach Hause gehen'; then he warns of terror to come: 'Mein Anblick bringt Schrecken und Grauen'; and at last, in stanzas added only in the *Romanzero* version of this poem,[1] his words shatter entirely the carnival atmosphere of light, colour, gaiety and whirling movement:

Der Nacht und dem Tode gehör ich.

Yet in face of all this, the duchess remains what she had been from the beginning: the woman laughing at the brink of an abyss. The image is familiar from *Ein Weib*; it had been suggested again by

[1] An earlier version of the poem had appeared in the *Kölnische Zeitung* of 31 May 1846. There is a survey of its subsequent evolution in vol. III of the 'Insel' edition of Heine, pp. 466–7.

the laughing princess of *Rhampsenit* and is to recur in *Pfalzgräfin Jutta*. Is laughter perhaps (as *Rhampsenit* had suggested) the answer to the terrors, the menace of life?

Now, as speech is about to issue into action, the dancer and the lady become generic, archetypal. No longer are they called 'ein schlanker Fant' and 'die schöne Herzogin':

> Wohl sträubt sich *der Mann* mit finsterm Wort,
> *Das Weib* nicht zähmen kunnt er.

They are Man and Woman *tout court*, performing a symbolic act, an act of great significance not only for this poem, but for the whole *Romanzero* and for Heine's poetry generally: the act of unmasking. The verse movement, with its strong stresses and hard finals ('zule*tzt*', 'Gewa*lt*') makes us re-experience that action almost physically:

> Sie riß zuletzt ihm mit Gewalt
> Die Maske vom Antlitz herunter.

Horror, death, has been unveiled in the midst of a carnival: to this, laughter is *no* answer.

The next line brings a precipitate cry ('Das ist der Scharfrichter von Bergen!') made more memorable by the line-division

> . . . so schreit
> Entsetzt . . . ;

followed by a slow backing away (transformed, by the verse movement, into something analogous to physical experience) which leaves the central pair isolated. And then, at the last, comes the duchess's headlong flight to the protection of her husband—again the line-division helps the words to *do* what they say:

> . . . die Herzogin
> Stürzt fort . . . .

This is the climax of the poem. The black executioner, belonging to night and death, stands alone in the midst of a motley crowd.

But for once, disaster can be averted, the gulf between the gay nobles and the sinister outcast, between joyous, colourful life and black death, can be bridged. And as the duke bridges that gulf, the poem slips imperceptibly from the present into the past tense:

> Der Herzog *ist* klug, er *tilgte* die Schmach....

A fairytale glamour is retrospectively thrown over the story:

> So ward der Henker ein Edelmann
> Und Ahnherr der Schelme von Bergen;

and then, as in *Rhampsenit* and *Der weiße Elefant*, the whole episode recedes into the distance:

> Ein stolzes Geschlecht! Es blühte am Rhein.
> Jetzt schläft es in steinernen Särgen.

In the end, night and death *did* conquer, as they must; and an image of stony death (the word 'blühte' helps, by contrast, to throw into relief the cold rigidity of those stone sarcophagi) fittingly ends the poem.

One must guard, however, as always in reading Heine, against over-simplification. The effect of the concluding lines of *Schelm von Bergen* is more complex than has just been suggested—for the word 'blühte' does not *merely* serve to emphasise the rigidity that follows, and the stone sarcophagi do not *merely* represent extinction. Life has somehow prospered, in that remote world the poet has conjured up; it has somehow refused to be terrorised by night and death and has left an impressive monument of itself. Perhaps it was all a trick, perhaps it was all make-believe—but somehow it has been 'managed'. Heine's tone is at once sardonic and tender, at once destructive of illusion and conscious of a hope that is born out of despair.

The central theme of *Schelm von Bergen* is also the central theme of the *Romanzero*—a theme summed up in a famous phrase from Heine's *Lutetia*: 'We are here dancing on a volcano—but we are dancing.'[1] The poem begins (like the *Romanzero*!) with the gayest of carnival atmospheres, into which intrude (as into the *Romanzero*!) intimations of something else, of something dark and menacing; intimations at once smothered by jubilation, light and swirling movement. Then follow the central stanzas (7–10)

[1] *SW*, VI, 294.

arresting music and movement, leading up to that blinding moment when 'otherness', night and death, stands alone in the midst of the horrified dancers. Life, however, in the person of the duke, here finds the compromise it could not find in Poe's related *Masque of the Red Death*. Or rather, life *was* able to find a compromise—for now the past tense replaces the present and the whole story recedes into the past. The life which then came to terms with 'otherness' and death has long since been conquered by time, and sleeps now in those coffins of stone which represent time's victory and on which the mind's eye lingers at the end of the poem. But there has been a triumph just the same. 'We are here dancing on a volcano—*but we are dancing*.'

This apparently so simple ballad associates with its main theme—gay life and 'otherness', the unmasking of horror in the midst of merry-making and dancing, the 'managing' of night and death—a number of subsidiary themes no less important in Heine's later work; themes which emerge clearly only if the poem is read in its *Romanzero* context. The juxtaposition of an aristocratic society and an executioner who strikes terror into it links *Schelm von Bergen* to *Karl I*; the insistence on the disreputable origin of a proud family recalls *Rhampsenit* and looks forward to *Valkyren*; and the portrait of an insatiable and insistent woman, the laughing woman, will be familiar to all readers of the later Heine. Above all, *Schelm von Bergen* presents most convincingly an outcast of a special kind: a man who fits perfectly into the best society—

Ihr Tänzer ist ein schlanker Fant,
Gar höfisch und behendig —

but from whom everyone shrinks away once his real nature and calling are known. That figure had fascinated Heine ever since he first presented it in *Donna Clara*[1]—we meet it in this study, with significant variations, in *Begegnung* and *Der Apollogott*.

Even the most cursory study of Heine's biography will show that the themes so subtly suggested by *Schelm von Bergen* have for the poet an immediate personal relevance. But neither this

[1] Cf. my account of *Donna Clara* in *Heine's 'Buch der Lieder'* (London, 1960), pp. 33–4.

poem nor any other in the *Romanzero* depends for its effect on a knowledge of biographical facts. Heine has succeeded in transforming his experience into generally accessible sensation: in conveying in perfectly organised language modes of experience peculiarly his own, which yet somehow belong to his century and are not foreign to ours. And what is more, he has learnt to speak (despite an occasional stridency and lapse of taste) without the self-pity, the posings and the over-dramatisation which so often mar his poetry.

Above all, *Schelm von Bergen* supplies the image which gives us a key to the *Romanzero*: the image of peering behind a mask, which is supplemented in *Maria Antoinette* by the complementary image of peering behind a façade. At the opening of that later poem Heine presents the gay spectacle of the windows of the Tuileries gleaming and sparkling in the sun:

> Wie heiter im Tuilerienschloß
> Blinken die Spiegelfenster...;

he then takes the reader behind that façade, where the ghosts of the past perform their half disgusting and half ridiculous ceremonies; and at last he returns to the opening spectacle to show that what looked like a joyous sparkle was in reality a horrified recoil:

> Wohl durch die verhängten Fenster wirft
> Die Sonne neugierige Blicke,
> Doch wie sie gewahrt den alten Spuk,
> Prallt sie erschrocken zurücke.

The *Romanzero* presents flights into illusion while knowing of their futility. It presents illusions and destroys them: it shows masks in order to tear them off, façades in order to break them down. It ruthlessly explores concepts dear to Romantic poetry and dear to Heine himself: sacred concepts like nobility, heroism and love. Heroes turn out, on closer inspection, to be either vulgarians or cowards (*Valkyren*, *Schlachtfeld bei Hastings*, *König David*, *Vitzliputzli*); love proves itself venal (*Pomare*, *Solidität*) or allied to cruelty and death (*Pfalzgräfin Jutta*, *Der*

Asra). Yet, strangely enough, these words do not lose their meaning: on the contrary, the *Romanzero* demonstrates again and again that true heroism *does* exist, though it shows itself more clearly in defeat than in victory, and that love, whether as *agape* or as *eros*, has power to ennoble and console.

3. FAIBISCH APOLLO

There's a most surprising lot of layers!
Are we never coming to the kernel?
Peer Gynt

HEINE had often depicted, in verse and prose, the transformation of the Greek pantheon into a pandaimonion—the degradation of classical gods and goddesses into devils after the coming of Christianity. *Die Nordsee*, *Zur Geschichte der Religion und Philosophie in Deutschland*, *Die romantische Schule* and, especially, *Die Götter im Exil* had dealt at length with this theme. Among these fallen and degraded gods two had engrossed the poet's attention with especial force: Venus, the 'Teufelinne' of *Der Tannhäuser*; and Apollo, the god of poetry and song. In the *Romanzero*, we see Apollo forced to pawn his lyre before Love will yield to him (*Solidität*); and we meet him again in one of the most disturbing poems of the whole collection—in *Der Apollogott*, in which the Greek, the Romantic-Germanic-Christian and the Jewish elements of Heine's inspiration meet and clash more violently than they had done in the 'Wild Hunt' sections of *Atta Troll*.

Der Apollogott is preceded, in the *Romanzero*, by the tetralogy *Pomare*, which tells of the corruptions and the heartlessness of modern cities; which presents the rise and fall of a famous cocotte who began in the mire—

Gestern noch fürs liebe Brot
Wälzte sie sich tief im Kot—

and after a brief moment of glory ended in a pauper's grave. Even that was a merciful end:

When I consider how this kind of comedy ends in reality: in the gutter of prostitution or the hospitals of Saint-Lazare or on the anatomical slab, where the medical student often sees the body of his former partner in love cut up for his instruction...then laughter dies in my throat.

So Heine had written in *Über die französische Bühne*.[1] His Pomare too is threatened with an end in which she is confounded with the animals that now draw her carriage:

Ach, es wird dich dieser Wagen
Nach dem Hospitale tragen,
Wo der grausenhafte Tod
Endlich endigt deine Not,
Und der Carabin mit schmierig
Plumper Hand und lernbegierig
Deinen schönen Leib zerfetzt,
Anatomisch ihn zersetzt —
Deine Rosse trifft nicht minder
Einst zu Montfaucon der Schinder;

she is saved from this fate only by the intervention of her old mother and her Father in heaven.

Arme Königin des Spottes,
Mit dem Diadem von Kot,
Bist gerettet jetzt durch Gottes
Ewge Güte, du bist tot.

Wie die Mutter, so der Vater
Hat Barmherzigkeit geübt,
Und ich glaube, dieses tat er,
Weil auch du so viel geliebt.

The irony of that last stanza—the absurd rhyme 'Vater'–'tat er' and the assimilation of God's love to the venal love of a courtesan —does little to alleviate the images of physical degradation and decomposition which had preceded it.

[1] *SW*, IV, 504.

Der Apollogott, however, opens as far as possible away from the 'Kot' in which Pomare had begun and ended. It opens with the vision of a secluded place of refuge, raised high above the turmoil of everyday life, firmly built on rock; with a vision of permanence and solidity that is mirrored in the regular, heavy stresses of the opening line:

> Das Kloster ist hoch auf Felsen gebaut.

Below this secluded convent flows the river which Heine held in special affection, whose majestic flow can be heard in the heavy stresses, the repeated *r* and the full vowels of the second line:

> Der Rhein vorüberrauschet.

But these suggestions of seclusion, solidity, majestic beauty soon turn into suggestions of another kind: suggestions of imprisonment, of insurmountable barriers. The stately, self-contained lines of the opening give way to straining enjambment; instead of the regularly constructed opening clause we have inversion, hurrying towards the subject:

> Wohl durch das Gitterfenster schaut
> Die junge Nonne....

A young nun looking through a barred window—an archetypal image of longing, well known to folk-song and German Romantic poetry. Folk-song is of course suggested also by the archaic use of 'wohl' and by the ballad metre in which this section of the poem is written.

The second stanza passes from the nun herself to what she sees and hears, and isolates one key-word. That word is 'märchenhaft', which ends the first line and is preceded by a pause; a word which stands in obvious relation to the folk-song elements of *Der Apollogott*, adding suggestions of the strange, unexpected, delightful and consciously regressive that are reinforced by hypnotic assonance:

> Da f*ä*hrt ein Schifflein, m*ä*rchenhaft
> Vom Abendrot beglänzet.

The reader can hardly fail to recognise the familiar situation. A fairytale atmosphere; a maiden on a rock; a boat on the Rhine as the sun goes down; golden hair, hypnotic allure, an irresistible song—all the elements of the most famous poem in the whole of the *Buch der Lieder* are here reproduced. But in *Der Apollogott*, the 'Lorelei' situation is strangely and characteristically inverted. The allure comes, not from above, but from below; the lonely figure imprisoned on her rock is attracted downwards, down to the world, by the colourful boatman.

And here we become conscious of a significant contrast. The opening suggestions of grey or black, of rigidity and asceticism are here confronted by suggestions of splendour and glitter, scarlet and gold, luxurious gaiety—suggestions of something which is at once beautiful and not 'respectable'.

> Ein schöner blondgelockter *Fant*
> Steht in des Schiffes Mitte;
> Sein goldgesticktes Purpurgewand
> Ist von antikem Schnitte.
>
> Zu seinen Füßen liegen da
> Neun marmorschöne *Weiber*;
> Die hochgeschürzte Tunika
> Umschließt die schlanken Leiber [my italics].

That is how 'Hellenic' allure enters a 'Nazarene' world; an allure which crystallises in the liquid consonants and the long *ie* and *ei* vowels of the fifth stanza and leads to the mingled pain and joy of the sixth:

> Sie schlägt ein Kreuz, und noch einmal
> Schlägt sie ein Kreuz, die Nonne,
> Nicht scheucht das Kreuz die süße Qual,
> Nicht bannt es die bittre Wonne.

With their insistent tunefulness and obtrusive oxymora, these lines, which end the first section of this tripartite ballad, read like a pastiche of Heine's own earlier poetry.

The second section, which purports to give the actual song that 'Apollo' sings as he sails down the Rhine, brings a striking change of tone. The tone is now that of a street minstrel, a *Bänkelsänger* who entertains the crowds in the market-place—witness popular forms of classical names like 'Musika', 'Gräcia', 'Artemisia' and so on. At the same time, modern Paris is allowed to intrude disconcertingly into reminiscences of ancient Greece:

> Mein Tempel hat in Gräcia
> Auf *Mont-Parnaß* gestanden.
>
> *Vokalisierend* saßen da
> Um mich herum die Töchter... [my italics].

If the first section had played with pastiche, the second plays with parody. Yet the effect of this most musical section of the poem is not, in the end, one of parody—it allows, rather, through its suggestions of a Parisian background beyond the German scene, the face of the exiled Heine to peep through his *personae*.

The second part of *Der Apollogott* speaks of a harmonious existence in which poetry comes as naturally as leaves to a tree; of a happy intoxication in a sylvan scene in which the world still appears apparelled in celestial light.

> Ich sang — und wie von selbst beinah
> Die Leier klang, berauschend;
> Mir war, als ob ich Daphne sah,
> Aus Lorbeerbüschen lauschend.
>
> Ich sang — und wie Ambrosia
> Wohlrüche sich ergossen,
> Es war von einer Gloria
> Die ganze Welt umflossen.

'Ergossen', 'umflossen'—the words characterise the rhythm, too. There are no harsh contours; all is drowned in sweet waves of sound. This imagined world knows no conflicts between Nazarene and Hellene, between beauty and morality—it presents an impossible existence (the elements of parody gently remind us of its impossibility!), a dreamland of childhood, a golden age, a Garden of Eden from which men are for ever banished and for which they long in vain.

And so the final stanza of this section opens with lines that flow irresistibly towards the word 'verbannt'—the bitter realisation of exile, driven home in the isolated 'vertrieben'; while the last lines of this stanza catch up and repeat caressingly the name 'Gräcia'. Around this name, with its historical and legendary associations, all the regressive longings of the poem crystallise; it is charged, in the end, with almost unbearable nostalgia.

Wohl tausend Jahr aus Gräcia
Bin ich verbannt, vertrieben —
Doch ist mein Herz in Gräcia,
In Gräcia geblieben.

Trembling on the edge of parody, the poem manages nevertheless to convey powerfully the longings of an exile for his home, of a poet for effortless life issuing in effortless poetry, of a man for that harmony which he dimly remembers in his own life or in the life of the world. There is no check to this regressive longing and feeling of grief and loss; no balancing insistence—such as we find, for instance, in Hölderlin, who had this same vision of Greece as the lost paradise of mankind—on the poet's mission to help the modern world to regain the harmony it has lost. The exiled god has become a dangerous will o' the wisp leading men to waste themselves in hopeless longing—he has become the beautiful, degraded Apollo of *Die Götter im Exil*:

Before his execution he asked to be allowed to play once more on his zither and to sing a song. But his playing was so moving and his singing so enchanting, and he was so beautiful to look at, that all the women wept and that later many of them even fell into a sickness because they had been so moved.[1]

He has become a demon who tempts men to waste themselves in the sort of dreams that Heine's Doktor Faust also knows—

. . . a limitless longing for the purely beautiful, for Greek harmony, for the selflessly pure figures of Homer's vernal world. . . .[2]

—sentimental dreams which *must* be followed by a harsh awakening.

The third section of *Der Apollogott* brings such an awakening. Rhyme (so insistent in the previous section) disappears as the nun

[1] *SW*, VI, 79. [2] *SW*, VI, 489.

leaves her high vantage-point and descends into the world to seek her newly found ideal; as the Nazarene frantically ('hastig' is a key-word) seeks sensual Hellenic beauty in the modern world. The change of atmosphere is unmistakable. No longer is the world 'märchenhaft / Vom Abendrot beglänzet'; no longer is it 'von einer Gloria . . . umflossen'. The world is viewed in clear cold daylight and found grotesque, in a section dominated by the voice and gestures of an undignified Jewish pedlar:

Doch des Wegs herangetrottelt
Kommt ein schlottrig alter Mensch,
Fingert in der Luft, wie rechnend,
Näselnd singt er vor sich hin. . . .

Here the search for Apollo, the Hellenic ideal, grotesquely ends. There *is* no Apollo, no 'Phoebus'—there is only 'Faibisch', the renegade cantor whose degraded life the pedlar now lovingly details.

Aus dem Amsterdamer Spielhuis
Zog er jüngst etwelche Dirnen,
Und mit diesen Musen zieht er
Jetzt herum als ein Apollo.

Eine dicke ist darunter,
Die vorzüglich quiekt und grünzelt;
Ob dem großen Lorbeerkopfputz
Nennt man sie die grüne Sau.

We are back in the world of *Pomare*, which had also assimilated prostitute and pig:

Gestern noch fürs liebe Brot
Wälzte sie sich tief im Kot . . .;

and we have not far to go to that image which Heine borrowed from the Grimms' fairytales[1] for the opening of the next poem in the *Romanzero*:

In einem Pißpott kam er geschwommen,
Hochzeitlich geputzt, hinab den Rhein. . . .

[1] *Kinder- und Hausmärchen*, no. 19: 'Von dem Fischer un syner Fru.'

The effect of *Der Apollogott* has been memorably described by Walther Killy in a recent book:

This...tale is intended to disillusion. The fable is frivolously simple, it gathers together in balladesque fashion the three great worlds which nourished the imagination of educated Germans: the Catholic and the Greek world and that world of the Old Testament to which Heine himself owed a double allegiance. But these turn out to be meaningless, a thousand years of exile from their country of origin have not left them unaffected, and what is left reveals itself as a chain of grotesque misunderstandings. The mythological figure is revealed as the cliché which graces every theatre curtain. Apollo—or rather the emancipated mountebank mistaken for someone else because of a philological error—has become a dubitable buffoon. He is wholly secularised and historicised into the present in which he tremulously sings his songs. ...In this way Apollo ends in the gutter in the middle of a century which saw at its beginning Goethe's and Hölderlin's use of Greek mythology and the mythologemes of Görres and Creuzer....Just as he conceived nature as cliché, so Heine had to conceive mythology as literature. In both he was no longer able to sense the truth which had been covered over by the rubble of time.[1]

Professor Killy has rightly seen the *disillusion* behind this disconcerting poem which leads its readers so steeply down from the remoteness of a mountain fastness to the sordid world below. He has rightly seen Heine's secularisation of Greek myth and his playing with the myths of Judaism and Christianity. Yet he has not seen deeply enough: he has not recognised that *Der Apollogott* is neither cynical nor hopeless, and that the myths that Heine uses with such sovereign freedom are not *all* shown up as mere 'literature'. Above all, he has not seen the complexity of the structure of this poem and its shifting angles of vision.

The three parts of the poem make the reader look at the same phenomenon—at the poet in the modern world—from three distinct points of view. First, in a section that slides again and again into pastiche, we share the point of view of a romantic maiden, who sees and hears the poet for a moment, in the distance, and feels in his song something colourful, gay, beautiful,

[1] W. Killy, *Wandlungen des lyrischen Bildes* (Göttingen, 1958), pp. 113–14.

daring, infinitely alluring—something which makes her feel her own existence as cramping and drab. She makes the mistake, however, of identifying 'Apollo' the *poet* with 'Apollo' the *man*; and so she comes up against another vision, that of the pedlar, who knows little about 'Apollo's' song, but all about the history of his family, the cost of his coat and the nature of the company he keeps.

Seinen Vater Moses Jitscher
Kenn ich gut. Vorhautabschneider
Ist er bei den Portugiesen.
Er beschnitt auch Souveräne.

Seine Mutter ist Cousine
Meines Schwagers, und sie handelt
Auf der Gracht mit sauern Gurken
Und mit abgelebten Hosen.

This is a contrast Heine had presented many times—notably in a famous passage of *Die romantische Schule*:

O how sad it is to see the stars on our literary firmament from close proximity! Perhaps the stars of heaven appear to us so beautiful only because we stand at a distance from them and do not know their private life.[1]

At the same time, however, Heine ever insisted that an artist cannot be judged merely by examining his origins and associates—'some people', he mocks in his notebooks, 'think they know the bird exactly because they have seen the egg out of which it has slipped'; and so he interposes between the vision of the nun and that of the pedlar a section which allows the reader to hear 'Apollo' for himself. The central section of *Der Apollogott* presents directly, with undeniable beauty, a song in which Romantic melody blends strangely with classical inspiration; in which the face of an exiled German poet in modern Paris peeps out incongruously from behind a classical mask; in which a moving lament is uttered in the tones of a market entertainer; in which genuine grief is not invalidated by suggestions of parody.

The reader is thus made to feel directly that the central figure of

[1] *SW*, v, 297.

Der Apollogott is *at once* Phoebus and Faibisch; at once a god and a vulgar street singer; at once a great poet and a sordid man.

What is more: the central section of the poem suggests an explanation of this dual state. 'Apollo' feels himself exiled, fallen from a former glory.

> Wohl tausend Jahr aus Gräcia
> Bin ich verbannt, vertrieben....

It is a lament we often hear in the *Romanzero*—in *Der Mohrenkönig*, for instance, or at the end of *Vitzliputzli*—and its autobiographical relevance is obvious. But what Heine is here presenting is not only his feeling that he himself did not 'belong'; not only his feeling that poets were necessarily exiles in the modern world. He has here re-formulated, in terms of his own experience, that great Judaeo-Christian myth whose relevance he had so often denied but whose truth he was now painfully experiencing. *Der Apollogott* presents ultimately the myth of the Fall, of man created noble and in God's image, but now tainted by sin and fallen from grace; of man's kinship with the angels and with the beasts; of man as at once, in Pascal's phrase, 'gloire et rebut de l'univers'.

In one way *Der Apollogott*, like *Schelm von Bergen*, is a poem of unmasking. It shows the danger of prying too closely, of pursuing the truth too far. But despite the sordid and disillusioned end of *Der Apollogott*, the reader must feel—as Helene Herrmann long ago pointed out[1]—that the pedlar's vision is just as partial as that of the nun and that the whole truth is there, for all who wish to hear it, in Faibisch Apollo's song.

[1] H. Herrmann, *Studien zu Heines 'Romanzero'* (Berlin, 1906), pp. 71–2.

4. ECHOES OF THE OUTSIDE WORLD

Bin ich es noch, der da unkenntlich brennt?
Erinnerungen reiß ich nicht herein.
O Leben, Leben: Draußensein.
Und ich in Lohe. Niemand, der mich kennt.

RILKE

HEINE's world, after 1848, was that of the sick-room and the fantasies and memories that peopled it—and as a true lyric poet, he used such material as came to him from his reading to symbolise and distance his own plight and problems. This holds good even in apparently remote instances. What parallel, one is inclined to ask, can there be between the sick man in the Rue Amsterdam and nuns that have broken their vows and are doomed to haunt the convent walls that saw their sin? How, in other words, can *Himmelsbräute* be regarded as 'personal confession'? Yet in a conversation with Fanny Lewald Heine used the central image of *Himmelsbräute* to describe his own plight:

My love of life is like the ghost of a tender nun in old convent walls; it only haunts the ruins of my self.[1] (22 March 1848)

Even in the most exotic ballads of the *Romanzero*—as *Vitzliputzli* serves to show—the reader is brought close to the sick poet and his experience of the world.

That experience, naturally enough, was no longer one continually fed by the outer world and normal social intercourse. Dimly the *Romanzero* seems conscious of the Paris outside:

Draußen Nacht und Schneegestöber
Und das Rollen von Fiakern, (*Zwei Ritter*)

while within reality is distorted and waking and dreaming seem hardly distinguishable. There is much in the *Romanzero* that recalls De Quincey's 'dreams of oriental imagery and mythological tortures', in which 'buildings, landscapes, etc. were exhibited in proportions so vast as the bodily eye is not fitted to receive', and the opium-eater's faculty, again described by De Quincey,

[1] *Gespräche*, p. 609. The image was probably suggested to Heine by Meyerbeer's *Robert le Diable*.

of painting, as it were, on the darkness all sorts of phantoms.... This faculty became positively distressing to me: at night, when I lay awake in bed, vast processions passed along in mournful pomp.... A theatre seemed suddenly opened and lighted up within my brain, and presented mighty spectacles of more than earthly splendour....[1]

This has obvious relevance to *Vitzliputzli*, for instance. Readers of the *Romanzero* will also recognise many of the features of anxiety-dreams listed by Ernest Jones in his book *On The Nightmare*:

The sudden transformation of one person into another or into an animal; the occurrence of phantastic and impossible animal forms; the alternation of the imagined object between extreme attractiveness and the most intense disgust...; the idea of flying or riding through the air; and the apprehension of sexual acts as torturing assaults.[2]

Mysteriously figures from books—historical, like Charles I and Marie Antoinette, or imaginary, like the Asra—mingle with shadowy dream-figures (the three voyagers of *Nächtliche Fahrt*) and the figures of Heine's waking life, strangely transformed. Mathilde's parrot, for instance, screeches in *Präludium* and *Jehuda ben Halevi*:

Auf den Baumesästen schaukeln
Große Vögel. Ihr Gefieder
Farbenschillernd. Mit den ernsthaft
Langen Schnäbeln und mit Augen

Brillenartig schwarz umrändert,
Schaun sie auf dich nieder, schweigsam —
Bis sie plötzlich schrillend aufschrein
Und wie Kaffeeschwestern schnattern. (*Präludium*)

Mathilde herself walks in *Gedächtnisfeier* and her perfumes bring torturing memories in *Präludium*. The poet's sick-nurses appear too. Here is Henri Julia's description of an incident in the Rue Amsterdam:

The poet, who wanted to have only fresh and charming faces about him, took pleasure in seeing himself served and nursed by young Marietta, who was attractive to look at and had such pleasant manners.

[1] *Confessions of an English Opium Eater*, ed. Sharp, pp. 83, 88, 96.

[2] *On the Nightmare* (London, 1931), pp. 238–9.

Unfortunately Madame Heine would not agree to this, and Dr Gruby was instructed to dismiss Marietta. This was done, although poor Marietta had performed her duties admirably and had been of impeccable behaviour. Dr Gruby replaced her with an old and ugly nurse whom the poor poet could not stand and of whom he spoke with rage years afterwards. He once said to me, pulling a pitiful face: 'No, the old guard (*Vieille Garde*) of Napoleon could not have struck more terror into me than the old nurse (*vieille garde*) of Dr Gruby.'[1]

Transformed and transfigured, Marietta and the 'vieille garde' appear in the motto of *Lamentationen*:

Das Glück ist eine leichte Dirne,
Und weilt nicht gern am selben Ort;
Sie streicht das Haar dir von der Stirne
Und küßt dich rasch und flattert fort.

Frau Unglück hat im Gegenteile
Dich liebefest ans Herz gedrückt;
Sie sagt, sie habe keine Eile
Setzt sich zu dir ans Bett und strickt —

and again, more recognisably, in *Frau Sorge*:

An meinem Bett in der Winternacht
Als Wärterin die Sorge wacht.
Sie trägt eine weiße Unterjack,
Ein schwarzes Mützchen, und schnupft Tabak,
Die Dose knarrt so gräßlich,
Die Alte nickt so häßlich....

Later, a mulatto nurse will become the grotesque Kaka of *Bimini*. Dream, reality and remembered reading are all sea-changed into powerful symbols, communicating a poet's experience of the nature of the world.

Politics, however, no longer seemed real. In the revolution of 1848 Heine could see nothing but a crazy farce, 'God's madness become visible'. 'I say nothing', he wrote to Campe on 9 July 1848, 'about what is happening in these times; it is universal anarchy, the world turned upside down, divine madness made

[1] *Gespräche*, pp. 867–8. Cf. Heine's letter to Dr L. Wertheim, 21 March 1850 (*Briefe*, III, 201).

visible! If this goes on, the Old One will have to be locked up. The atheists are to blame for all this, they have driven Him out of His wits.' The blasphemy is characteristic; yet the whole of this letter to Campe bears out what Alfred Meissner saw when he visited the poet in 1849: 'Heine had given up politics; his literary work was now most important to him and religious questions gradually insinuated themselves into his mind.'[1]

From this new position the *Romanzero* looks back at the heroes of liberty. There are, first, the heroic Poles who had so stirred up the sympathy and the conscience of Europe in the 1830's—Platen had likened them to the band of Leonidas, Herwegh had called on all people to avenge 'the death-rattle of poor murdered Polonia', Lenau had celebrated their tragic fortitude, and Maltitz, in his now forgotten *Polonia*, had expressed clearly what was in all German minds: that these Polish heroes of freedom had done in the real world what German liberals did only in imagination. Now, in the 1850's, Heine thinks of the survivors of that heroic rebellion whom he had met in Paris—and he sees them as soft and corrupt, as addicted to creature comforts no less whole-heartedly than the meanest Philistine.

Hätt ich doch hier in Paris
Meinen Bärenpelz, den lieben
Schlafrock und die Katzfell-Nachtmütz,
Die im Vaterland geblieben!

Zwei Ritter, from which these lines come, is one of Heine's funniest poems—but it is also, as J. P. Stern has rightly pointed out,[2] a 'horrid' poem. It is horrid precisely because Heine was here for once voicing views which were not unfashionable; because he was providing, half unconsciously, ammunition for those aggressive German nationalists who sought to compensate themselves for concessions at home by looking down on their Slav neighbours. He was helping to build up the picture of Poland and the Poles which was to appear with such frightening clarity in Gustav Freytag's *Soll und Haben* of 1855 and was to take the political forms we have experienced in our own times.

[1] *Gespräche*, p. 637.

[2] *Cambridge Journal*, November 1953.

Unlike Gustav Freytag, however, Heine does not invest the German *Bürgertum* with the mission of civilising the 'backward and effete' Poles. He looks at German liberalism with a no less jaundiced eye—sees Herwegh as *Der Ex-Lebendige*, Dingelstedt as *Der Ex-Nachtwächter*, whose ideas were always cloudy and who have now made their peace with the Philistines with whom they always, in spirit, belonged.

Ihr schautet manchmal in die Höh,
Wo die dunklen Wolken jagen —
Viel dunklere Wolke war die Idee,
Die Ihr im Herzen getragen.

Brutus, wo ist dein Cassius?
Er denkt nicht mehr ans Morden!
Es heißt, er sei am Neckarfluß
Tyrannenvorleser geworden....

(*Der Ex-Lebendige*)

Seven years after Heine's death, in 1863, Herwegh himself summed up Heine's attitude in a poem that cleverly uses a metre, images and phrases borrowed from the *Romanzero* itself:

Mit uns allen geht es *ex*;
'Trägst du noch so hoch den Scheitel',
Spricht ein alter Versifex,
'Unter der Sonn ist alles eitel'.

Brutus, Cassius sind *ex*,
Die es einst so toll getrieben,
Und ich hab an meinen *Rex*
Keine Briefe mehr geschrieben.

Mit dem stolzen Flug ist's *ex*,
Aus ist's mit den Sturmgesängen;
An dem Leim des goldnen Drecks
Bleiben jetzt die Spatzen hängen.

Einer nach dem andern schleicht
Sich vom Tanze — die Poeten
Werden klug — man kann so leicht
Einen Fuß sich übertreten. (*Heinrich Heine*)[1]

[1] Herwegh, *Werke*, ed. H. Tardel, III, 83.

The 1848 revolution had shown up the feebleness of German liberals in a way which seemed to justify all Heine's jests at their expense in *Atta Troll* and *Zeitgedichte*.

As for Gustav Freytag's real hero, the industrious and fundamentally unpolitical *Bürger*—Heine takes a look at him at the beginning of the most powerful political poem of the *Romanzero*: *Im Oktober 1849*.

Gelegt hat sich der starke Wind,
Und wieder stille wird's daheime;
Germania, das große Kind,
Erfreut sich wieder seiner Weihnachtsbäume.

Wir treiben jetzt Familienglück —
Was höher lockt, das ist vom Übel —
Die Friedensschwalbe kehrt zurück,
Die einst genistet in des Hauses Giebel.

Gemütlich ruhen Wald und Fluß,
Von sanftem Mondlicht übergossen;
Nur manchmal knallt's — Ist das ein Schuß? —
Es ist vielleicht ein Freund, den man erschossen.

Heine here mocks the programmatic self-limitation of the *Biedermeier* ('Wir *treiben* jetzt Familienglück') which was to find such moving and uncompromising expression in the later work of Adalbert Stifter; he presents a caricature of the ideals of the German 'Poetic Realists', with their search for a provincial idyll in an unquiet world:

Kaum zittert durch die Mittagsruh
Ein Schlag der Dorfuhr, der entfernten;
Dem Alten fällt die Wimper zu,
Er träumt von seinen Honigernten. —
Kein Klang der aufgeregten Zeit
Drang noch in diese Einsamkeit.[1]

(Theodor Storm, *Abseits*)

Behind the *gemütlich* idyll lurks violence and repression; the 'sound of the unquiet times' which dimly penetrates into the idyllic scene of Heine's poem may be just fireworks in celebration of Henriette Sontag's return to the stage, but it is just as likely to be a gunshot

[1] The poem is readily accessible in the *Oxford Book of German Verse* (no. 396).

fired by the forces of reaction against some unusually bold friend of liberty:

Vielleicht mit Waffen in der Hand
Hat man den Tollkopf angetroffen
(Nicht jeder hat so viel Verstand
Wie Flaccus, der so kühn davongeloffen).

The mention of Horace in this context is significant. Heine is no longer measuring the failures of his own times against past greatness or at least past superiority; he now believes

that the world goes on like the plays of Gozzi, in all of which the same characters appear with the same intention and the same fate. It is true that motives and events are different in each piece, but the spirit of the events is the same. The persons in one play know nothing of their predecessors in the other, in which they themselves played a part: therefore, after all their past experiences, Pantalone has become no more agile and open-handed, Tortaglia no more conscientious, Brighella no more courageous and Colombine no more moral.

These sentences come from Schopenhauer's *Die Welt als Wille und Vorstellung*,[1] but they express much of the spirit of Heine's *Romanzero*.

The menacing gunshots that break into the caricatured *Biedermeier* world of *Im Oktober 1849* go unregarded; the good burghers are more interested in celebrating the Goethe centenary, or the return of Henriette Sontag, or the advent of a new virtuoso: Franz Liszt. Liszt, of course, was a Hungarian, and his fame contrasts with the unrecorded and unregarded death of those heroic countrymen of his who had lately revolted against Habsburg sovereignty and had been crushed with Russian help.

Es klirrt mir wieder im Gemüt
Die Heldensage, längst verklungen,
Das eisern wilde Kämpenlied —
Das Lied vom Untergang der Nibelungen.

Es ist dasselbe Heldenlos,
Es sind dieselben alten Mären,
Die Namen sind verändert bloß,
Doch sind's dieselben 'Helden lobebären'.

[1] Schopenhauer, *Sämtliche Werke*, 2. Aufl. (Leipzig, 1877), II, 215–16.

Es ist dasselbe Schicksal auch —
Wie stolz und frei die Fahnen fliegen,
Es muß der Held, nach altem Brauch,
Den tierisch rohen Mächten unterliegen.

The *Nibelungenlied* is not only talked about; it is there, concretely, in the stanza form, with its extra foot in each final line.[1] Once again, Heine insists on the endless repetitions of history—once again he broaches the theme of *Valkyren* and *Schlachtfeld von Hastings*: the necessary defeat of the better man. And then, in the last line of the stanzas just quoted, the insistent *animal* imagery of the *Romanzero* recurs, applied here to the enemies of liberty.

Und diesmal hat der Ochse gar
Mit Bären einen Bund geschlossen —
Du fällst....

The ox, of course, is Schwarzenberg's Austria, the bear is the Russia of Czar Nicholas I; and the imagery suggests, horrifyingly, the spectacle of noble men senselessly mauled and trampled to death. Yet even this is not the end. The ox and the bear deserve some respect—the forces of reaction have some nobility, which Heine had saluted on more than one occasion, often to the astonishment and discomfiture of his liberal friends. A worse fate awaits those lovers of liberty who did not perish in Hungary:

Du fällst; doch tröste dich, Magyar,
Wir andre haben schlimmre Schmach genossen.

Anständge Bestien sind es doch,
Die ganz honett dich überwunden;
Doch wir geraten in das Joch
Von Wölfen, Schweinen und gemeinen Hunden.

This is an image of a *Verkehrte Welt* more disturbing than any in the poem of that name: an image of an Animal Farm in which beasts reverse the order of nature by laying a yoke on men. The poem ends with suggestions of the cacophonously triumphant cries and the noisome stench of the victorious animals and with a

[1] The longer and weightier final line is, of course, one of the most striking features of the *Nibelungenstrophe*.

return to the sick singer of the song, the Lazarus who would do better to keep silent, husband his strength and cease provoking the enemies he cannot crush:

> Doch still, Poet, das greift dich an —
> Du bist so krank, und schweigen wäre klüger.

The beasts that dominate the final stanzas of *Im Oktober 1849* represent the new aristocracy of wealth which had come to dominate French and was creeping also into German society. They stand for the powers that had opposed Heine himself in the quarrel with Salomon Strauss and Jeanette Wohl; the powers that had recently tried their strength with him in the struggle over Salomon Heine's inheritance. They stand for the financiers and virtuosos that controlled and corrupted the French press in their own interests and for the French and German journalists, spies and claqueurs that served their ends. All these creatures turn up again and again in Heine's correspondence, conversations and journalistic reports under the guise of rapacious or filthy beasts—in later years the 'bed-bug' image is to assimilate them all, while the image of the 'donkey' turns up more and more frequently to suggest their dupes and tools. To them—to dirty beasts and insects sitting on money-bags—the present belongs: they have imposed, as *Weltlauf* suggests with powerful irony, their perverted values on modern society:

> Hat man viel, so wird man bald
> Noch viel mehr dazu bekommen.
> Wer nur wenig hat, dem wird
> Auch das Wenige genommen. (*Lazarus* 1)

The corrupting and soiling power of money is one of the principal themes of the whole *Romanzero*. During the inheritance quarrel Heine had experienced it all too painfully in his own mind and soul.

The power of money is suggested also at the beginning of an earlier poem which Heine first published in Püttmann's *Album* of 1847 under the title *Zur Doktrin*. This poem was written soon after the already ailing poet's first exhilarating encounter with the

Socialist Ferdinand Lassalle; an encounter which drew from him the comment (in a letter to Lassalle's father): 'In this youth I see the Messiah of the century' as well as the slightly more equivocal recommendation of Lassalle to his old friend Varnhagen von Ense:

Herr Lassalle is definitely the son of the new age, who wants to have nothing to do with the renunciation and diffidence with which we, in *our* time, have more or less hypocritically loafed and gabbled our way along. This new generation wants to enjoy itself and make its presence felt in the visible world; we, the older generation, bowed down humbly before the invisible, aspired to shadowy kisses and the scent of blue flowers, renounced and wept and were, perhaps, happier than these hard gladiators who go so proudly to meet their death in battle.... Like myself, you have helped to bury the old times and have played midwife to the new—yes, we have helped to bring the new age to the light of day and now we are afraid. We are like the poor hen that has hatched a duck's eggs and is horrified to see her young brood plunge into the water and swim comfortably! (Letter of 3 January 1846)

By the time the *Romanzero* was published, Lassalle had become, for Heine, 'one of the most terrible villains' (to Gustav Heine, 21 January 1851); but the poem he had earlier helped to inspire found a place in the *Romanzero* in spite of all.

It is now entitled *An die Jungen* and encourages a new generation to avoid the mistakes of the old:

Laß dich nicht kirren, laß dich nicht wirren
Durch goldne Äpfel in deinem Lauf!
Die Schwerter klirren, die Pfeile schwirren,
Doch halten sie nicht den Helden auf.

One recalls the promise of the traveller of *Deutschland. Ein Wintermärchen*:

Es wächst heran ein neues Geschlecht,
Ganz ohne Schminke und Sünden,
Mit freien Gedanken, mit freier Lust —
Dem werde ich alles verkünden. (Caput XXVII)

An die Jungen proclaims, through the myth of Atalanta and Hippomenes, the danger of corruption through gold; and in the stanzas that follow, the story of Alexander the Great is used to illustrate the success that awaits the bold, fearless and incorruptible. The internal rhymes, so unusual in Heine, suggest a martial music, a quick dealing of blow for blow:

> Ein kühnes Beginnen ist halbes Gewinnen,
> Ein Alexander erbeutet die Welt!
> Kein langes Besinnen! Die Königinnen
> Erwarten schon knieend den Sieger im Zelt.

In the original version of this poem, the final stanza had intensified this martial music, had ended with gestures of extravagant enjoyment and defiance even of the prospect of death:

> Wir sind die Erben. Wir schlagen in Scherben
> Die Becher, woraus wir getrunken schon!
> Und müssen wir sterben, zuletzt wir erwerben
> Den schönen Triumphtod in Babylon.[1]

The *Romanzero* version retains the sudden shift of perspective implied in the use of *wir*, this sudden speaking with the very voice of the new generation—but it intensifies the sexual suggestions which had been only dimly present in the version of 1847:

> Wir wagen, wir werben! besteigen als Erben
> Des alten Darius Bett und Thron;

and then it breaks out into what can only be called a paean to death:

> O süßes Verderben! O blühendes Sterben!
> Berauschter Triumphtod zu Babylon!

Nothing could be more unlike the martial janissary-music of the rest of the poem than these superbly melodious lines. With their suggestions of the sweetness and intoxication of death and their intensified sexual imagery they recall nothing so much as the music of Wagner's *Tristan und Isolde*. Death is no longer something to be just accepted ('Und müssen wir sterben...'); death is a desirable goal, a fulfilment, if it comes in the midst of battle and sexual conquest—if it is 'ein blühendes Sterben' and not the slow, miserable dying of a Lazarus prostrate among dogs.

[1] *SW*, I, 556.

5. LAZARUS

Death destroys a man, but the idea of death saves him—that is the best account of it that has yet been given.

E. M. FORSTER

TRAGICALLY ambivalent figures—the executioner of *Schelm von Bergen*, Faibisch of *Der Apollogott*, the Shah and the poet of *Der Dichter Firdusi*, the mad 'saviour' of *Nächtliche Fahrt*, Cortez of *Vitzliputzli*—are at the heart of the first section of the *Romanzero*. Their equivalent in the second section is the Biblical character who gives his name to the most impressive group of poems: Lazarus.

There was a certain rich man, which was clothed in purple and fine linen, and fared sumptuously every day:

And there was a certain beggar named Lazarus, which was laid at his gate, full of sores,

And desiring to be fed with crumbs which fell from the rich man's table: moreover the dogs came and licked his sores.

(Luke xvi. 19–21)

It is easy to see what attracted the sick poet to the Lazarus figure presented by St Luke. The beggar's sores could stand as a symbol of his own disease; the prostration among dogs would suggest at once the helplessness of a lamed man and the bad company to which (as Heine so often lamented) the exiled and the indigent were condemned; while the opposition of the helpless beggar and the rich man clothed in purple offered a tempting analogy to the place of an unbusinesslike poet in a commercial world:

Wenn du aber gar nichts hast,
Ach, so lasse dich begraben —
Denn ein Recht zum Leben, Lump,
Haben nur die etwas haben.

That stanza comes from the opening poem of the *Lazarus* cycle in the *Romanzero*, and it speaks with the very voice of Dives—a voice that curiously resembles the voice of Thomas John at the opening of Chamisso's *Peter Schlemihl*: 'Whoever cannot command at least a million is—if you will excuse the expression—a rogue!'[1] And if the first *Lazarus* poem assumes the accent of Dives, the second speaks unmistakably with that of Lazarus himself; it alludes obliquely to that subsequent fate of Dives and his like which St Luke has so powerfully painted:

Lebt wohl! Dort oben, ihr christlichen Brüder,
Ja, das versteht sich, dort sehn wir uns wieder.

With this figure from St Luke's gospel other figures merge in the *Romanzero*: Job, that other Biblical sufferer whose sores were licked by the dogs, and the Wandering Jew, who laments his immortality:

Lange schon, jahrtausendlange
Kocht's in mir. Ein dunkles Wehe!
Und die Zeit leckt meine Wunde
Wie der Hund die Schwären Hiobs.

Dank dir, Hund, fur deinen Speichel —
Doch das kann nur kühlend lindern —
Heilen kann mich nur der Tod,
Aber, ach, ich bin unsterblich! (*Jehuda ben Halevi*)

And finally, the Lazarus of St Luke coalesces with another Lazarus—that of St John who rears his head so terrifyingly in Eliot's *Lovesong of J. Alfred Prufrock*:

I am Lazarus, come from the dead,
Come back to tell you all, I shall tell you all.

The Lazarus of St John's gospel has seen the secrets of another world and in this he resembles the poet of *Romanzero*, who seems, as Berlioz realised, to speak with the voice of one who belongs already to the kingdom of the dead:

Il a l'air d'être à la fenêtre de sa tombe pour regarder encore ce monde dont it ne fait plus partie.[2]

Heine's choice of this composite Lazarus figure for his last great *persona* was thus a happy one. It suggests deepest humiliation and most abject suffering—but it suggests also insight and triumph. It conveys the triumph of a beggar who was destined to rest,

[1] *Chamissos Werke*, ed. M. Sydow (Goldene Klassiker Bibliothek), III, 162.
[2] *Briefe*, VI, 110.

ultimately, in Abraham's bosom; and the triumph of a man who had been declared dead and yet returned to sit beside his Lord (John xii. 2).

The *Lazarus* cycle of the *Romanzero* unites poems of many kinds and moods. There are expressions of hatred and rage—in controlled indictments of commercial values (the world of Dives!) like *Weltlauf* and *Lumpentum*; in ironical compliments to former loves like *Unvollkommenheit*; and in the savage curses on personal enemies in *Vermächtnis*. We hear a muted music of death: sometimes, as in *Fromme Warnung*, with satirical overtones; and the prospect of death dominates every poem. At the end of *Rückschau* death seems to be anticipated as a relief from suffering and disillusion; but even here the anticipation is tinged with irony. More often, death comes as 'der böse Thanatos' who drags men away from what they love:

> Er reißt mich fort, Mathilden soll ich lassen,
> O, den Gedanken kann mein Herz nicht fassen!
> (*An die Engel*)

or he comes in a shape that is undignified and unwelcome:

> Mancher leider wurde lahm
> Und nicht mehr nach Hause kam —
> Streckt verlangend aus die Arme,
> Daß der Herr sich sein erbarme! (*Sterbende*)

The *Lazarus* cycle is full of such images of paralysis and physical and mental suffering:

> Jetzt lieg ich auf feuchtem Rasen,
> Die Glieder sind mir rheumatisch gelähmt,
> Und meine Seele ist tief beschämt... (*Rückschau*)

> Ach, ich liege jetzt am Boden,
> Kann mich nimmermehr erheben.
>
> Und Ade! sie sind zerronnen,
> Goldne Wünsche, süßes Hoffen!
> Ach, zu tödlich war der Faustschlag,
> Der mich just ins Herz getroffen...;
> (*Verlorene Wünsche*)

images from which the reader escapes for a moment to wish-dreams of other, happier, more protected and cherished modes of existence (*Salomo*) or to memories of a comparatively happy past (*Rückschau*, *Verlorene Wünsche*, *Frau Sorge*, *Wiedersehen*, *Böses Geträume*). Such memories, however, serve only to illustrate the truth that Dante's Francesca had learnt in the second circle of Hell:

> Nessun maggior dolore,
> che ricordarsi del tempo felice
> nella miseria;[1]

and they are followed, inevitably, by a harsh awakening:

> Was sie zur Antwort gab, das weiß ich nimmer,
> Denn ich erwachte jählings — und ich war
> Wieder ein Kranker, der im Krankenzimmer
> Trostlos daniederliegt seit manchem Jahr.
>
> (*Böses Geträume*)

There are, it is true, glances at a world beyond death, visions of resurrection and judgment. *Auferstehung*, for instance, presents an impressive vision of the Last Judgment and rings with the trumpet-notes of which it speaks; but the vision is consciously archaic, 'folk-like', and commands no real assent. *Auferstehung* therefore ends with a parody of heavenly justice—

> Der Himmel dem Schäfchen fromm und brav,
> Dem geilen Bock die Hölle! —

which prepares for the presentation of heaven as a Philistine's pipe-dream in *Fromme Warnung*. It is not to death and a problematical world beyond that this new Lazarus feels most strongly drawn: he yearns rather for earthly pleasures he will never taste again (*Der Abgekühlte*), is full of tender concern for those he must leave behind (*An die Engel*, *Gedächtnisfeier*), looks again at the political scene in which he will never more act (*Im Oktober 1849*) and tries to survey, in retrospect, his own contribution to the political and social battles of his time (*Enfant Perdu*).

The most moving of these poems at the threshold of death is

[1] *Inferno*, Canto v, ll. 121–3.

Gedächtnisfeier, rightly one of Heine's best-known and best-loved poems.

Keine Messe wird man singen,
Keinen Kadosch wird man sagen,
Nichts gesagt und nichts gesungen
Wird an meinen Sterbetagen.

That opening stanza, with its many incantatory repetitions, its heavy measured tread and its alliterative ritual formulae, speaks with the voice of a man who has, in spirit, already left this earth: who looks on at the anniversaries of his own death from a point beyond time. What he sees is utter desolation and emptiness; for he is shut out alike from the ritual of the Christian and that of the Jewish community, and shut off too from those Germanic traditions that are suggested by the phrase 'singen und sagen'. Again and again the stress crashes down on the words 'kein' and 'nichts', intensifying the prevailing sense of deprivation and loss to a point that is almost unbearable. But then the tone changes:

Doch vielleicht an solchem Tage,
Wenn das Wetter schön und milde,
Geht spazieren auf Montmartre
Mit Paulinen Frau Mathilde.

Mit dem Kranz von Immortellen
Kommt sie mir das Grab zu schmücken,
Und sie seufzet: Pauvre homme!
Feuchte Wehmut in den Blicken.

Heine's tone is now at once tender and humorous—a bourgeois genre-picture is seen *sub specie aeternitatis* and presented with the gentlest irony. The irony, of course, lies mainly in the unexpressed contrast between the impressive ceremonies of the Catholic mass and of the Jewish prayer for the dead, and Mathilde's 'Pauvre homme'. The mention of Mathilde by name makes it quite clear that Heine is here speaking in his own proper person—that he has dropped the mask of Lazarus and wishes his readers to think of the fate of Heinrich Heine, the sick man of the Rue d'Amsterdam. And is not Mathilde's 'Pauvre homme' a poor memorial to a great German poet? Yet it is good to be loved and remembered even by one human being; and *Gedächtnisfeier* is now invaded by a wave of tenderness.

Leider wohn ich viel zu hoch,
Und ich habe meiner Süßen
Keinen Stuhl hier anzubieten;
Ach! sie schwankt mit müden Füßen.

Süßes, dickes Kind, du darfst
Nicht zu Fuß nach Hause gehen;
An dem Barrièregitter
Siehst du die Fiaker stehen.

The object of love is seen for what she is—a stout and rather foolish child, whose tired gait is there in the very rhythms of the stanzas that speak of her; a child, moreover, to whom one cannot speak of one's deepest concerns, but to whom one must point out—even from beyond the grave—where she can get a *fiacre*. Yet this clear-sightedness is no bar to genuine love and concern; to an affection that speaks in simple human endearments ('Meiner Süßen', 'Süßes, dickes Kind...') and in simple human actions like offering a chair and calling a cab.

But the really striking feature of these final stanzas of *Gedächtnisfeier*, as Heinz Politzer has pointed out,[1] is the way in which divided and distinguished worlds here come together. A man regrets that he 'lives so high up' (the cemetery of Montmartre, it may be remembered, lies on a hill) that he cannot 'offer a chair' to his wife; and these common phrases acquire a new resonance because of what is left unspoken, because the poet speaks already from a world beyond that of time and change, in which his wife still lives. The drama of the *Lazarus* cycle is played out on the frontiers of these two realms.

The poet of *Gedächtnisfeier* looks back with tenderness on the world he has already proleptically left—but there are other ways of looking back, as three stanzas of *Vermächtnis* may serve to show:

Diese würdgen, tugendfesten
Widersacher sollen erben
All mein Siechtum und Verderben,
Meine sämtlichen Gebresten.

[1] H. Politzer, 'Heinrich Heine', in *Die neue Rundschau*, December 1948, p. 28.

Ich vermach euch die Koliken,
Die den Bauch wie Zangen zwicken,
Harnbeschwerden, die perfiden
Preußischen Hämorrhoiden.

Meine Krämpfe sollt ihr haben,
Speichelfluß und Gliederzucken,
Knochendarre in dem Rücken,
Lauter schöne Gottesgaben....

What is new here is not the note of almost hysterical hatred; readers of *Die Bäder von Lucca*, certain portions of *Ludwig Börne* and the *Lobgesänge für König Ludwig* will have heard that already. What is new, rather, is the uncompromising way in which Lazarus–Heine tears away the veil from portions of the human experience which other poets have tended to ignore.

We divert our attention from disease and death as much as we can; and the slaughter-houses and indecencies without end on which our life is founded are huddled out of sight and never mentioned, so that the world we recognise officially in literature and society is a poetic fiction far handsomer and cleaner and better than the world really is.[1]

(William James, *The Varieties of Religious Experience*)

The *Lazarus* cycle, like the *Romanzero* as a whole, refuses to have anything to do with such a cult of 'healthy-mindedness'. It insists on details of disease, on the less savoury portions of the human body, on squalor and filth; insists on the pitiful helplessness of naked, unaccommodated man (the *Romanzero* ends, indeed, with a suggestion of stench, the smell of unwashed, sweating bodies). The heroic play—to use one of Heine's own favourite images—is over, the audience departs, and what is left is an empty auditorium whose silence is broken by a sudden discordant sound like the snapping of a string, while amid the scurrying of rats and the all-pervading smell of rancid oil the last poor lamp gutters out its flame:

Doch horch! ein schollernd schnöder Klang
Ertönt unfern der öden Bühne; —
Vielleicht daß eine Saite sprang
An einer alten Violine.

[1] Mentor Books (New York, 1958), p. 85.

Verdrießlich rascheln im Parterr
Etwelche Ratten hin und her,
Und alles riecht nach ranzgem Öle.
Die letzte Lampe ächzt und zischt
Verzweiflungsvoll, und sie erlischt.
Das arme Licht war meine Seele. (*Sie erlischt*)

Yet all this deflation of conventional heroism does not impair the dignity of man in face of death—it serves rather to enhance it, because it shows the obstacles of squalor and wretchedness he has to surmount. Like the besieged Spaniards in Peru (*Vitzliputzli*), like the Moorish king before Granada (*Der Mohrenkönig*) and like Jehuda ben Halevi in Jerusalem, Lazarus snatches victory out of defeat, nobility out of the squalid business of dying. He is a key-figure in the *Romanzero*, that strange collection of disturbing poems which has been so well called, by Jules Legras, 'the Golden Book of the Vanquished'.[1]

6. PRODIGAL SON

. . . Till there was no place left where they could still pursue him
Except that exile which he called his Race. W. H. AUDEN

THE parable of Lazarus is preceded, in St Luke's gospel, by that of the Prodigal Son—and here too, in the story of the man driven to throw himself at his father's feet by extremes of want, Heine saw an analogy with his own situation. In the long prose 'Postscript' to the *Romanzero* he himself pointed to this analogy:

Yes, I have returned to God, like the Prodigal Son, after I had long kept swine among the Hegelians. Was it only misery that drove me back? Perhaps it was a less miserable cause. A heavenly nostalgia overcame me. . . .[2]

The parable of the Prodigal Son embodies a concept which is by no means specifically Christian—a concept central, indeed, to the

[1] *Henri Heine, Poète* (Paris, 1897), p. 337: 'une sorte de livre d'or des vaincus'.
[2] *SW*, I, 485.

religion of the Jews. This is the concept of the *Teshubah*, a Hebrew word generally translated by 'repentance' which literally, however, means 'return'. Exhortations to 'return' may be encountered everywhere in the Jewish liturgy:

Return, O my Soul, to thy God.

Teshubah, Prayer and Charity avert the impending doom.

For thou desirest not the death of the sinner, but that he turn from his way and live. And even until the day of his death Thou waitest for him; and if he return Thou dost straightway receive him.

A well-known Talmudic legend even affirms that the Teshubah, a possibility of return, was created before Man, before the Universe came into existence:

Seven things were created before the universe came into being: Torah (the Sacred Law), Teshubah, Paradise, Hell, the Throne of Glory, the Sanctuary, and the name of the Messiah. (Talmud: *Pesachim*, 54(2))

Behind and within the Christian parable Heine felt the Teshubah of the Jews.

The *Romanzero* postscript is not the only place in which the later Heine speaks of a 'return' to God. In his preface to the second edition of *Zur Geschichte der Religion und Philosophie in Deutschland*, in *Geständnisse* and in many of his letters and conversations he came back to this same confession:

Yes, I have returned to the lowly fold of God's creatures, and I acknowledge once again the omnipotence of a supreme being.[1]

(*Geständnisse*)

I have deserted German atheism and am on the eve of returning to the most commonplace beliefs.

(Letter to François Mignet, 17 January 1849)

Tired of all atheistic philosophy, I have returned to the common man's humble belief in God. (Letter to Heymann Lassalle, 30 April 1850)

Heine is careful to stress that he has returned to no positive religion ('My religious views', we read in the *Romanzero* postscript, 'have remained free from the bondage of every Church');[2] but from 1848 onwards he frequently refers to himself as a 'Jew'.

[1] *SW*, VI, 50. [2] *SW*, I, 487.

I am no longer a divine biped, I am no longer 'the freest German after Goethe', as Ruge called me in healthier days; I am no longer the Great Pagan No. 2...; I am no longer a Hellene...who laughed contemptuously at gloomy Nazarenes—I am now only a poor Jew sick unto death, a withered picture of misery, an unhappy man.[1]

(*Berichtigung*, April 1849)

His God is the God of Moses:

Einer nur, ein einzger Held
Gab uns mehr und gab uns Bessres
Als Kolumbus, das ist Jener
Der uns einen Gott gegeben.

Sein Herr Vater, der hieß Amram,
Seine Mutter hieß Jochebeth,
Und er selber, Moses heißt er,
Und er ist mein bester Heros (*Vitzliputzli*)

and bears the features of the deity of that Old Testament which Heine so often reads and so often quotes in these later years.[2]

It was not only despair of the body which impelled Heine towards a return to God—he seems to have experienced a genuine revulsion against atheism. He who had once proclaimed the death of the old God as an esoteric secret, now found God denied, not by the enlightened few, but by the vulgar; and he who had never ceased to feel himself, even in his most rebellious days, as a 'Knight of the Holy Spirit' found atheism associated with the grossest materialism. In 1855 he writes, in his imperfect French, to Michel Chevalier:

Mon engouement à réclamer les droits de la matière a cessé depuis que je vois combien cette matière devient envahissante, après s'être vu un peu réhabilitée; elle ne se contente plus d'être établie sur un pied d'égalité avec l'esprit, non, d'usurpation en usurpation elle va jusqu'à insulter l'esprit. Ah, Madame la matière, c'est très bête à vous, et vous êtes une sotte!

Worse still: atheism went hand in hand with communism, whose progress Heine watched with fascinated loathing. 'I saw', he tells

[1] *Briefe*, III, 170.

[2] Heine uses Hebrew invocations of God in *Nächtliche Fahrt* and refers, in *Lazarus* 15, to the 'Shem Hamforesh', the Hebrew name of God that only the High Priest was allowed to pronounce on solemn occasions.

the readers of *Geständnisse*, 'that atheism had made a more or less secret pact with a horribly naked communism that has shed its last fig-leaf.'[1] In face of this threat, Heine turned to God as to established authority; in a fragment found among his papers after his death, he refers to God as the Louis Philippe of Heaven.

But more than this: a return to God meant returning home, home to the comfort and relative security of childhood for which the mortally sick poet hopelessly longed. 'Das himmlische Heimweh überfiel mich' we read in the *Romanzero* postscript. It meant, in a literal sense, a return to the father—as is made quite clear by the characteristically double-edged philippic which Heine makes his father deliver at the end of the only fragment of his *Memoiren* that has come down to us:

> My dear son! your mother allows you to study philosophy with Rector Schallmeyer. That is her affair. I for my part do not love philosophy, for it is all superstition and I am a merchant and need my head for my business. You can be a philosopher as much as you like, but please do not say publicly what your opinions are, for it would harm my business if my customers came to know that I have a son who does not believe in God; the Jews especially would stop buying velveteen from me, and they are honest people who pay promptly and rightly keep to their religion. I am your father and therefore older than you and more experienced—and you can believe me if I make so bold as to tell you that atheism is a great sin.[2]

And the God of Heine's father, the God of his childhood, is the Jewish God of *Hebräische Melodien*.

These 'Hebrew Melodies'—the final section of the *Romanzero*—are not, like Byron's, exercises in 'interesting' local colour and Romantic orientalism; they represent a poet's attempt to return home, to return to his obscure origins. Where *Lamentationen* had ended with a backward glance at the struggles of the poet's maturity—

> Verlorner Posten in dem Freiheitskriege,
> Hielt ich seit dreißig Jahren treulich aus.
> Ich kämpfte ohne Hoffnung, daß ich siege,
> Ich wußte, nie komm ich gesund nach Haus —

[1] *SW*, VI, 42. [2] *SW*, VII, 511.

Hebräische Melodien opens with praise of an obscure life and simple pleasures:

> Fliegt dir das Glück vorbei einmal,
> So faß es am Zipfel.
> Auch rat ich dir, baue dein Hüttchen im Tal
> Und nicht auf dem Gipfel.

The poems that follow revive memories of youth: memories of synagogue melodies and prayers and of religious instruction in Rintelsohn's Jewish school; of Sabbath and Passover ceremonies in the home; of the characteristic 'Jerusalem' nostalgia of religious Jews; and last but not least of mother's *kasher* cookery, from the fish which begins the meal to the *shalet* which ends it. Above all, *Hebräische Melodien* is instinct with the beauty of Hebrew poetry: the post-Talmudic poetry of Yehuda Halevi, Gabirol and Ibn Ezra, the *Haggadah* part of the Talmud, and the poetry of the Hebrew Bible:

> In dem Urtext, dessen schöne
> Hieroglyphisch pittoreske
> Altchaldäische Quadratschrift
>
> Herstammt aus dem Kindesalter
> Unsrer Welt, und auch deswegen
> Jedem kindlichen Gemüte
> So vertraut entgegenlacht. (*Jehuda ben Halevi*)

Heine's actual knowledge of Hebrew was (to say the least) inadequate; the Hebrew poets of the Spanish period he knew only at second hand (notably through Michael Sachs's *Die religiöse Poesie der Juden in Spanien*, published in 1845), and the Bible he read invariably in Luther's translation. He had, however, been taught the rudiments of Hebrew in his youth, and therefore associates the *Hebrew* Bible—as the passage just quoted clearly demonstrates—with a return to childhood.

But even in the first two *Hebräische Melodien* the reader discerns a telling ambivalence. *Prinzessin Sabbath* conjures up that special Sabbath atmosphere which no one who has spent his childhood in a Jewish home can fail to recognise: that awed feeling of being in the presence of God which is made mysteriously actual in the ominous soughing of stanzas like:

> Durch das Haus geheimnisvoll
> Zieht ein Wispern und ein Weben,
> Und der unsichtbare Hausherr
> Atmet schaurig in der Stille.

The poem lovingly recalls the beautiful prayer on entering the synagogue ('Zelte Jakobs, eure heilgen / Eingangspfosten küßt mein Mund!'), the *Lecho Daudi* hymn with which the Sabbath is welcomed and the *Habdalah* ceremony with which it is ended; and it conveys a vivid impression of the Jew on the Sabbath, awed and yet proud ('Mit erhobnem Haupt und Herzen') in the presence of his God. It is a picture not only of spiritual exaltation but also of temporal happiness and contentment in the midst of a miserable life—of a mental and physical satisfaction that brings ancient Palestine into modern Europe:

> Schalet, schöner Götterfunken,
> Tochter aus Elysium!
> Also klänge Schillers Hochlied,
> Hätt er Schalet je gekostet.
>
> * * *
>
> Speist der Prinz von solcher Speise,
> Glänzt sein Auge wie verkläret,
> Und er knöpfet auf die Weste,
> Und er spricht mit selgem Lächeln:
>
> 'Hör ich nicht den Jordan rauschen?
> Sind das nicht die Brüsselbrunnen
> In dem Palmental von Beth-El,
> Wo gelagert die Kamele?
>
> Hör ich nicht die Herdenglöckchen?
> Sind das nicht die fetten Hammel,
> Die vom Gileathgebirge
> Abendlich der Hirt herabtreibt?

Heine's tone is at once ironic, tender and envious here, as it had been in the episode of *Die Bäder von Lucca* in which the comic

Hirsch Hyazinth had spoken of the Sabbath happiness of Moses Lump:

When he comes home on Friday evening he lays down his bundle and all his cares, and sits down at table with his mis-shapen wife and even more mis-shapen daughter, partakes with them of fish cooked in a tasty garlic sauce, sings the most splendid psalms of King David, rejoices whole-heartedly at the exodus of the Children of Israel from Egypt, rejoices also that all the miscreants who behaved wickedly towards them died in the end, that King Pharaoh, Nebuchadnezzar, Haman, Antiochus, Titus and all such people are dead, while *Lümpchen* is still alive and partaking of fish with his wife and child—And I tell you, Herr Doktor, the fish is delicious and the man is happy, he does not have to worry about culture, he sits wrapped contentedly in his religion and green dressing-gown like Diogenes in his tub, he gazes cheerfully at his candles....[1]

That is the Jew on the Sabbath. But what of the Jew on week-days?

Hund mit hündischen Gedanken
Kötert er die ganze Woche
Durch des Lebens Kot und Kehrricht....

A prince on the Sabbath, he turns into an animal—at once ridiculous, pathetic and disgusting—on week-days; just as the god Phoebus Apollo seemed to turn, at the end of *Der Apollogott*, into the renegade cantor Faibisch who roamed the country in the company of fat prostitutes. The boldly coined verb 'kötern' is the key-word here, suggesting the fawning humility of a cur and (as its proximity to 'Kot' in the next line might seem to suggest) the filth of the roads along which it sniffs its way.

Nor is *Jehuda ben Halevi*, the pearl of these *Hebräische Melodien*, free of such ambivalence. The music of the Hebrew psalms, as intoned by religious Jews, resounds through the whole poem:

'Lechzend klebe mir die Zunge
An dem Gaumen, und es welke
Meine rechte Hand, vergäß ich
Jemals dein, Jerusalem —'

[1] *SW*, III, 328.

Wort und Weise, unaufhörlich
Schwirren sie mir heut im Kopfe,
Und mir ist, als hört ich Stimmen,
Psalmodierend, Männerstimmen —

Manchmal kommen auch zum Vorschein
Bärte, schattig lange Bärte....

That clearly draws on memories, not only of Luther's translation of the Bible, but of Hebrew *kinoth* or songs of lamentation; and it is interesting to find the Yiddish equivalent of the word *kinah* turning up in a deleted passage of *Jehuda ben Halevi*:

Auf des Tempels Trümmern saß er,
Singend seine große Kinne,
Das berühmte Klaglied 'Zion'....[1]

The poem passionately extols the Babylonian Talmud, in a passage which speaks of 'die blühende Haggada',

Wo die schönen alten Sagen,
Engelmärchen und Legenden,
Stille Märtyrerhistorien,
Festgesänge, Weisheitssprüche,

Auch Hyperbeln, gar possierlich,
Alles aber glaubenskräftig,
Glaubensglühend....

Most of all, *Jehuda ben Halevi* is a paean to the Hebrew poets of the twelfth century, who are seen against their background of Israel's great and tragic history:

Ja, er ward ein großer Dichter,
Stern und Fackel seiner Zeit,
Seines Volkes Licht und Leuchte,
Eine wunderbare, große

Feuersäule des Gesanges,
Die der Schmerzenskarawane
Israels vorangezogen
In der Wüste des Exils.

[1] *SW*, I, 559.

But whenever Heine mentions modern Jews, he feels at once inclined to ridicule. Chamisso's friend Julius Eduard Hitzig, for instance, is credited with a dream-vision in which he sees his original—and patently Jewish—name 'Itzig' traced in the heavens and preceded by the letter *H*:

'Was bedeutet dieses H?'
Frug er sich — 'etwa Herr Itzig
Oder Heilger Itzig? Heilger
Ist ein schöner Titel — aber

In Berlin nicht passend' — endlich
Grübelnsmüd nannt er sich Hitzig,
Und nur die Getreuen wußten
In dem Hitzig steckt ein Heilger;

while members of the Rothschild family are treated with elaborate and patently ironical courtesy:

Perlen, reiner noch als jene,
Die der Königin Atossa
Einst geschenkt der falsche Smerdis,

Und die späterhin geschmücket
Alle Notabilitäten
Dieser mondumkreisten Erde,
Thais und Kleopatra,

Isispriester, Mohrenfürsten,
Auch Hispaniens Königinnen,
Und zuletzt die hochverehrte
Frau Baronin Salomon.

What is ambivalence in the first two poems turns into rank dissonance in the spirited *Disputation* which ends the *Hebräische Melodien*. Here Heine delightedly seizes every opportunity of venting his spleen not only on the Catholic religion (towards which he had been emotionally attracted in younger days) but also on the Jews; and in lines which end the whole *Romanzero*, the Rabbi is rejected along with the monk, dogmatic Judaism together with dogmatic Christianity.

Heine's 'return' to his people, it would seem, was not a great success. He spoke occasionally, in these later years, of accesses of pride in his Judaism:

I see now that the Greeks were only beautiful youths, but that the Jews were always men—strong, unyielding men—not only in the past, but to this very day, in spite of eighteen centuries of persecution and suffering.... Were not all pride of ancestry a silly inconsistency in a champion of the revolution and its democratic principles, the writer of these pages would be proud that his ancestors belonged to the noble house of Israel, that he is a descendant of those martyrs who gave the world a God and a morality, and who have fought and suffered on all the battlefields of thought. (*Geständnisse*)[1]

That mood finds expression in *Hebräische Melodien* too; but these suggest just as powerfully a dilemma on which a fragment in Heine's notebooks throws startling light.

B. If I belonged to the tribe which produced our Lord, I would be inclined to boast of the fact rather than be ashamed of it.

A. So would I, if our Lord were the only one who has sprung from this tribe—but it has also produced such a rascally mob (*so viel Lumpengesindel*) that one may well scruple to acknowledge the relationship.[2]

Deeply impressed as he was by Jewish history and Jewish cultural achievement, by Bible, Talmud and liturgy, by Jewish tenacity and endurance, he found it impossible to make any real Jewish friends. Prepared to 'return' to his people, he found among the Weills, Wohlwills and Friedlands who surrounded his sick-bed, among the Rothschilds who patronised and the Strauss's and Wohls who attacked him, more to deter than to attract him.

Heine never 'returned' to his people, because though he was prepared to revere Judaism and Jews in the abstract he could not find, even in his own family, a Jewish friend whom he could love and respect as he had once loved and respected Moses Moser. It might be said, in the same way, that he never 'returned' to his God, because he could not find it in his heart to trust implicitly in His goodness and in His justice. And without such love and trust

[1] *SW*, VI, 55. [2] *SW*, VII, 407–8.

there can be no Teshubah. 'Thou shalt *love* the Lord thy God' (so reads the *Shema*, a prayer the Jewish child learns before any other), 'with all thy heart and with all thy soul and with all thy might.'

Yet Heine, as the *Hebräische Melodien* and the whole Romanzero demonstrate, really did long to 'return', to find a God he could love, to find a people, a community, with whom he could identify himself. Again and again he shows the beauty of religious gesture and ceremony, which links an individual grief to that of the community and submits it to God. The final procession in *Schlachtfeld bei Hastings*, the 'Miserere' of the doomed Spaniards in *Vitzliputzli*, the synagogue and home ceremonies of *Prinzessin Sabbath*, the death and apotheosis of Jehuda ben Halevi—these are unforgettable instances. And on the reverse side he again and again laments his own outcast state; in *Jetzt wohin?* for example:

Traurig schau ich in die Höh,
Wo viel tausend Sterne nicken —
Aber meinen eignen Stern
Kann ich nirgends dort erblicken.

Hat im güldnen Labyrinth
Sich vielleicht verirrt am Himmel,
Wie ich selber mich verirrt
In dem irdischen Getümmel,

or most clearly of all in the opening stanza of *Gedächtnisfeier*. If only he *could* submit—if only he *could* identify himself with something or somebody! If only he were not always forced to see the ridiculous and sordid side of everything, to stray from the beauty of the Jewish Sabbath and the religious ecstasy of Yehuda Halevi to the absurd 'visions' of Kriminalrat Hitzig, to the undignified gait and gestures of Jewish pedlars, to the ostentation of Jewish *nouveau-riches* and to the bigotry of so many of the rabbis:

Gilt nichts mehr der Tausves-Jontof,
Was soll gelten? Zeter! Zeter!
Räche, Herr, die Missetat,
Strafe, Herr, den Übeltäter!

Denn der Tausves-Jontof, Gott,
Das bist du! Und an dem frechen
Tausves-Jontofleugner mußt du
Deines Namens Ehre rächen! (*Disputation*)

But this is just what Heine could never do. He could not 'return' in this sense to his people or to his God. And the painful conflict between his desire to 'belong' and his inability to conform, between his desire to submit and his indomitable intellectual pride, informs all his later poetry, giving sting to his saddest and point to his wittiest things.

Alfred Meissner records that shortly before the completion of the *Romanzero* Heine said to him: 'It would be tasteless and petty if it could be said of me that I had ever been ashamed of being a Jew, but it would be just as ridiculous if I were to assert that I am one.'[1] Yet it did seem to Heine on occasions that there was no need for him to 'return' because he was already there. 'I make no secret of my Judaism', he said to Ludwig Kalisch in 1850, 'to which I have not returned because I have never left it.'[2] The condition of the Jews that he presented so powerfully and disturbingly he could recognise as his own:

You see, my dear Meissner, how I mock and pity the Jews almost in the same breath; and they do indeed seem to me to be as ridiculous as they are worthy of veneration.[3]

That is a dualism he had often seen in himself—a dualism, moreover, which the *Romanzero* everywhere shows to be implicit in human existence. The Arabian Nights' tale at the opening of *Prinzessin Sabbath* is but another version of the degradation of Apollo in *Der Apollogott*:

In Arabiens Märchenbuche
Sehen wir verwünschte Prinzen,
Die zu Zeiten ihre schöne
Urgestalt zurückgewinnen:

Das behaarte Ungeheuer
Ist ein Königsohn geworden;
Schmuckreich glänzend angekleidet,
Auch verliebt die Flöte blasend.

[1] *Gespräche*, p. 693. [2] *Ibid.* p. 668. [3] *Ibid.* p. 692.

Doch die Zauberfrist zerrinnt,
Und wir schauen plötzlich wieder
Seine königliche Hoheit
In ein Ungetüm verzottelt.

The rest of the *Romanzero* demonstrates again and again that this is true, not only of Israel, but of humanity as a whole, through whose baseness and absurdity an inextinguishable glory continues to shine. Heine could therefore see in the Wandering Jew, as he proclaimed in the French edition of *Elementargeister*,[1] the 'melancholy symbol' of all mankind.

7. THE GRAND DESIGN

Oh! Blessed rage for order, pale Ramon,
The maker's rage to order words of the sea,
Words of the fragrant portals, dimly starred,
And of ourselves and of our origins,
In ghostlier demarcations, keener sounds.

WALLACE STEVENS

LIKE so many of Heine's works, the *Romanzero* falls into three sections: *Historien*, *Lamentationen* and *Hebräische Melodien*; and this triadic rhythm seems to have played a remarkable part in Heine's life, thought and art.

The tripartite division of Heine's life corresponds to a favourite form of his poetry: the trilogy. Netoliczka noticed and Legras considered at length Heine's tendency to arrange his poems in the manner of a triptych; exposition, crisis, solution are the ever-recurring motifs which impose form on his ballads. *Almansor*, *Die Wallfahrt nach Kevlaar*, *Tragödie*, *Ritter Olaf*, *Der Tannhäuser*, *Der Apollogott*, *Der Dichter Firdusi*, *Vitzliputzli*—all these are tripartite....It was Hegel who had imported the triadic rhythm into all the manifestations of this world.[2]

(Oskar Walzel, Introduction to the 'Insel' edition of Heine's works)

The tripartite structure of the *Romanzero* does indeed suggest something like a Hegelian triad—with a first section stressing the

[1] *SW*, IV, 616. [2] Vol. I, xlii.

world-order and its flaws, a second stressing the sufferings of an individual poet, and a third seeking to synthesise the two by finding a place for the poet in a community, to regress to the Judaism into which Heine himself had been born. Such regression was, however, doubly impossible in the case of a poet who felt that he could

> perhaps more easily than other mortals do without positive religious dogma. He is in possession of grace, and the symbols of heaven and earth unlock themselves to his spirit; he does not need the keys of any church.[1] (*Geständnisse*)

The attempt to 'return' proved a failure; and instead of culminating in a synthesis, the *Romanzero* ends with the rank dissonance of *Disputation.*

Such human failure is not, however, paralleled by a failure of artistry. It is true that the *Romanzero* suffered a little from the haste with which it was published and from the paralysed poet's occasional inability to give all his work that final polish which is so characteristic of his earlier collections. *Hebräische Melodien*, as Heine's correspondence with Campe amply attests, was worst affected by his haste to get the manuscript to the printer—so that even *Jehuda ben Halevi*, which in a letter of 21 August 1851 the poet called 'the most beautiful of my poems', remained a fragment and was allowed to degenerate at times into a loosely organised gossip. *Lamentationen* suffered too; a handful of lyrics had to be unceremoniously ejected from this section just before the book was due to leave the press, and Heine found himself hard put to it to fill the resulting lacunae. Towards the end of September 1851 he sent the following particularly revealing note to Campe:

> If the sheet that contains *Plateniden* has not yet been printed, then you may print immediately after that poem the above verses *Symbolischer Unsinn*, in order to fill a few more pages. But if that sheet is already in the press, please throw the poem in the fire.

This seems a somewhat haphazard way for a 'great master of arrangement' to make up his collections; and Heine's own artistic

[1] *SW*, VI, 56.

conscience was far from satisfied. 'I am only too well aware', he wrote to Campe on 10 September 1851, 'that my book is not all flowers, that here and there the grass has come up too', and in a letter to his mother and sister he even called the whole *Romanzero* 'a very weak book'. Yet it is not only in its individual poems that the *Romanzero* equals anything Heine had ever written before: as a collection too it has a *grande ligne* which few of the world's great books of poetry can rival and which none have surpassed. Of this over-all arrangement Heine came to be justifiably proud:

> You know that a feeling for significant order is one of my main characteristics. You will have noticed this again recently, when the *Romanzero* was published, which would surely have lost infinitely much if I had not given a great deal of time and thought to its external arrangement. The collections of many German poets would attract the public more if they did not betray, in the anarchy of their arrangement, the barbarous spirit of their authors;
>
> (Letter to Campe, 18 March 1852)

and no appreciation of the *Romanzero* can be adequate if it fails to take full account of its *grande ligne*.

Historien—the opening section—begins with the consciousness of betrayal (a consciousness that was always with Heine after the inheritance quarrel); betrayal that brings in its train a sadness and rage which can be momentarily allayed by poetry but will vanish only with death.

Wenn man an dir Verrat geübt,
Sei du um so treuer;
Und ist deine Seele zu Tode betrübt,
So greife zur Leier.

Die Saiten klingen! Ein Heldenlied,
Voll Flammen und Gluten!
Da schmilzt der Zorn, und dein Gemüt
Wird mild verbluten.

From this realisation the *Historien* seek escape into faerie and masquerade worlds (*Rhampsenit*, *Der weiße Elefant*, *Schelm von Bergen*), into the world of Offenbach's operettas, into that 'vaudeville' world which Barker Fairley has so brilliantly analysed and related to Heine's own life and art. *Schelm von Bergen*, however, and the poem *Valkyren* that follows it, mark a turning-point: the world of legend and fantasy gives way to that of history. History, as *Schlachtfeld bei Hastings* serves to show, is a chronicle of injustice, cruelty and suffering that confounds men and beasts:

Viel tausend Leichen lagen dort
Erbärmlich auf blutiger Erde,
Nackt ausgeplündert, verstümmelt, zerfleischt,
Daneben die Äser der Pferde.

Its victors are invariably contemptible ('Der schlechtre Mann gewinnt'); and though its vanquished have, like the doomed king of *Karl I*, a certain dignity born out of defeat, they can also present the scabrous and ridiculous spectacle that is afforded by the—literally—headless aristocracy of *Maria Antoinette*. *Pomare* links the historical scene with the present; its heroine is victor and vanquished in one, and pity at her fall mingles with bitter satisfaction at the thought of pride humbled and brought to dust. This leads over into the ambiguous centre-piece of the *Historien*—*Der Apollogott*, that supreme test of any appreciation of the later Heine. Here we see to the full the danger of prying too deeply and looking too closely, already announced in *Schelm von Bergen*, *Schlachtfeld bei Hastings* and *Maria Antoinette*: the sordidness behind the most attractive façade, the degradation which is somehow inherent in exile and suffering. Yet all this does not invalidate the strange beauty of Apollo's song, a beauty which cannot be explained away in terms of the fish-market and the old clo' shop. The nun's vision and that of the pedlar are but two strands in the strangely mingled yarn of life.

The end of *Der Apollogott*, however, for all the ambivalence of this poem, leaves the reader in the mire, leaves him with an impression of sordid squalor which the poems that follow do little to alleviate. All the clogs of the modern world seem now to be dragging down the poet's spirit; the narrow meanness of the Philistine (*Kleines Volk*), the baseness of revolutionary 'heroes' (*Zwei Ritter*), the corrupting power of money (*Das goldne Kalb*) and the vileness of absolutism, which has not changed in three thousand years of recorded history (*König David*). From this constricting atmosphere, *König Richard* seems at first sight to offer a welcome escape.

> Wohl durch der Walder einödige Pracht
> Jagt ungestüm ein Reiter;
> Er bläst ins Horn, er singt und lacht
> Gar seelenvergnügt und heiter.

This is a different laughter from any heard in the *Romanzero* so far—the carnival merriment of *Rhampsenit*, with its grain of horror like the sesame seed in nougat, the ignorant peals of the duchess in *Schelm von Bergen*, the frenzied gaiety of the dancers around the idol of *Das goldne Kalb*; different too, to anticipate for a moment, from the cruel laughter of *Pfalzgräfin Jutta* and the bitter laughter of the disappointed poet of *Der Dichter Firdusi*. King Richard's laughter marks joy and relief, relief at escaping from a stuffy prison to the 'freie Luft' of the lonely forest. The olfactory image of the penultimate line, so characteristic of Heine, makes the relief explicit:

> Er denkt an Oestreichs Festungsduft —
> Und giebt seinem Pferde die Sporen.

The combination of 'Oestreich' and 'Festung' would of course have associations for nineteenth-century liberals which are not altogether those of the newly freed Cœur de Lion.

It will hardly escape the reader's notice, however, that *König Richard*, the most exhilarating poem of the whole *Romanzero*, is also one of the most deliberately stylised. A 'Bänkelsänger' tone has again crept in, with skipping rhythms that not only render the gay cavorting of Cœur de Lion's horse but also mock the dignity of which they speak:

> Das ist Herr Richard Löwenherz,
> Der christlichen Ritterschaft Blüte.

And when, in the third stanza, the trees begin to speak with 'green tongues', the reader begins to suspect parody: parody of those *Buch der Lieder* anthropomorphisations which had been earlier mocked in *Der weiße Elefant*.

Yet the effect of such images in *König Richard* is not quite parodistic. The poem presents itself rather as a nostalgic evocation of earlier dreams—as a regretful, half-ironic contemplation of an escape clearly recognised as impossible. Its image of a ride through the lonely forest represents the wish-dream of a lame man in a stuffy room; a vision of carefree existence and rebirth that could never become reality in a world poisoned not only by 'Oestreichs Festungsduft' but also by a wasting and constricting disease.

Der Asra begins with another wish-dream, a vision of undisturbed harmony in a setting of Eastern luxury; but it soon turns into yet another 'instance' of the danger of prying too deeply. Behind love and within it lurks death—a theme elaborated, in different ways, by *Himmelsbräute* and *Pfalzgräfin Jutta*. *Der Mohrenkönig*, a poem of exile and longing, breaks out of the nightmare atmosphere created by the final stanza of *Pfalzgräfin Jutta*, and sings of the fame that awaits the vanquished as well as the victor; while *Geoffroy Rudel und Melisande von Tripoli* seeks to lull the reader with melancholy music, with a vision of posthumous love that is not without its ironical overtones:

> ...posthume Galantrie
> Aus des Minnesanges Zeiten...
>
> Also kosen, also wandeln
> Jene zärtlichen Gespenster...

Der Dichter Firdusi returns again to the theme of treachery, of the deceptiveness of appearances, of the pitiful weakness of the apparently noble. It is Heine's clearest dramatisation of the inheritance quarrel, with Uncle Salomon raised to the dignity of an oriental despot—

> Schach Mahomet hat gut gespeist,
> Und gut gelaunet ist sein Geist[1] —

and Heine himself transmogrified into the poet-priest who keeps alive, in his poetry, the finest traditions of his country and who

[1] Cf. Heine's remark about his uncle in *Briefe*, II, 41: 'In der Fütterungsstunde ist er immer sehr zahm' (15 July 1833).

yet shows himself tainted by some of the same greed that animated the dancers around the golden calf:

Der Poet riß auf die Säcke
Hastig, um am lang entbehrten
Goldesanblick sich zu laben....

The heavy stress on 'hastig' reveals a greed which all the dignified gestures of the rest of the poem cannot make us forget.

The slow procession of death that ends *Der Dichter Firdusi* is followed by the mystery and horror of *Nächtliche Fahrt*, the opium dream of a poet in pain who seems to sense—in a delirious second self—that only death can wash off the 'Unfläterei' inseparable from the business of living. From this, *Präludium* presents yet another attempt to escape; a thwarted attempt which ends in the inferno of *Vitzliputzli*, with its senseless alternation of murder and revenge, its sense of constriction, its tortures, its song of vengeance and hatred arising from wounded love, in the midst of which—suddenly, somehow—'a terrible beauty is born'.[1]

Und sie nahmen ab die Helme
Von den Häuptern, knieten nieder,
Stimmten an den Psalm der Toten
Und sie sangen: De profundis!

Unter jenen, welche starben,
War auch Raimond de Mendoza,
Sohn der schönen Abbatissin,
Cortez' erste Jugendliebe.

Als er auf der Brust des Jünglings
Jenes Medaillon gewahrte,
Das der Mutter Bildnis einschloß,
Weinte Cortez helle Tränen —

Doch er wischt' sie ab vom Auge
Mit dem harten Büffelhandschuh,
Seufzte tief und sang im Chore
Mit den andern: miserere!

This *miserere* had already resounded through *Himmelsbräute*; but there it had been nothing but a hopeless wailing, while in *Vitzli-*

[1] W. B. Yeats, 'Easter 1916', *Collected Poems*, 2nd edition (London, 1950), p. 202.

putzli it is a communal prayer that brings consolation and unites—as Helene Herrmann has shown—an individual with a group in the hour of his grief. The slow and stately verse movement, the full vowels and soft consonants of these stanzas underline the significance of this religious act: they show directly how the human mind may transmute even horror into beauty. The hour of doom reveals the beauty of religious ceremony and the unquenchable nobility of man. No animal images, so intrusive in the rest of the poem, disturb us here; man has spiritual treasures revealed only by extremity of suffering and grief that lift him far above those beasts whom he seems so often to resemble.

The pattern of the *Romanzero* should now have become clear. It presents a poet's consciousness of betrayal, of pain and horror, and his ever renewed attempts to escape into fantasy worlds, and into illusion. Such illusions, as the frequently ironic mode of presentation shows, are from the first experienced *as* illusions, though they are none the less cherished for that; and again and again they dissolve, to let an absurd or tragic reality starkly appear. And paradoxically, it is within that reality, within human baseness and grief and pain, that beauty and dignity are born. The *Romanzero* exhibits no vulgar pessimism—it bears witness rather to a tragic view of life.

The *Historien* have also stated, and begun to develop, the main themes of the *Romanzero*. They have presented the image of the mask or façade behind which it is dangerous and attractive to peer—the face belies the mask, the interior belies the façade, but in no simple, one-way fashion. Every human face has its own complexity. 'Apollo' may be shown as a renegade cantor and mountebank, the 'hero' Cortez as a mere robber-chief; but even in their degradation they have a sort of beauty or of dignity. Yet 'degradation' is of course another of the main themes of these *Historien*: their many animal images are relevant here (juxtapositions of men and animals in common besottedness or common suffering), and so are the many passages that insist on filth and squalor, on man's animal appetites and on his greed. Gold plays a prominent part as an agent of such degradation—it tempts man to be untrue to his nobler self in *Das goldne Kalb*, for instance, and in *Der Dichter Firdusi*, and in *Vitzliputzli*. In his constant indictment of gold Heine is indicting the commercial values of his own society, the society he found in Paris no less than that which he had left behind in Hamburg. Linked with gold is the dance, that favourite motif to which Heine returns again and again in *Lutetia*: the cancan, which seemed to him at once an image of sexual temptation, a persiflage of human ideals and a means of overcoming fear in Dionysiac ecstasy. But even this does not exhaust the complexity of this 'dance' motif; for it represents also, in the *Romanzero*, the wish-dream of a paralysed man. It is linked with other images of movement—images of riding and flying—that bear an interesting relationship to the images of impeding, shackling and laming that abound in the *Romanzero*, reflecting the poet's actual situation and serving him, at the same time, as a symbol for the condition of mankind. Many other of such themes or motifs are first stated in the *Historien*: that of exile, for instance, which binds together such varied poems as *Der Mohrenkönig*, *Der Apollogott*, *Der Dichter Firdusi* and *Vitzliputzli*, and that of the special relation in which poets stand to God and the traditions of their people (*Der Dichter Firdusi* I). All these motifs are intertwined, illuminate each other mutually, modify each other, and make up a whole as complex as life itself. Each poem, to use Yeats's beautiful image, flickers with the light of many symbols 'as a sword-blade may flicker with the light of burning towers'.[1]

'It will not be easy', Barker Fairley has well said, 'to spot another writer with a mind thus constituted—so extremely discursive, so irresponsible—looking on the surface, so easily held together by the flexible ramifications of images inside'.[2]

The *grande ligne* of *Historien* is then continued in *Lamentationen*. After an opening attempt to regress to the *Waldeinsamkeit* of youth, this second section of the *Romanzero* plunges its reader into horror, sordidness and pain. *Spanische Atriden* tells once again of the inhumanity of man to man even within one and the

[1] W. B. Yeats, *Essays* (London, 1924), p. 192.

[2] Barker Fairley, *Heinrich Heine. An Interpretation* (Oxford, 1954), p. 163.

same family and leads over into poems of more overtly personal recollection: memories of liberals who deserted their cause, of Munich personalities, of Platen, of proud young women whose scornful disdain has melted away too late. Some of these poems breathe a hatred and rage that are terrifying: Heine never wrote anything more savage than the passages on Görres and Döllinger in *Der Ex-Nachtwächter*; than *Alte Rose*; or than the poem *Vermächtnis* at the end of the *Lazarus* cycle. But here too he allows flashes of beauty to illuminate, again and again, the darkness of the world: the death-intoxicated exaltation that ends *An die Jungen*, the dreamy love of *Salomo* with its memories of Hebrew night-prayers and the *Song of Songs*, the tenderness of *Gedächtnisfeier* (that most bitter-sweet of all Heine's poems), and the proud consciousness of the fighter for freedom in *Enfant Perdu*. And in the final section—*Hebräische Melodien*—a last attempt is made to regress, to forget a terrible present through excursions into a picturesque past.

Jahre kommen und vergehen,
Menschentränen träufeln, rinnen
Auf die Erde, und die Erde
Saugt sie ein mit stiller Gier —
Tolle Sud! Der Deckel springt —
Heil dem Manne, dessen Hand
Deine junge Brut ergreifet
Und zerschmettert an der Felswand.

Gott sei Dank! Die Sud verdampfet
In dem Kessel, der allmählich
Ganz verstummt. Es weicht mein Spleen,
Mein westöstlich dunkler Spleen —

Auch mein Flügelrößlein wiehert
Wieder heiter, scheint den bösen
Nachtalp von sich abzuschütteln,
Und die klugen Augen fragen:

Reiten wir zurück nach Spanien
Zu dem kleinen Talmudisten,
Der ein großer Dichter worden,
Zu Jehuda ben Halevi?

Jehuda ben Halevi, that centre-piece of the *Hebräische Melodien* from which the stanzas just quoted have been taken, presents wish-dream images of a poet animated by a burning faith in his God, the destiny of his people and his own poetry; a poet who lives in a colourful world and who dies a death which has something fitting and beautiful about it. Yet ever and again modern Europe may be discerned through the oriental trappings; ever and again the actual situation of a paralysed and disillusioned poet is half-revealed.

Still davon — gebrochen liegt
Jetzt mein stolzer Siegeswagen,
Und die Panther, die ihn zogen,
Sind verreckt, so wie die Weiber,

Die mit Pauk und Zimbelklängen
Mich umtanzten, und ich selbst
Wälze mich am Boden elend,
Krüppelelend — still davon —

Still davon.... (*Jehuda ben Halevi* III)

Animal images (men and beasts confounded in a common doom), dance images, and the image of someone lying on the ground unable to rise combine into a terrible and (by now) familiar picture. Regression, escape into oriental fantasies, are recognised as ultimately impossible. Heine could not, would not console himself with comfortable illusions; if consolation was to be found at all, it had to be found within a fully apprehended reality. The discordant *Disputation* is therefore allowed to end *Hebräische Melodien* and the whole *Romanzero*.

Heine's last great volume of poetry has been well compared to a sonata[1]—its intricate interweaving of themes and their development make the comparison appropriate. It possesses, moreover, as I have tried to show, what Aaron Copland demands of every fine piece of music:

The form must have what in my student-days we used to call *la grande ligne*....Every good piece of music must give us a sense of flow—a sense of continuity from first note to last.[2]

[1] R. M. Meyer, *Die deutsche Literatur des 19. Jahrhunderts* (Berlin, 1912), p. 107.
[2] Aaron Copland, *What to Listen for in Music* (New York, 1939), p. 32.

It is, of course, a composition that ends on a dissonance, without a comforting return to the tonic; yet it leaves the listener with admiration for the greatness of the human spirit that could so defy its recurrent desire to escape into worlds of make-believe and could retain its dignity even in baseness, degradation, terror and pain.

8. THE POET'S WORKSHOP

Alle Großen waren große Arbeiter, unermüdlich nicht nur im Erfinden, sondern auch im Verwerfen, Sichten, Umgestalten, Ordnen. NIETZSCHE

WITH the exception of *Altes Lied*, a version of which had appeared as early as 1824, all the poems in the *Romanzero* were written in the space of five years—between 1846 and 1851. Towards the end of that period Heine's secretary was Karl Hillebrand, who has left an interesting account of the way in which the poet worked on the *Romanzero* poems:

In his sleepless nights he would compose his loveliest lyrics. He dictated the whole of the *Romanzero* to me. Every poem was quite complete in the morning. But then there began a process of polishing which went on for hours and in which...he used my inexperienced youth much as Molière used the ignorance of Louison by asking my opinion about melody, tone, clarity and so on. Every present and imperfect tense was carefully considered, the suitability of every archaic or unusual word was tested, every elision was resolved, every unnecessary adjective struck out, and here and there corrections were made whose purpose was to give the appearance of carelessness.[1]

A modern reader may occasionally feel that Heine did not blot quite enough and may sigh for the terseness of his *Buch der Lieder* manner. Is he not sometimes too insistent and too explicit in these later poems? In the central section of *Schlachtfeld bei Hastings*, for instance, he evokes perfectly the eerie silence, the

[1] *Gespräche*, p. 656.

long monotony of Edith's search for her lover amid the horrors of the battlefield—a silence suddenly broken by a single cry:

Sie suchte schon den ganzen Tag,
Es ward schon Abend — plötzlich
Bricht aus der Brust des armen Weibs
Ein geller Schrei, entsetzlich.

The emotional comment—'entsetzlich'—impairs the effect of such a passage instead of strengthening it. The same may be said of other poems in which Heine yields to a fatal weakness for talking emotions instead of generating them:

Nicht allein der Triumphator,
Nicht allein der sieggekrönte
Günstling jener blinden Göttin,
Auch der blutge Sohn des Unglücks,

Auch der heldenmütge Kämpfer,
Der dem ungeheuren Schicksal
Unterlag, wird ewig leben
In der Menschen Angedenken. (*Der Mohrenkönig*)

Und des Knaben edles Herze
Ward ergriffen von der wilden,
Abenteuerlichen Süße,
Von der wundersamen Schmerzlust

Und den fabelhaften Schauern
Jener seligen Geheimwelt,
Jener großen Offenbarung,
Die wir nennen Poesie. (*Jehuda ben Halevi*)

The obtrusively emotional adjectives make it impossible to read such passages aloud without embarrassment.

These are, however, only isolated lapses, in which Heine's favourite self-idealisations (the heroic fighter for freedom, the tragic exile and the divinely inspired poet) assume control at the expense of the coolly weighing craftsman. For the most part the latter is in complete command, controlling rhythms and images so that experiences and attitudes are communicated with maximum economy, immediacy and force. This becomes unmistakably plain if we compare the *Romanzero* poems with the earlier manuscript and printed versions that are so conveniently reprinted in editions by Ernst Elster and Jonas Fränkel.

Such a comparison reveals first of all Heine's concern to eliminate from his later work a feature that had been prominent in his earlier: that sliding speech-rhythm which puts no weight on individual words; the rhythm, say, of *Lyrisches Intermezzo* 9 ('Auf Flügeln des Gesanges...'). Again and again his later versions isolate a word, give it greater prominence, counterpointing grammatical and metrical pause. We read, for instance, in a manuscript version of *Rhampsenit*:

Sintemal des Manns Adresse,
Unsres Eidams, noch zur Stunde
Unbekannt uns, bringt der Aufruf
Hierdurch unsrer Gnade Kunde.[1]

In the *Romanzero* this long sentence is allowed to flow on, unimpeded, over all the line-divisions, until it comes to a halt on the word 'unbekannt', which now appears ironically isolated at the beginning of the third line:

Sintemal uns die Adresse
Unsres Eidams noch zur Stunde
Unbekannt....

Similarly, the reader will hardly notice how inevitably the stress falls on the three key-words ('Auge', 'Dolch', 'gezücket') in the third stanza of *Schelm von Bergen*, unless he contrasts it with an earlier version. In the *Romanzero* the final lines of this stanza read:

Daraus gar freudig blicket
Ein Auge, wie ein blanker Dolch,
Halb aus der Scheide gezücket.

This supersedes the version published in the *Kölnische Zeitung* in 1846, in which the irrelevant associations of 'Scheide' seem to obtrude themselves to an unwarranted degree:

Draus blitzt hervor, mit Freude,
Ein Auge, wie ein blanker Dolch,
Gezogen halb aus der Scheide.[2]

[1] With the exception of the variants specified in note two below and note one on p. 218, all the early readings discussed in this chapter are to be found in *SW*, I, 551–61.

[2] *Heinrich Heines Sämtliche Werke* (Insel edn., 1911), III, 467.

Lines projected for stanza 10 of *Himmelsbräute*,

> Büßend jene Schuld, die schwere,
> Gehn wir um in diesen Mauern...,

appear lifeless and dull beside the final version, with its startling stress on 'Irre gehn':

> Müssen büßend wir nunmehre
> Irre gehn in diesen Mauern....

The words which bear the strongest emphasis in the sentence here coincide with the first stress of a verse-line, after an enjambment: this makes all that goes before appear like an *Auftakt* to these two words.

Perhaps the most impressive instance of Heine's tendency, in the *Romanzero*, to throw the heaviest possible stress on single important words will be found in the final stanza of *Spanische Atriden*: a stanza in which the narrator, after hearing of the unnatural wickedness of the king whose banquet he has just attended, is politely asked whether he enjoyed his meal. Here the word 'höflich' (its original etymological connection with 'Hof' firmly restored) is preceded by a line that has one verse-foot less than any other line in the poem and followed by a grammatical pause:

> Don Diego stockte plötzlich,
> Denn der Seneschall des Schlosses
> Kam zu uns und frug uns
> Höflich: ob wir wohl gespeist?

The pause before and after 'höflich' points the irony: it forces the reader to read this word with the kind of emphasis he would give to words in inverted commas.

It is passages such as these (and they are many) which determine the characteristic music and movement of the *Romanzero*—passages in which the poet, through his rhythms and the interplay of grammatical and metrical stress, forces the reader to concentrate on particular words and their oscillation of meaning. Only occasionally does he introduce a poem in his earlier, more obviously 'melodious' manner: *Der Mohrenkönig*, for instance, or *Geoffroy Rudel*, or the beginning of *Der Asra*; and then the effect is one of gentle but deliberate stylisation.

A study of variant readings reveals at every point the rhythmic subtlety of these often apparently careless poems. Time after time, the alteration, or addition, or omission of a single word or even syllable attests Heine's delicate ear for correspondences, and that painstaking attention to detail for which we have not only Karl Hillebrand's testimony but also Heine's own. 'I have *worked*, really worked at my poems',[1] he told Adolf Stahr and Fanny Lewald in 1850. Even so slight a piece as *Kleines Volk* bears witness to this. In the Stuttgart *Morgenblatt* of 4 September 1846, the third stanza began: 'Da ist es puppenniedlich und nette....' For the *Romanzero* Heine added a single monosyllable, which somehow transformed the whole line into a representation of the fussy, tripping gait and speech of the undignified wooer:

> Da ist es so puppenniedlich und nette....

Similar instances may be found in *Geoffroy Rudel*, where the slow walk of the two 'tender ghosts' becomes actual in the lines

> Also kosen, also wandeln
> Jene zärtlichen Gespenster...

(the manuscript has 'Also kosen sie und wandeln'); in the thirteenth stanza of *Schlachtfeld bei Hastings*; and in *Maria Antoinette*. In this last poem, the line

> Ja, sie die mit turmhohem Toupet...

arrests attention by two strong opening stresses and then makes the reader look up as it were, to a great capillary edifice by hurrying him to 'turmhoch'. The lame manuscript version ('Die Fürstin, die mit turmhohem Toupet...') demonstrates Heine's success.

Maria Antoinette also reveals that the poet's mimic gift has not been impaired by time and sickness. He parodies the courtier and

[1] *Gespräche*, p. 743.

his absurd view of life and of history in stanzas that skip mockingly along:

Sie haben alle keinen Kopf,
Der Königin selbst mankieret
Der Kopf, und Ihre Majestät
Ist deshalb nicht frisieret.

* * *

Das sind die Folgen der Revolution
Und ihrer fatalen Doktrine;
An allem ist schuld Jean Jacques Rousseau,
Voltaire und die Guillotine.

Absurd, of course, yet somehow, motions of assent and dissent are curiously balanced here. Is not the courtier right in a way? Does not Heine himself proclaim, again and again, that the guillotine *belongs* to Voltaire and Rousseau, that Robespierre was only the midwife who brought to birth what the philosophers of the past had engendered? A revolution begins in the solitude and cleanliness of the study and ends with the bloody horrors of the market-place. The mocking tone—in vocabulary as in verse movement—conceals a telling ambivalence of feeling and attitude.

The parodistic section of *Maria Antoinette* that has just been quoted is preceded, in Heine's manuscript, by a stanza which reads:

Die Taille ist schmal, der Reifrock bauscht,
Darunter lauschen die netten
Und niedlichen Füßchen so klug hervor —
Ach, wenn sie nur Köpfe hatten!

The poet soon noticed, however, that the adjective 'niedlich' did no work in this stanza, added nothing to 'nett', and he therefore replaced it in the *Romanzero* by another that gives the passage truth and life:

Darunter lauschen die netten
Hochhackigen Füßchen....

This is only one instance of a process of tightening up, in expression as well as in rhythm, which makes Heine's occasional lapses into adjectival insistence all the more surprising. Unnecessary adjectives disappear: 'die gekrönte Ratten-Kön'gin' becomes simply 'Rattenkön'gin' (*Vitzliputzli* III), and 'Unsers teuern

Briten Martin' turns into 'Unsers Briten Henri Martin' (*Vitzli-putzli* II).[1] Throughout, colourless or conventional terms are replaced by terms that are more expressive and charged with meaning. In stanza 4 of *Der Mohrenkönig*, for instance, the anthropomorphic 'wimmern' replaces 'klingeln' with great effect:

Nur des Maultiers Silberglöckchen
[Klingeln] schmerzlich in der Stille;
Wimmern

and the addition of the word 'trällernd' in stanza 7 of *Zwei Ritter* makes concrete the vision of a light-hearted grisette:

Auch dieselbe Henriette
Dient als Wäscherin den Polen;
Jeden ersten Tag des Monats
Kommt sie, Wäsche abzuholen [Manuscript version].

Auch dieselbe Henriette
Wäscht für beide edle Polen;
Trällernd kommt sie jeden Monat,
Um die Wäsche abzuholen [*Romanzero* version].

Such changes may seem small and unimportant in themselves: yet it is often words added in this way which make Heine's lines both memorable and true. They act as 'needlehooks of experience' of which Evelyn Waugh has spoken in a Proustian passage of *Brideshead Revisited*: 'those needlehooks of experience which catch the attention when larger matters are at stake, and remain in the mind when they are forgotten, so that years later it is a bit of gilding, or a certain smell, or the tone of a clock's striking, recalls one to a tragedy'.[2]

Sometimes such tiny changes may add a whole new dimension of meaning to the poem within which they are made. The final stanza of *Der Mohrenkönig* had originally ended melodiously, with a dying fall:

Nimmer wird sein Ruhm verhallen,
Ehe nicht die letzte Saite
Schnarrend losspringt von dem letzten
Zitherspiel der Poesie.

[1] Heine means the painter John Martin (1789–1854).
[2] *Brideshead Revisited*, Book I, ch. 6.

In the *Romanzero* the last two lines appear as:

Schnarrend losspringt von der letzten
Andalusischen Guitarre —

a version which has not only the virtue of greater concreteness, but which also transforms the melody of the whole stanza. The high, light vowels of the earlier ending are replaced by darker ones, and the dying fall is superseded by something more appropriately dissonant. 'Guitarre' harks back to 'schnarrend' and conveys, concretely, the snapping of a string. The end of *Der Mohrenkönig* now casts some doubt on the consolations of fame and looks forward to the disillusion of *Sie erlischt*:

Doch horch! ein schollernd schnöder Klang
Ertönt unfern der öden Bühne, —
Vielleicht daß eine Saite sprang
An einer alten Violine....

In the same way, the change of a single word in the third section of *Vitzliputzli* opens up new perspectives. The dethroned idol threatens his conquerors with pursuit to their own country:

Nach der Heimat meiner Feinde,
Die Europa ist geheißen,
Will ich flüchten, dort beginn ich
Eine neue Lebensweise.

So Heine had written originally; but in the *Romanzero* 'Lebensweise' becomes 'Karriere', a word which transports us immediately out of the vividly evoked fantasy-world to the careerist Europe of the nineteenth century and suggests some of the things that *Vitzliputzli* symbolises. The passage now recalls others in which the level of style had suddenly changed in this way:

Sterbend sprach zu Salomo
König David: A propos.... (*König David*)

Mein Tempel hat in Gräcia
Auf Mont-Parnaß gestanden.... (*Der Apollogott*)

Different historical worlds coalesce, and modern Paris peeps out from behind legendary façades.

An examination of variant readings of these *Romanzero* poems will also reveal Heine's endeavour to eliminate lines that referred too tearfully and too crudely to his own situation. He tones down in this way the ending of *Verlorene Wünsche*:

Bin ein hoffnungsloser Krüppel,
Der sich krümmt am Boden elend.

Qualvoll sterb ich hin, die Wurzel
Meines Lebens ist verletzt—
Ach, das kommt von einem Fußtritt,
Den man mir ins Herz versetzt,

(Manuscript version)

changes 'Gelähmt am Boden liegt seit manchem Jahr' at the end of *Böses Geträume* to: 'Trostlos daniederliegt seit manchem Jahr' and cuts out 'Weckt in mir die Hodenkrämpfe' from *Jetzt wohin?* Again and again he sacrifices words that seemed on reflection too mannered or too crude. The neologism of 'Solchem Freveltum zu steuern' (*Rhampsenit*) gives way to: 'Um zu steuern solchem Diebstahl'; the transferred epithet of 'Die verstorbenen Manieren' is replaced by the more normal: 'Der Verstorbenen Manieren' (*Präludium*); and the obtrusive compound: 'In dem Tagessonnenstrahle' (*Geoffroy Rudel*) resolves itself into: 'In des Tages Sonnenstrahle'. Crass onomatopoeic effects are given up—the lines 'Trompeten blasen, Schnedderedengh' and 'Und es kam mir diese Nacht / Ha ha ha! ein Schatz abhanden' are projected for *Schelm von Bergen* and *Rhampsenit* respectively, but do not appear in the final version. Other crudities—such as the projected line 'Hahnerei ward unser Heiland'—are toned down (*Himmelsbräute*, stanza 8); a process that may be well observed in three successive versions of a line from *Zwei Ritter*, which pass from coarse caricature through plain statement to mock-heroic parody:

Fraßen in derselben Kneipe...

Aßen in derselben Kneipe...

Speisten in derselben Kneipe....

It is this same endeavour which made Heine on more than one occasion change an exclamation into a statement.

Another group of changes attests the poet's fine ear, not only for subtleties of rhythm, but also for balance of vowels and consonants and for expressive word-music. In stanza 30, for instance, of *Der Dichter Firdusi* III, Heine seems to have felt that two long *o* sounds made too solemn a music for his purpose—he therefore changed

Mit einer roten Führerfahne
Zog er voran der Karawane

into the more jaunty:

Mit einer roten Führerfahne
Ritt er voran....

More interesting are the changes Heine made in the refrain of *Pfalzgräfin Jutta*. The manuscript[1] shows clearly that Heine had originally written:

Die Toten schwimmen so traurig.

This seemed to constate too soberly, and the line is transformed into an exclamation:

Wie traurig schwimmen die Toten!

With that refrain, *Pfalzgräfin Jutta* appeared in the Stuttgart *Morgenblatt* of 2 September 1846. But even then the poet's ear was not satisfied; feeling, perhaps, that the opening 'Wie' was too high and light in sound as well as too eagerly demonstrative, he changed the line yet again before republishing his poem in the *Romanzero*:

So traurig schwimmen die Toten!

Only now, after this almost imperceptible change in its sound-pattern, does the refrain make its full effect.

A study of manuscript and printed sources will yield many similar instances, of which one might say, with Dr Johnson: 'Of these specimens every man who has cultivated poetry, or who delights to trace the mind from the rudeness of its first conceptions to the elegance of its last, will naturally desire a great number; but

[1] Reproduced in facsimile in the *Romanzero* volume of *Heines Werke in Einzelausgaben* (1923), p. 59.

most other readers are already tired, and I am not writing only to poets and philosophers.'[1] One further group of changes, however, must not go unnoticed—a group which attests the later Heine's fondness for magical incantation and obsessive repetition. Instances occur in *Der Apollogott*, where the line

> Das kann nicht scheuchen die süße Qual...

is transformed into:

> Nicht scheucht das Kreuz die süße Qual...;

and in the opening stanza of *Pfalzgräfin Jutta*, where Heine had at first written

> Siehst du die Menschenleichen nicht...

and then altered one word, with uncanny effect:

> Siehst du die sieben Leichen nicht....

What strikes one most about such musical effects is that they all have definite work to do in the poem within which they occur. Heine does not often, in his *Romanzero* period, indulge in verbal 'music-making' for its own sake.

To sum up, then, our final impression of the style of the *Romanzero*. The composition of individual poems (*Der weiße Elefant*, *Der Dichter Firdusi*, *Vitzliputzli*, *Spanische Atriden*, *Jehuda ben Halevi*) is looser than in any collection since the earliest *Traumbilder*—often one feels that Heine is spinning the poem out to dull the consciousness of pain:

> I work out many verses and some amongst them allay my pain like magic melodies when I sing them over to myself,
>
> (Letter to Campe, 30 April 1849)

or that he is forging for himself the sort of form that W. H. Auden has cultivated in our own day:

> I want a form that's large enough to swim in,
> And talk on any subject that I choose,
> From natural scenery to men and women,
> Myself, the arts, the European news.[2]

[1] *Lives of the Poets*, 'Pope'.

[2] Auden, *Letter to Lord Byron*.

But again and again in the course of such loosely flowing poems the reins suddenly tighten, a vision flashes vividly on the consciousness, an image obtrudes itself with startling force—Firdusi tearing open the money-bags, the torture of the Spaniards, Cortez kneeling down to intone the Miserere, and so on. Exactly the same process may be observed within the individual stanzas. The rhythm is that of natural speech, the word order as close to that of conversational prose as possible—until suddenly an inversion startles the reader, or he is arrested by a particularly prominent word or phrase on which the whole stress is thrown, and to which all that comes before seems merely an *Auftakt*:

Spricht ein Lump von einem Thoman,
Ist die Rede nur von Silber,
Ist gemeint ein Silberthoman.

Doch im Munde eines Fürsten,
Eines Schaches, ist ein Thoman
Gülden stets; (*Der Dichter Firdusi*)

Nur dem Gotte steht er Rede,
Nicht dem Volke — In der Kunst
Wie im Leben kann das Volk
Töten uns, doch niemals richten.[1]
(*Jehuda ben Halevi*)

There is little play with word-music for its own sake—like the counterpointing of speech stress and metrical stress, like all rhythmic deviations and irregularities, so 'musical effects' have generally a definite function in the economy of the poem. The same is true of all the prominent stylistic eccentricities of the *Romanzero*: the introduction of aggressively modern expressions into passages where they seem (superficially) inappropriate, and the curious mixture, in poems like *Der Apollogott*, of the exalted and the vulgar. For this curious mixture precisely conveys Heine's experience of a world in which the sublime and the ridiculous are close neighbours; just as the mingling of archaic and modern expressions conveys his sense of shifting time, of

[1] Cf. Helene Herrmann's introduction to the 'Goldene Klassiker Bibliothek' edition of Heine, I, 45.

'now' and 'then' contained in one another, of the mutual illumination of present and past.

In short: at every point the form of the *Romanzero* is inseparable from its content. Heine has forged for himself, in his later work, a perfect instrument for the expression of his particular and individual experience of life. We may not like that experience, with its dissonances and its sudden descents. We may not like the co-presence of almost cloying sweetness and extreme bitterness, of magical incantation and savage abuse, of grief and laughter, of historical re-evocation and sudden swoops into the present. We may not like the world the *Romanzero* presents, the world of a sick-room filled with half-seen and remembered shapes:

> Bin ich im Fieber? Ist das ein Spuk
> Der nächtlichen Phantasei?
> Äfft mich ein Traum? Es träumet mir
> Grausame Narretei. (*Nächtliche Fahrt*)

We may not like those *personae* that have a disconcerting way of disintegrating and revealing the features of their creator. We may wish that Heine had broken away from the four-line stanza he had made his own in his youth and evolved new and larger forms in which the conversational tone of so much of his later poetry would sound less strange. We may even wish he had been less easy to imitate or that he had led his followers along better paths than those indicated by Karl Kraus in *Heine und die Folgen*. But all this would be beside the point. In the *Romanzero* Heine presented genuine human possibilities—possibilities of the post-Romantic era in Europe—in a form adequate to them, in a language as contradictory and (sometimes) as worn as the experience of which it speaks. Whatever we may think of his imitators, we cannot but find his own later poetry *true*; we cannot fail to hear in it that authentic voice of which George Eliot has spoken: 'No echo, but a real voice, and therefore, like all genuine things in this world, worth studying.'[1]

[1] George Eliot, 'German Wit: Heinrich Heine', *Westminster Review*, LXV (1856), p. 33.

III

LAST POEMS

Imagine, then, by miracle, with me,
(Ambiguous gifts, as what gods give must be)
What could not possibly be there,
And learn a style from a despair.

WILLIAM EMPSON

1. OLLA PODRIDA

These fragments I have shored against my ruins

T. S. ELIOT

In the same year as the *Romanzero* Heine published his ballet, or 'Tanzpoem', *Der Doktor Faust*, in which the Mephistopheles of the old legend and of Goethe's play became a Mephistophela and Helena turned in a moment from the most beautiful of women into an enshrouded skeleton. As so often, Heine here describes experience of life in terms of experience of love. This experience is now one of insufficiency, of being unable to respond to ardours that seem to belong to another world —a theme already treated by *Die Beschwörung* (in *Neue Gedichte*) which is now given its classical formulation by the motto prefixed to *Der Doktor Faust*:

Du hast mich beschworen aus dem Grab
Durch deinen Zauberwillen,
Belebtest mich mit Wollustglut —
Jetzt kannst du die Glut nicht stillen.

Preß deinen Mund an meinen Mund,
Der Menschen Odem ist göttlich!
Ich trinke deine Seele aus,
Die Toten sind unersättlich.

Heine's 'vampire' poems merge feelings of insufficiency in face of experience with feelings of life ebbing out of the body, memories of love with consciousness of present sickness.

Es hatte mein Haupt die schwarze Frau
Zärtlich ans Herz geschlossen,
Ach! Meine Haare wurden grau,
Wo ihre Tränen geflossen.

Sie küßte mich lahm, sie küßte mich krank,
Sie küßte mir blind die Augen,
Das Mark aus meinem Rückgrat trank
Ihr Mund mit wildem Saugen. (*Zum Lazarus* 2)

Here the physical facts of sickness, implicit in the *Doktor Faust* motto, are made explicit: here the Helena of the Faust legend turns unmistakably into the figure of Death, the more terrible because she apes the motions of love. Novalis had used this vampire image before Heine:

O! sauge, Geliebter,
Gewaltig mich an,
Daß ich entschlummern
Und lieben kann.
Ich fühle des Todes
Verjüngende Flut,
Zu Balsam und Äther
Verwandelt mein Blut —
Ich lebe bei Tage
Voll Glauben und Mut
Und sterbe die Nächte
In heiliger Glut. (*Hymnen an die Nacht* 4)

But Novalis's ecstatic welcome of such death-in-love contrasts at every point with Heine's recoil; just as the transformation envisaged by Novalis—death as a rejuvenating flood, changing blood to balsam and aether—contrasts with the transparent references, in Heine's *Zum Lazarus* poems, to the symptoms of his own wasting disease.

The motto of *Der Doktor Faust* was reprinted under the title *Helena* in a new edition of *Neue Gedichte* published in 1852. *Neue Gedichte* now appeared without *Deutschland. Ein Wintermärchen*, and it was necessary to swell its size. In order to do this, Heine added the old cycle *Diana*, once rejected as too immoral, to the section entitled *Verschiedene*—times and manners had changed, and what had once seemed over-bold would now cause hardly an eyebrow to be raised; and he added eleven poems from his more recent period, of which ten (including *Helena*) were united in the section *Zur Ollea*. This section of new poems was intercalated between *Romanzen* and *Zeitgedichte*.

Zur Ollea did not and does not increase Heine's reputation as a poet. Its title proclaims a hodge-podge, a Spanish stew or *olla podrida* such as had been celebrated in *Vitzliputzli*:

> Eine Ollea-Potrida,
>
> Dick verschmoret mit Garbanzos,
> Unter welchen, schalkhaft duftend,
> Auch wohl kichernd, sich verbergen
> Die geliebten Knoblauchwürstchen.

But the ingredients here offered represent the scrapings of the barrel. For the most part, the poems of *Zur Ollea* had been considered and rejected for the *Romanzero*; and though there are good satirical lines in *Maultiertum* and *Hoffart*, though *Altes Kaminstück*[1] is a convincing presentation of dream and disillusion, there is nothing here which has not been done, and done better, in the *Romanzero* itself. The most striking new poem added to this new edition of *Neue Gedichte* is not in *Zur Ollea* at all. Heine added it to the cycle of *Schöpfungslieder* which connect *Der Tannhäuser* to *Friedrike*; and there it forms a strange contrast, in mood and in tone, with the six poems that precede it. As so often, Heine is here creating a God in his own image—but now the sick poet in search of consolation and fulfilment in poetry imagines, strangely, a sick God healed through the very act of creation.

> Warum ich eigentlich erschuf
> Die Welt, ich will es gern bekennen:
> Ich fühlte in der Seele brennen,
> Wie Flammenwahnsinn, den Beruf.

[1] The adjective 'alt' in the title is fully justified—a version of this poem had appeared as early as 1824.

Krankheit ist wohl der letzte Grund
Des ganzen Schöpferdrangs gewesen;
Erschaffend konnte ich genesen,
Erschaffend wurde ich gesund.

That, like *Helena*, belongs to the world of *Zum Lazarus*; it is part of that great dialogue with God which Heine conducts in his poetry after the *Romanzero*.

Curiously enough, however, Heine did not reprint in *Zur Ollea* the poem which most modern readers will recognise as the most striking of all those removed from the *Romanzero*. This is *Morphine*, a bold tribute to the opium drugs which alone could relieve the poet's pain; a tribute which begins with a characteristic variation of an image from Lessing's *Wie die Alten den Tod gebildet*,[1] and ends with a reference to a passage from Sophocles[2] that Heine found himself tempted to quote more than once in these terrible last years. The end of *Morphine* brings a paean to death, to not-being, which sounds all the more terrible in the mouth of this lover of life and all its sensual pleasures.

Groß ist die Ähnlichkeit der beiden schönen
Jünglingsgestalten, ob der eine gleich
Viel blaßer als der andre, auch viel strenger,
Fast möcht ich sagen viel vornehmer aussieht
Als jener andre, welcher mich vertraulich
In seine Arme schloß — Wie lieblich sanft
War dann sein Lächeln, und sein Blick wie selig!
Dann mocht es wohl geschehn, daß seines Hauptes
Mohnblumenkranz auch meine Stirn berührte
Und seltsam duftend allen Schmerz verscheuchte
Aus meiner Seel — Doch solche Linderung,
Sie dauert kurze Zeit; genesen gänzlich
Kann ich nur dann, wenn seine Fackel senkt
Der andre Bruder, der so ernst und bleich. —
Gut ist der Schlaf, der Tod ist besser — freilich
Das Beste wäre, nie geboren sein.

[1] Lessing, *Wie die Alten den Tod gebildet. Eine Untersuchung*, in *Werke*, ed. F. Muncker (Stuttgart, 1890), x, 233f.

[2] Sophocles, *Oedipus at Colonus* (transl. E. F. Watling): 'Say what you will, the greatest boon is not to be; / But life begun, soonest to end is best, / And to that bourne from which our way began / Swiftly return.'

The whole of Heine's post-*Romanzero* poetry may be regarded as an attempt to come to terms with the exaltation of death, unconsciousness and unbeing which informs this strange and revealing poem.

2. THE CALL OF DEATH

Though wise men at their end know dark is right,
Because their words had forked no lightning they
Do not go gentle into that good night.

DYLAN THOMAS

IN October 1854 appeared Heine's last publication in book form: three volumes of *Vermischte Schriften*, of which the second and third were entirely given over to a prose account of French politics, art and life (*Lutetia*), while the first contained a section headed: *Gedichte 1853 und 1854*. These poems do not make up as impressive a collection as the *Romanzero*: their arrangement, though it has a definite logic and consistency, does not exhibit the grand line of development, the rhythm, of that great work. Yet individually these new poems too can stand with the best of Heine, while collectively they introduce into German poetry a note which had never been heard there before. 'What kind of poems are these!', Alfred Meissner exclaimed when Heine first showed them to him; 'You have never written anything like this before.' 'It is true', replied the poet; 'Yes, I know it well, they are beautiful, terrifyingly beautiful. They are like a lament from a grave, a cry through the night by one who has been buried alive, or by a dead man, or even by the grave itself. Yes, such notes as these German lyric poetry has never heard before—has never been able to hear because no poet has ever been in such a predicament.'[1]

To make their full effect these poems ought to be read, not only in the order in which Heine arranged them, but also in the context

[1] *Gespräche*, p. 897 (August 1854).

of the prose works between which they appear in *Vermischte Schriften*. The poet himself makes this point in a letter to Campe of 15 July 1854:

> They are, as it were, a continuation of *Geständnisse*. The poems form a connecting-link between these 'Confessions' and *Die Götter im Exil*; in making my selection I had this in mind.

Three days later he impresses on Campe once again that the poems

> must appear in the position assigned to them, for otherwise the harmony of my book is disturbed; they are the 'nose' of the book; they must not be moved from their place; they are a continuation of my Confessions, and at the end of the book I return to the same theme.

Modern editors, alas, never preserve this sequence; some, including Ernst Elster, even saw fit to break up the poetry section of *Vermischte Schriften* altogether and distribute the poems under various headings in an arrangement of their own.

If the poems are read in *Vermischte Schriften* it will be seen that they are preceded by one of Heine's most striking presentations of a poet's dilemma—by his imaginative retelling and application of a legend from the Limburg chronicles.

> The chronicle recounts that in the year 1480 songs were whistled and sung throughout Germany which were sweeter and lovelier than any that had ever been known in Germany before, and that young and old —but women especially—were quite infatuated with them and sang them from morning till night; but these songs, the chronicle adds, had been composed by a young cleric afflicted with leprosy who lived in a wilderness concealed from all the world....(He) sat sadly in the desert of his loneliness, while all over Germany his songs were being jubilantly and exultingly sung and whistled....Sometimes in my sad nocturnal visions I seem to see before me the cleric of the Limburg chronicle, my brother in Apollo, and his suffering eyes stare strangely out of his cowl; but in the selfsame moment he flits past, and I hear the grating sounds of the Lazarus-rattle dying away like the echo of a dream.[1]

That establishes the *persona* of the poems which are to follow— the poet dedicated to delight and joy who is himself cut off for

[1] *SW*, VI, 73–4.

ever from the pleasures he heightens and inspires. It establishes also the ultimate tribunal before which the poet will now plead his case. For the fate of the poet-monk of Limburg is not presented as fortuitous; it is seen rather as a jest such as God, 'the Aristophanes of Heaven', allows himself from time to time.

O this fame—what was it but the mockery we know so well, God's cruel jest, which was the same then as now, though dressed up in the more Romantic trappings of the Middle Ages?[1]

These covert accusations are clearly relevant to that central group among the poems of *Vermischte Schriften* which Heine entitled *Zum Lazarus.*

The poem which immediately follows the story of the monk of Limburg is headed: *Ruhelechzend.* This opens with an almost Baudelairean evocation of the voluptuous pleasure to be found in pain and sorrow itself. But Heine is no Baudelaire, and irony soon intrudes; an irony which becomes obvious, characteristically, when God is first mentioned.

Auch danke hübsch dem lieben Gott,
Wenn Zähren deine Wangen netzen.

Such lines as these irresistibly recall Heine's mockery of identical attitudes in his earlier *Zeitgedichte.* The simple piety he had claimed for himself in the *Romanzero* postscript was not really for him.

Suddenly I now find myself taking my stand on the Bible, like Uncle Tom, and I kneel with an equal devotion beside my black brother in prayer.[2] (*Geständnisse*)

In the original German, this passage too is not without its hidden irony: the phrase 'schwarzer Betbruder' can suggest an African Mr Stiggins as easily as a 'brother in prayer'. And as for taking his stand on the Bible—it is necessary to recall, not only the praise of this Book of Books in *Geständnisse*, but also the irreverent use made of Biblical characters in the very *Romanzero* postscript in which Heine first announced his 'conversion'.

[1] *SW*, VI, 73–4.

[2] *SW*, VI, 54.

Ruhelechzend, however, is not in the main concerned either with the voluptuous pleasure to be drawn from agony itself or with the question of God's goodness. It presents rather a contrast between the garishness of day and the peace of night—that old contrast which had often served the German Romantics (and Heine himself in such poems as 'Der Tod, das ist die kühle Nacht') as an image for the bustle of life and the peace of death. Here, however, the contrast is sharpened by particulars. Heine's material is clearly his own recurrent experience: the intrusion of fools and knaves into his sick-room; the tinkling pianoforte whose sounds, penetrating from an adjoining flat, maddened his solitude; and suggested by this, memories of the vain and venal musical virtuosos he had so often described in his reports for the *Augsburger Allgemeine Zeitung*. From such shameless noise and bustle, the grave seems a welcome refuge:

O Grab, du bist das Paradies
Für pöbelscheue, zarte Ohren —
Der Tod ist gut....

But this unalloyed death-wish is no more possible for Heine than a voluptuous relishing of sorrow; and so the final lines return, with powerful effect, to the end of *Morphine*, to the wisdom proclaimed by Theognis and Sophocles: 'Best of all things upon earth is not to be born nor to behold the splendour of the sun.'[1]

'Splendour of the sun', in fact, is the theme of the next poem in *Gedichte 1853 und 1854*. *Im Mai* presents the contrast, not between the garish world of the living and the peace of death, but between a beautiful world outside and misery and heartbreak within. Its very rhymes ('jungfräulich'–'abscheulich', 'mailich'–'abscheulich') point the contrast. The poem seems to praise death; yet when the idea of death is translated into music, we find, not the intoxicating sweetness of Hofmannsthal's *Erlebnis*:

Das ist der Tod. Der ist Musik geworden,
Gewaltig sehnend, süß und dunkelglühend,
Verwandt der tiefsten Schwermut...,[2]

[1] Theognis, 425–8.
[2] *Die Gedichte und kleinen Dramen* (Leipzig, 1912), p. 5.

but rather a monotonous soughing, discordantly broken by shrieks, shrill singing and barking.

> Für leidende Herzen ist es viel besser
> Dort unten am stygischen Nachtgewässer.
>
> Sein melancholisches Geräusch,
> Der Stymphaliden ödes Gekreisch,
> Der Furien Singsang, so schrill und grell,
> Dazwischen des Cerberus Gebell —
>
> Das paßt verdrießlich zu Unglück und Qual....

In guise of praising death at the expense of life, Heine expresses horror of death and love of the sights and sounds of this imperfect earth. And as is hardly surprising in a man half blind, he is using more and more acoustic rather than visual images: images reinforced, as they should be in great poetry, by the sounds and rhythms of the words themselves.

The opening poem had spoken of the grave as a paradise, a paradise of quiet for one whose ears had been assailed too much by the noise of the vulgar; while the second had implicitly contradicted this conception, presenting a Hades filled with shrill and unmusical sounds. The third poem, *Leib und Seele*, turns from this to the Christian conception of heaven—and again, the opening impression is one of revulsion rather than desire to enter it. Soul and body must part, and the soul clings to its body:

> Weh mir! Jetzt soll ich gleichsam nackt,
> Ganz ohne Körper, ganz abstrakt,
> Hinlungern als ein sel'ges Nichts
> Dort oben in dem Reich des Lichts,
> In jenen kalten Himmelshallen,
> Wo schweigend die Ewigkeiten wallen
> Und mich angähnen — sie klappern dabei
> Langweilig mit ihren Pantoffeln von Blei.
> O das ist grauenhaft....

Here the realm of death is presented in an image that involves more senses than one: impressions of empty spaces, of cold, of yawning figures walking slowly and in silence, of a quiet broken only by a monotonous clacking as of leaden slippers—and over it all a sense of dragging boredom conveyed by the very rhythms of the passage. Again, be it noted, Heine is using the materials of his own present experience of life to suggest a future beyond the grave: slippers, silence punctured by monotonous ticking or knocking, boredom, a sense of the slow passing of time of which he is to complain more than once:

Wie langsam kriechet sie dahin,
Die Zeit, die schauderhafte Schnecke!

(*Zum Lazarus* 3)

The resulting picture of a Christian heaven is no more attractive than the vision of Hades in the preceding poem.

Leib und Seele is a strange reversal of the traditional role of the two protagonists in a 'Dialogue of the Body and the Soul'; for in Heine's poem it is the body, doomed to die, which offers consolation to the immortal guest that inhabits it. Yet the body's stoic consolation can do little to alter the image of heaven which the soul has already presented:

Vielleicht auch amüsiert man sich
Im Himmel besser als du meinst.

What these 'amusements' are likely to be, we learn from later poems: from *Himmelfahrt*, for instance, which tells of the vanity of the angels and the great 'Weltkapellenmeister' himself, of their aversion to philosophy, of eternal 'Flanieren / Auf edelsteingepflasterten Gassen'; or from *Zum Lazarus* 11:

Auf Wolken sitzend Psalmen singen,
Wär auch nicht just mein Zeitvertreib.

The impulsion towards death with which the poems began turns more and more into an impulsion toward life. Life is seen with a clear eye in all its imperfection and yet pronounced desirable in Heine's inimitably wry and unsentimental manner:

Ich weiß, es ist voll Sünd und Laster
Die Welt; jedoch ich bin einmal
Gewohnt, auf diesem Erdpechpflaster
Zu schlendern durch das Jammertal.

Genieren wird das Weltgetreibe
Mich nie, denn selten geh ich aus;
In Schlafrock und Pantoffeln bleibe
Ich gern bei meiner Frau zu Haus.

A Philistine, a Biedermeier ideal, which Heine had so often ridiculed and which could never, we know, have satisfied his restless spirit. There is self-mockery here; but there is also bitterness, for death is coming and even the creature comforts of the Philistine are for ever beyond the reach of the dying poet. And in face of death, as the final poem of *Gedichte 1853 und 1854* unmistakably proclaims, the meanest life may seem desirable. Had not Achilles proclaimed this very truth to Odysseus in the underworld?

Der Pelide sprach mit Recht:
Leben wie der ärmste Knecht
In der Oberwelt ist besser
Als am stygischen Gewässer
Schattenführer sein, ein Heros,
Den besungen selbst Homeros.[1]

This final poem of *Gedichte 1853 und 1854, Epilog*, speaks openly of sensual delights even of the lowest kind as infinitely desirable in face of death: a theme which found its most complete expression in the fourth and fifth poems of *Zum Lazarus*. In these poems, Lazarus shows himself tortured by the memory of gratifications spurned, gratifications of the senses which are now for ever beyond his reach; and here the vampire motif of *Helena* and *Zum Lazarus* 2 finds its last and most powerful variation. The vampire is now an emissary not of death but of the remembered past, of a life left for ever behind—a phantom of pleasures for ever barred yet for ever desired.

O zärtliches Phantom, umschließe
Mich fest und fester, deinen Mund
Drück ihn auf meinen Mund — versüße
Die Bitternis der letzten Stund! (*Zum Lazarus* 5)

[1] *The Odyssey*, transl. E. V. Rieu, Book XI: 'Put me on earth again, and I would rather be a serf in the house of some landless man, with little enough for himself to live on, than king of all these dead men that have done with life.'

That is the authentic note of Heine's last poetry. The stanza has a full sweet music that conveys an unmistakable urgency: all the lines except the last are broken in the middle, all flow restlessly on into the next until they issue, at the end of the stanza and the poem, in suggestions of bitterness and approaching death. Bitterness and approaching death are reality, and the 'tender phantom' is known to be nothing but a feverish dream; yet conjuring repetitions—'fest und fester', 'deinen Mund...auf meinen Mund'—and a controlled stress that falls heavily on the verbs that make the impossible appeal—'umschließe', 'drück ihn', 'versüße'—bring a serious and moving plea that it might not be so, that dream and reality might change places. This is not the sighing of a living, suffering man who yearns for death, but the cry of one already entombed who longs for the most tangible delights life has to offer and knows that his longing can never be assuaged.

3. COLLOQUY WITH GOD

Now his wars on God begin;
At stroke of midnight God shall win.

YEATS

THE new 'Lazarus' poems which Heine placed at the centre of his last collection of lyrics begin and end with an address to the personal God to whom Heine claimed to have 'returned'. Alfred Meissner, when confronted with the first of these poems and told it was 'religious', confessed himself horrified. '*That* you call religious?', he asked the poet, only to receive the answer: 'Yes, religious—blasphemously religious.' And it would indeed seem as though Heine saw in his return mainly an opportunity for blasphemy. 'Thank God that I now have a God again!', he had written to Heinrich Laube in February 1850. 'Now I can permit myself a few blasphemies when my sufferings get too much for me. The atheist has no such relief.' The newly found deity becomes a heavenly substitute for Uncle Salomon. As in the letters to Salomon Heine so we find in the poet's references to God downright submission to His will ('May His sacred will be done!': letter to Dr L. Wertheim of 15 March 1850) alternating with half-ironical cajolery:

> Gesundheit nur und Geldzulage
> Verlang ich, Herr..., (*Zum Lazarus* 11)

and that again with wry abuse: 'I will lodge a complaint against *der liebe Gott*, who treats me so cruelly, with the Society for the Prevention of Cruelty to Animals' (Letter to Elise Krinitz, November 1855). 'Der liebe Gott'—how ironical that phrase sounds whenever Heine uses it! How impossible he found it, despite his protestations of kinship with Uncle Tom (whose acquaintance he had recently made in Harriet Beecher Stowe's famous book), to return to any simple faith! *Vermächtnis* in the second book of the *Romanzero* and *Testament* among the posthumously published poems are sufficient proof, if any was needed, that Heine's religion included in it little of Christian charity. But neither could Heine return whole-heartedly to the Jewish God of his childhood. Recognising his power, he could not love Him, he could not accept the notion of His goodness and benevolence.

> With great love hast Thou loved us, O Lord our God, and with great and exceeding pity hast Thou pitied us. Our Father, Our King, for our fathers' sake, who trusted in Thee, and whom Thou didst teach the statutes of life, be also gracious unto us and teach us.

These words, from one of the earliest prayers in the Hebrew liturgy, sum up the attitude of the religious Jew to his God—an attitude which is diametrically opposed to that of the later Heine.

Yet the questions Heine so powerfully asks in the first poem of *Zum Lazarus* are questions with which prophets and religious thinkers have had to wrestle from the first. 'Wherefore', Jeremiah had asked his God, 'doth the way of the wicked prosper? Wherefore are they happy that deal treacherously?' And Heine:

> Laß die heilgen Parabolen,
> Laß die frommen Hypothesen —
> Suche die verdammten Fragen
> Ohne Umschweif uns zu lösen.

Warum schleppt sich blutend, elend,
Unter Kreuzlast der Gerechte,
Während glücklich als ein Sieger
Trabt auf hohem Roß der Schlechte?

Woran liegt die Schuld? ist etwa
Unser Herr nicht ganz allmächtig?
Oder treibt er selbst den Unfug?
Ach, das wäre niederträchtig.

Also fragen wir beständig,
Bis man uns mit einer Handvoll
Erde endlich stopft die Mäuler —
Aber ist das eine Antwort?

That is not the poetry of a repentant prodigal. There is no sense of sin, no willing submission, no sense of standing in need of divine grace. The tone is proud and peremptory; the impersonal construction of the final stanza ('Bis *man* uns...') and its quasi-rhyme ('Handvoll'–'Antwort') even smack of contempt, the contempt of the creature for its unjust maker. But neither is this poetry self-sufficiently defiant, the work of a man who feels no need of God and refuses to acknowledge His existence. It is rather the work of a poet lost in the dark night of the soul, unable to find his way back to the peace which submission to God's will can give.

T. S. Eliot, in words strikingly reminiscent of Heine's own to Alfred Meissner, has said in his *Dialogue on Dramatic Poetry*: 'It is only the irreligious who are shocked by blasphemy. Blasphemy is a sign of faith.'[1] This is a paradox of which we have rightly learnt to be sceptical. Heine never sinned his way to Jehovah; he never *found* a faith; but he did search for a way towards that divine being whose hand he felt upon himself.

The poet's tone is not always as peremptory as that of the 'Laß die heilgen Parabolen'. *Zum Lazarus* ends with a poem which appeals to God in a very different way:

O Herr! Ich glaub, es wär das Beste
Du ließest mich in dieser Welt;
Heil nur zuvor mein Leibgebreste,
Und sorge auch für etwas Geld...,

[1] T. S. Eliot, *Selected Essays* (London, 1932), p. 45.

a poem which has clear affinities with the posthumously published *Miserere*. *Miserere* begins seriously and impressively, with a construction reminiscent of Luther's Bible ('Die Söhne des Glückes') which yet blends naturally into the characteristically conversational tone of Heine's later poetry.

> Die Söhne des Glückes beneid ich nicht
> Ob ihrem Leben, beneiden
> Will ich sie nur ob ihrem Tod,
> Dem schmerzlos raschen Verscheiden.

The meaningful rhyme of this opening stanza points to a central paradox; and the adjectives of the final line conjure up the negative co-presence of the slow agony of the mattress grave. In the stanzas that follow, a happy life and painless death are suggested through images that remind the reader of an earlier Heine: of the poet who had demanded, in *Deutschland. Ein Wintermärchen*,

> Rosen und Myrten, Schönheit und Lust

for all mankind, and who had transformed the classical Hades (in the opening sections of *Unterwelt*) into a parody of his own domestic life. In *Miserere* too parody and humour intrude, as Fortuna becomes a fickle monarch and Proserpine a Czarina:

> Im Festkleid und mit Rosen geschmückt,
> Die noch wie lebend blühten,
> Gelangen in das Schattenreich
> Fortunas Favoriten.
>
> Nie hatte Siechtum sie entstellt,
> Sind Tote von guter Miene,
> Und huldreich empfängt sie an ihrem Hof
> Zarewna Proserpine;

but soon the opening melody and the opening seriousness return. The fifth stanza throws the stress once again on the word 'beneiden', and supplements the negative suggestions of the first stanza ('schmerzlos rasch') with overtly autobiographical suggestions of prolonged agony:

Wie sehr muß ich beneiden ihr Los!
Schon sieben Jahre mit herben
Qualvollen Gebresten wälz ich mich
Am Boden, und kann nicht sterben!

The trochee at the beginning of the third line brings pain vividly before us, while the passage from the third line to the fourth makes actual the effort implied by the word 'wälzen'. From these agonies the sick man turns to the God of the Judaeo-Christian rather than the Greek and Roman tradition—and as he does so, humour once again intrudes into the poem.

O Gott, verkürze meine Qual,
Damit man mich bald begrabe;
Du weißt ja, daß ich kein Talent
Zum Martyrtume habe.

Ob deiner Inkonsequenz, o Herr,
Erlaube, daß ich staune:
Du schufest den fröhlichsten Dichter, und raubst
Ihm jetzt seine gute Laune.

Der Schmerz verdumpft den heitern Sinn
Und macht mich melancholisch,
Nimmt nicht der traurige Spaß ein End,
So werd ich am Ende katholisch.

Ich heule dir dann die Ohren voll,
Wie andre gute Christen —
O Miserere! Verloren geht
Der beste der Humoristen!

The assumption that for martyrdom one needs a special kind of 'talent', that if one becomes melancholy one is inclined to turn Catholic, that good Christians try the Lord's patience by continual howling, that the man who could write this poem is himself a 'good Christian' or likely to become one—these are amusing notions which make the 'O Miserere' of the penultimate line a parody of the earlier 'O Gott'. Yet the prayer introduced by that invocation—

O Gott, verkürze meine Qual,
Damit man mich bald begrabe... —

has behind it the pressure of the previous stanzas with their unmistakably earnest presentations of envy and of pain. Its seriousness is unimpaired by the persiflage that follows.

The tone Heine adopts towards his God, in poems like *Miserere*, is ironically reverential; and while it would be foolish and insensitive to miss the irony, it would be no less wrong to miss the reverence, or at least the wish to revere. There was no danger of Heine's turning Catholic or losing his sense of humour. But a new element has been added to his poetry: it is now a cosmic drama played out before a God who is at once cruel, capricious and paradoxically just; a God whom the poet acknowledges but before whom he cannot and will not abdicate the pride of his reason.

Yet it was precisely because he felt horrified at the spread of atheism and materialism in Europe, at the increasing stress on the rational rather than the spiritual faculties of man, that Heine so often emphasises his own problematical 'return' to his God. He scoffed at the fashion for rationalistic exegesis of Biblical miracles:

Nicht *von* Raben, nein *mit* Raben
Wurde Elias ernähret —
Also ohne Wunder haben
Wir die Stelle uns erkläret.

Ja, anstatt gebratner Tauben
Gab man ihm gebratne Raben,
Wie wir deren selbst mit Glauben
Zu Berlin gespeiset haben.

(*Rationalistische Exegese*)

He constantly extolled the Bible as a repository of spiritual truth, though here again he would not scruple to use Biblical characters and events for humorous effects. And he saw in God a 'maker' of beauty whose kinship with those other 'makers'—the poets—appeared at every step.

Des Weibes Leib ist ein Gedicht,
Das Gott der Herr geschrieben
Ins große Stammbuch der Natur,
Als ihn der Geist getrieben.

Ja, günstig war die Stunde ihm,
Der Gott war hochbegeistert;
Er hat den spröden, rebellischen Stoff
Ganz künstlerisch bemeistert. (*Das Hohelied*)

Because of this affinity, poets stand in a special relation to their God: they see in him, as *Jehuda ben Halevi* had proclaimed, their only judge.

Wie im Leben, so im Dichten
Ist das höchste Gut die Gnade —
Wer sie hat, der kann nicht sündgen,
Nicht in Versen, noch in Prosa.

Solchen Dichter von der Gnade
Gottes nennen wir Genie:
Unverantwortlicher König
Des Gedankenreiches ist er.

Nur dem Gotte steht er Rede,
Nicht dem Volke — In der Kunst,
Wie im Leben, kann das Volk
Töten uns, doch niemals richten.

That was Heine's own special *hubris*. He felt that God could be recreated in the image of the poet and that a God so conceived would forgive him his many irreverences and blasphemies because He held His fellow-poets in special affection.

As for the terrible questions he had asked in 'Laß die heilgen Parabolen'—these too Heine justified in a striking passage at the end of the volume of *Vermischte Schriften* in which *Zum Lazarus* first appeared.

Why do the just have to suffer so much on this earth? Why must talent and honesty perish while boastful buffoons . . . stretch themselves on beds of fortune and almost stink of well-being? The Book of Job does not solve this evil question. On the contrary, this book is the Song of Songs of scepticism, in which the terrible serpents hiss out their eternal: 'Why?' How comes it then that at the return from Babylon the pious Commission of the Temple-Archives, whose president was Ezra, accepted this book into the canon of the Holy Scriptures? I have often asked myself this question. I think that these divinely enlightened men did this not because they did not know any better, but because they were well aware that doubt is deeply and justifiably rooted in human nature, and that it must not be clumsily suppressed, but rather healed. They embarked on this cure as homoeopaths who cure like with like; but instead of administering a tiny homoeopathic dose they increased it enormously. The Book of Job is a tremendously strong dose of Doubt; this poison *had* to be there in the Bible, that great medicine-cupboard of mankind. Just as man must weep his fill when he is suffering so he must also doubt his fill when he feels cruelly disappointed in his claims to happiness; and like the most violent fit of weeping, so that highest degree of doubt (*Zweifel*) which the German language rightly calls despair (*Verzweiflung*) brings on the crisis of moral healing.—But happy are they who are healthy and need no medicine.[1]

Out of his doubts and accesses of despair, out of his scepticism and his need for faith, Heine fashioned the uniquely ambivalent poetry of his later years. In his colloquy with God he presents to his readers conflicts typical of the nineteenth century which had never been so perfectly and so honestly transmuted into 'images of feeling': conflicts such as that between temperamental nonconformity and the desire to 'return', between pride of intellect and the prodigal's need to say 'Father, I have sinned against heaven and before thee, and am no more worthy...'. His uncompromising presentation of such dualism gives Heine's last poetry its symbolic power and its bitter truth.

4. SATIRES AND FABLES

This poem will rid me of these insects!

POPE

IN the *Romanzero* political satire had played a small but important part in conveying the poet's disillusion and accesses of despair. *Zwei Ritter* had shown the disappointment in store for those who look too closely at the heroes of liberty; *Im Oktober 1849* had contrasted the comfort and complacency of German and Austrian 'Bürger' with the actions committed by the

[1] *SW*, VI, 126.

governments they sanctioned; and *Disputation*, without being overtly political, had mocked at the inadequacy of organised religion and the church militant of any faith. Even in his most serious mood, Heine was never far from satire—it was the mode that expressed his world-view most adequately; and in the poetry of his last years as in that of his 'middle period' he again and again slips into satiric mockery.

Few readers would dispute, however, that the political poems of *Gedichte 1853 und 1854* are the weakest feature of that collection. Poems like *Hans ohne Land* and *Kobes I*, which ridicule the Frankfurt parliament of 1848, or like *Simplicissimus I*, which seeks to contrast the older Herwegh with the younger, bear painful witness to the extent to which Heine had lost contact with the political scene. They try to make up in inordinate length and garrulity for what they have lost in incisiveness and clear vision. It is only when Heine returns to the Germany of the early forties, the Germany he had revisited just before composing *Deutschland. Ein Wintermärchen*, that his old sparkle shows itself undimmed. At the last moment he decided to omit *Simplicissimus I* and to write another satire which would glance only at the younger and not at the older Herwegh—and from this decision resulted the only poem in Heine's last collection worthy to stand with the best of his earlier *Zeitgedichte*. *Die Audienz* caricatures, with inimitable verve and *brio*, Herwegh's famous interview with Frederick William IV. It shows up the mixture of simplicity and love of theatrical effect which Herwegh and the king had in common; it introduces, through constant reference to the Bible and to folksong, a standard of judgment by which the deficiencies satirised can be measured; and it produces, by its sudden modulation from 'Sauerkraut und Rüben' to a scene from Schiller's *Don Carlos*, an effect so shatteringly incongruous that only quotation can do it justice.

> Der König sprach: 'Es pflegt der Schwab
> Sein Vaterland zu lieben —
> Nun sage mir, was hat dich fort
> Aus deiner Heimat getrieben?'

Der Schwabe antwortet': 'Tagtäglich gab's
Nur Sauerkraut und Rüben;
Hätt meine Mutter Fleisch gekocht,
So wär ich dort geblieben.'

'Erbitte dir eine Gnade', sprach
Der König. Da kniete nieder
Der Schwabe und rief: 'O geben Sie, Sire,
Dem Volke die Freiheit wieder!

'Der Mensch ist frei, es hat die Natur
Ihn nicht geboren zum Knechte —
O geben Sie, Sire, dem deutschen Volk
Zurück seine Menschenrechte!'

Der König stand erschüttert tief —
Es war eine schöne Szene; —
Mit seinem Rockärmel wischte sich
Der Schwab aus dem Auge die Träne.

Der König sprach endlich: 'Ein schöner Traum! —
Leb wohl, und werde gescheiter;
Und da du ein Somnambülericht,
So geb ich dir zwei Begleiter,

'Zwei sichre Gendarmen, die sollen dich
Bis an die Grenze führen —
Leb wohl! ich muß zur Parade gehn,
Schon hör ich die Trommel rühren.'

So hat die rührende Audienz
Ein rührendes Ende genommen.
Doch ließ der König seitdem nicht mehr
Die Kindlein zu sich kommen.

Die Audienz is Heine's wittiest and most incisive presentation of the weakness of German liberalism, with its literary inspiration and its incapacity for practical politics, and of the *gemütlich* tyranny which proved too strong for it. It is also the best portrait ever painted of Frederick William IV, that puzzling mixture of weak expansiveness, Romantic aspirations, theatricality and parade-ground Prussianism.

In his satire on actual persons Heine was never again to reach the heights of *Die Audienz*, though there is an amusing farewell to his old butt Hans Ferdinand Massmann in *Die Menge tut es* and an uproarious welcome to a new butt in *Päan* and *Festgedicht*:

Beeren-Meyer, Meyer-Beer!
Welch ein Lärm, was ist der Mär?
Willst du wirklich jetzt gebären
Und den Heiland uns bescheren,
Der verheißen, der versprochen?
Kommst du wirklich in die Wochen? (*Festgedicht*)

All too often in this period Heine's personal satire was marred by hysterical hatred or, more often, by sheer incomprehension. The author of *Jung-Katerverein für Poesiemusik*, one cannot help feeling, understood nothing of Wagner and was concerned only to express his loathing for innovation, for virtuosos and (at this time of his life) for music as such. Music, in the shape of a tinkling piano that was constantly being practised near his sick-room, had become a torture to Heine; and as a species of revenge he hurled at Liszt and Wagner—who were then much in the news—shafts that failed egregiously to hit their mark.

More interesting than these exercises in pure mockery is a group of poems, in *Gedichte 1853 und 1854*, which characteristically mingle satire on oppressors with compassion for the oppressed. Such a poem is *Das Sklavenschiff*—a terrifying indictment of commercial values and the exploitation of man by man, which presents not only the folly and wickedness of slave-traders but also, movingly, the plight of the slaves. The same is true of *Der Philanthrop*, in which Heine contrasts public charity and private heartlessness; and of the later *Jammertal*, in which a heartrending and yet quite unsentimental description of the death of two 'poor souls' is thrown into relief by the uncomprehending officialese of the doctor who issues their death-certificate.

Die strenge Wittrung, erklärte er,
Mit Magenleere vereinigt,
Hat Beider Ableben verursacht, sie hat
Zum mindesten solches beschleunigt.

Wenn Fröste eintreten, setzt' er hinzu,
Sei höchst notwendig Verwahrung
Durch wollene Decken; er empfahl
Gleichfalls gesunde Nahrung.

Through his mockery of pompous professional language Heine here indicts a society that allows men to sever their 'official' from their private personality and to use words in order to escape from feelings.

These 'social' poems of Heine's last years have, however, a special flavour that the terms in which our analysis has hitherto been conducted are powerless to convey. *Erinnerung an Hammonia*, for instance, in which Heine recalls an annual feast-day in the life of Hamburg's municipal orphanage, ends with the following stanzas:

Leider kommt mir in den Sinn
Jetzt ein Waisenhaus, worin
Kein so fröhliches Gastieren;
Gar elendig lamentieren
Dort Millionen Waisenkinder.

Die Montur ist nicht egal,
Manchem fehlt das Mittagsmahl;
Keiner geht dort mit dem andern,
Einsam, kummervoll dort wandern
Viel Millionen Waisenkinder.

Social criticism here clearly turns into criticism of the world-order as a whole. The plight of those who are oppressed or neglected or abandoned by their fellow-men becomes a symbol for the plight of all mankind. Indictment of mankind gives way, once again, to a 'terrible question' asked of God.

What is directly stated at the end of *Erinnerung an Hammonia* is present obliquely but none the less powerfully in other 'social' poems of this period. The very title of *Jammertal*, for instance—'vale of tears'—gives universal application to the indictment of a particular society and places the drama played out in the poem *sub speciem aeternitatis*. And the central image of *Das Sklavenschiff*—the forced, hysterical dance of the negroes while the sharks are already waiting to devour them—recalls other images of 'dancing over an abyss' in Heine's work as well as an earlier stanza in which Heine had symbolised the plight of his own menaced soul:

Der Haifisch und der Roche,
Die schnappen hervor aus der See,
Es hebt sich, es senkt sich die Möwe;
Der Mond steht hoch in der Höh. (*Seraphine* 3)

The sufferings of the slaves of *Das Sklavenschiff* are only a more lurid exemplification of the plight of all mankind.

The later Heine does more than depict the weaknesses of a specific society or system—he shows up flaws in the world-order. Habitually, he now sees specific abuses in a cosmic setting. How constantly he does this may be gauged from a comparison between *Ein Weib* (in *Neue Gedichte*) and *Schnapphahn und Schnapphenne* (in *Gedichte 1853 und 1854*). *Ein Weib*, as has been shown, begins and ends in the lower depths of metropolitan society; but *Schnapphahn und Schnapphenne*, which begins in those same depths, ends with an ironic glance at another world:

Nach euch, ihr ehrlich reinen Seelen,
Die ihr bewohnt das Reich des Lichts,
Sehnt sich mein Herz. Dort braucht ihr nichts,
Und braucht deshalb auch nichts zu stehlen.

Once again, the poet's accusing eye strays from the realm of man to that of God.

Prominent among Heine's later poems of social criticism is a group of fables—a genre he had not greatly favoured in his earlier days. He hoped, in fact, to write a whole book of animal fables for Campe's young son, but never found sufficient leisure, peace of mind and physical strength to complete the collection. The animal world seemed now to become for him what the loving lotus-flowers and water-lilies had been in his *Buch der Lieder* period. It offered an escape from the unsatisfactory world of men—a letter to Campe of 7 September 1854 speaks of Heine's desire to lose himself 'in an innocent world of beasts'; it offered at the same time a means of satirising a world in which men (as the same letter has it) were behaving in a 'sufficiently beastly' way. When the poet was plagued by his squabbles with Joseph Dessauer, who felt insulted by Heine and accused him of pique because he had been refused a loan, he could find relief in writing *Der Wanzerich*:

Gemein und schmutzig, der Wanzerich,
Wie Wanzen pflegen, rächte er sich:
Er sagte, daß ihm der Zeisig grollte,
Weil er kein Geld ihm borgen wollte.

When he was visited by torturing memories of students who had treated him contemptuously in his 'Burschenschaft' days or of beautiful women who had spurned him and married for money, he would write poems like *Duelle* and *Die Libelle*, in which he at once purged his spleen and escaped into a fantasy-world.

Die Neger berichten: der König der Tiere,
Der Löwe, wenn er erkrankt ist, kuriere
Sich dadurch, daß er einen Affen zerreißt
Und ihn mit Haut und Haar verspeist.

Ich bin kein Löwe, ich bin kein König
Der Tiere, doch wollt ich erproben ein wenig
Das Negerrezept — ich schrieb dies Poem,
Und ich befinde mich besser seitdem.

In this epilogue to *Festgedicht* Heine reveals the force that gives life and strength to his fables.

It is significant, however, that Heine preferred, in these his later years, to transform men into beasts rather than into flowers. In the *Romanzero* too, it will be remembered, animal imagery had been (often painfully) prominent; and it is not irrelevant to recall that Thomas Rowlandson, in the bitterness of his final years, constantly drew the heads of men next to those of animals they seemed to resemble. To see men as beasts is the final nemesis of the caricaturist.

Of all Heine's fables the most successful is, undoubtedly, *Die Wanderratten*. In his reports for the *Augsburger Allgemeine Zeitung* he had constantly warned his contemporaries of the doctrines of communism, whose logic and social justice he admired while dreading the levelling of cultural values and standards it would inevitably bring in its train.[1] *Die Wanderratten* transforms these warnings into a picture, at once amusing and terrifying, of a horde of hungry rats advancing on a city while burgomaster and senate try to oppose them with guns, prayer and argument.

Nicht Glockengeläute, nicht Pfaffengebete,
Nicht hochwohlweise Senatsdekrete,
Auch nicht Kanonen, viel Hundertpfünder,
Sie helfen euch heute, ihr lieben Kinder!

Heut helfen euch nicht die Wortgespinste
Der abgelebten Redekünste.
Man fängt nicht Ratten mit Syllogismen,
Sie springen über die feinsten Sophismen.

Im hungrigen Magen Eingang finden
Nur Suppenlogik mit Knödelgründen,
Nur Argumente von Rinderbraten,
Begleitet von Göttinger Wurstzitaten....

That forceful last stanza, with its assimilation of the spiritual into the most grossly material, was to influence the Brecht of *Die Dreigroschenoper*, whose formulation—

Erst kommt das Fressen, dann kommt die Moral[2] —

seems to owe not a little to Heine.

Yet these fables too, like the other poems of social criticism written in Heine's last years, reflect more than just our familiar human world. *Rote Pantoffeln* for instance, which E. M. Butler has described as 'one of the most enchanting examples of the cautionary tale',[3] has at its centre a vision that can hardly be referred to any 'cautionary' intention:

Mein Mäuschen, du bist mausetot!
Jedoch die Pantöffelchen scharlachrot,
Die will ich stellen auf deine Gruft;
Und wenn die Weltposaune ruft

[1] E.g. *SW*, VI, 408f.

[2] Brecht, *Die Dreigroschenoper*, in *Stücke*, III (Berlin and Frankfurt, 1955), p. 99.

[3] E. M. Butler, *Heinrich Heine. A Biography* (London, 1956), p. 237; cf. my review of this work in *Modern Philology*, LVI (1959), pp. 209f.

Zum jüngsten Tanz, O weiße Maus,
Aus deinem Grab steigst du heraus,
Ganz wie die andern, und sodann
Ziehst du die roten Pantöffelchen an.

That recalls a dream of Heine's in which he saw—or purported to see—rows of shoes neatly ranged along rows of graves, as though awaiting the boot-black in some vast hotel.[1] The dream is amusing, as amusing as the transformation, in *Rote Pantoffeln*, of the Last Judgment into a Last Dance, 'Jüngster Tag' into 'Jüngster Tanz'; but beneath all the frivolity and all the fun there is seriousness. Ever and again the most common sights and sounds become, in Heine's later poetry, images of another world. Ever and again he seeks to convey, through such poor materials as this earth affords, his visions of a realm beyond and his hopes—to which he clung *quand même*—of the immortality of the soul and the resurrection of the body.

5. THE LAST CENSOR

Satiren, die der Zensor versteht, werden mit Recht verboten.

KARL KRAUS

AIDED by his publisher Campe, Heine had always found means of circumventing and outwitting the official censors of the various German states. He hoodwinked authority with ambiguities of phrasing that revealed their prime meaning only to the discerning; or he packaged his wares so cleverly that politically inflammable material slipped by under cover of more harmless goods. When all else failed, he always found in France journals that would publish his most overt attacks on the establishment, and could rest secure in the knowledge that *Die armen Weber* or *Lobgesänge auf König Ludwig* or *Schloßlegende* would soon find their clandestine way into Germany.

In his last years, however, Heine had to submit to a new kind of censorship. His cousin Karl, on whose bounty he was dependent

[1] *Gespräche*, p. 695 (Summer 1850).

after the death of his uncle Salomon, threatened to discontinue his allowance and that which was to be paid to Mathilde after his death if he published anything which might be interpreted as derogatory to members of the Heine or Furtado-Fould families. This measure was directed particularly against the Memoirs on which Heine was at that time engaged. Since not only his own allowance but also that of his wife was threatened, the poet had no choice but to submit; but he was deeply hurt by Karl's demand, and the bitterest poems of his last years are those that speak—in necessarily veiled and yet unmistakable fashion—of the 'treachery' of the family from whom he had expected love.

At first, in *Der Dichter Firdusi*, for instance, or *Spanische Atriden*, Heine had circumvented the new censorship by distancing the story in space or time, fitting it out with oriental or Spanish trappings, finding correlatives for it in legend or history. Even then he was careful to delete anything that might make the intended parallel too obvious. In *Spanische Atriden* he cut out, before publication, two stanzas that spoke of the relation of a powerful king with a poet cousin whose pen he feared:

> Er erzählte mir zum Beispiel,
> Wie der König dem Don Gaston,
> Seinem leiblich eignen Vetter,
> Abhaun ließ die beiden Hände —
>
> Einzig und allein, weil dieser
> Ein Poet war und der König
> Einst geträumt, der Vetter schreibe
> Gegen ihn ein Spottsirvente.[1]

This poem owes its very title to similar considerations—it had originally been entitled: *Familiengeschichte*.

Yet the hatred and bitterness in the poet's soul did not find sufficient release in these obliquities; and at the very end of his life he wrote a number of poems which deal with the blow his family had struck him in a more direct and personal way, though he kept to the letter of his agreement with Karl by mentioning no names. Three of these are once again played out on the cosmic

[1] *SW*, I, 555.

stage so characteristic of the later work. The sonnet 'Sie küßten mich mit ihren falschen Lippen' ends with mock-Christian forgiveness which turns into an appeal to God to damn and destroy those 'Magen und Sippen' who poisoned him; *Orpheisch* describes a descent into hell to unmask the villain who dealt this new Orpheus a poisoned blow while pretending to generosity; and 'Nicht gedacht soll seiner werden' ends with a vision of the Last Judgment. In all the poems it is clear that their special note of bitterness and hatred is due partly to a feeling of impotent weakness:

Nachts, erfaßt vom wilden Geiste,
Streck ich die geballten Fäuste
Drohend aus — jedoch erschlafft
Sinkt der Arm, mir fehlt die Kraft.

Leib und Seele sind gebrochen,
Und ich sterbe ungerochen... —

a feeling of weakness conspicuously absent from Heine's political and social poems; but even more it is due to a feeling of perverted love, of love gone sour and turned to rage. The cosmic setting has therefore a new part to play: it is an appeal to the newly found God to wreak the judgment the poet himself has been prevented from executing on enemies who might have been friends.

In the most powerful poem of this group, however, there is no appeal to God and only the faintest hint of a cosmic setting.

Wer ein Herz hat und im Herzen
Liebe trägt, ist überwunden
Schon zur Hälfte, und so lieg ich
Jetzt geknebelt und gebunden —

Wenn ich sterbe, wird die Zunge
Ausgeschnitten meiner Leiche;
Denn sie fürchten, redend käm ich
Wieder aus dem Schattenreiche.

Stumm verfaulen wird der Tote
In der Gruft, und nie verraten
Werd ich die an mir verübten
Lächerlichen Freveltaten.

Horrors which had been distanced in the *Romanzero*, told in a ballad form that had permitted intrusions of irony, are now suffered by a 'lyric I'. The images of gagging and fettering, of physical mutilation and of the rotting of a mutilated corpse strike the reader the more forcefully because they are introduced in an unhysterical, matter-of-fact way, without characterising adjectives. Only at the end, in the very last line, is there such an adjective—and then it is not the expected cry of horror, but something far more effective and far more true. The poem ends with the recognition that the horrors of the mind for which Heine has here found physical equivalents have their ridiculous side; they are inflicted by petty men not worth a moment's thought, they may be laughed at by those not immediately concerned. Yet this does not make the anguish they cause any the less keen; on the contrary, it heightens it, for it robs the sufferer even of his dignity. The word 'lächerlich', on which the stress crashes down at the end of the poem with such surprising inevitability, conveys most powerfully Heine's recognition of a truth formulated in our own day by Simone Weil in her essay *L'Amour de Dieu et le Malheur*: 'Le malheur est ridicule.'[1]

The poem which ends with this heartrending discovery of the indignity of suffering begins with a statement of the disabling and crippling power of love. The autobiographical truth behind this is not only the undoubted affection in which Heine had held the cousin who now wielded so tyrannous a power over him, who not only gagged his living body by censorship of immediate publications but also prevented him from speaking out after his death by inhibiting the appearance of all but a fragment of his memoirs. For what was it, after all, which made Heine submit to such posthumous mutilation? It was, of course, his tender affection for his wife, whose improvidence had to be shielded after the poet's death, whose allowance would be discontinued at once if anything appeared which infringed the agreement he had been forced to make with his cousin Karl.

[1] *Waiting on God* (London, 1951), p. 69.

Wer ein Herz hat und im Herzen
Liebe trägt, ist überwunden
Schon zur Hälfte....

Leicht erspäht Familienlist,
Wo der Held verwundbar ist.

The love which made the poet so vulnerable and inhibited his revenge was love of Mathilde.

Yet Heine *did* manage to take his revenge in a way more satisfying perhaps to his subtle spirit than any more direct attack could have been. In the first volume of *Vermischte Schriften*—of which Campe sent a copy to Karl Heine on the poet's own instructions—there are a number of poems which express, obliquely, feelings of hatred and contempt for members of the Heine family. No names are mentioned, of course; yet it is surely hard for anyone acquainted with the poet's biography not to recognise, in the setting of *Affrontenburg*, Salomon Heine's country-house at Ottensen, and in the animals that inhabit its garden relatives who played a baleful part in the poet's early life.

Vermaledeiter Garten! Ach,
Da gab es nirgends eine Stätte,
Wo nicht mein Herz gekränket ward,
Wo nicht mein Aug geweinet hätte.

Da gab's wahrhaftig keinen Baum,
Worunter nicht Beleidigungen
Mir zugefüget worden sind
Von feinen und von groben Zungen.

Die Kröte, die im Gras gelauscht,
Hat alles mitgeteilt der Ratte,
Die ihrer Muhme Viper gleich
Erzählt, was sie vernommen hatte.

Die hat's gesagt dem Schwager Frosch —
Und solcherweis erfahren konnte
Die ganze schmutzge Sippschaft stracks
Die mir erwiesenen Affronte.

Des Gartens Rosen waren schön,
Und lieblich lockten ihre Düfte;
Doch früh hinwelkend starben sie
An einem sonderbaren Gifte.

Zu Tod ist auch erkrankt seitdem
Die Nachtigall, der edle Sprosser,
Der jenen Rosen sang sein Lied, —
Ich glaub, vom selben Gift genoß er.

Heine had thrown to the winds the caution he had displayed in the changes made in *Spanische Atriden.* The references to Amalie Heine's early death and to his own sickness make the autobiographical background clear enough for the Friedländers and Halles and Karl Heines to have recognised their portraits in toad and viper and frog. Yet, insensitive to poetry and attentive only to journalistic prose, the family noticed nothing. 'What a light the publication of *Castle Contumely* throws on the darkness of their minds!', E. M. Butler rightly comments.[1] Heine had had a double revenge: he had expressed his feelings in a way posterity could not possibly mistake, and had demonstrated in the most forcible manner the obtuseness of his enemies. He had once again, brilliantly, outwitted the censor.

[1] E. M. Butler, *Heinrich Heine*, p. 238. Against this interpretation of *Affrontenburg* it may be objected that 'Rosen' implies more than one girl, and that while Amalie was dead, Therese was still alive. But this presses the demand for correspondence too far. 'Rosen', even in the plural, can suggest just one beloved—and the general drift of *Affrontenburg* is clear enough.

6. LAST LOVE

Her voice was like the voice of his own soul
Heard in the calm of thought; its music long,
Like woven sounds of streams and breezes, held
His inmost sense suspended in its web
Of many-coloured woof and shifting hues.

SHELLEY

THE daemonic poetry of hate examined in the last chapter is complemented by a new poetry of love. Notes of gentle tenderness such as had, in the past, been sounded only in poems which Heine addressed to his mother, now find their way into poems addressed to Mathilde—the child-like wife whom the poet feared to leave at the mercy of the world. In the thirties Heine had given Eugénie Crescence Mirat the name 'Mathilde' in the same ironic spirit in which he had called the women described in *Verschiedene* 'Seraphine', 'Angelique' and 'Diana'. He had seen in her then something very different from the aetherial Mathilde of *Heinrich von Ofterdingen*, that Blue Flower in human form. She had been for him akin to the heartless woman of *Ein Weib* and the earthy but irresistible Venus of *Der Tannhäuser*; she had even been stylised into Cleopatra in *Shakespeares Mädchen und Frauen*. But now all was changed. Now Mathilde had become for Heine what he first presented in *Gedächtnisfeier*: a 'süßes dickes Kind', naturally gay, clumsy and helpless, who saw in her husband not a great poet but only a 'pauvre homme' and who depended on this 'pauvre homme' for advice on even the simplest things. In the *Lazarus* cycle of the *Romanzero*, Mathilde had appeared as the one person who still needed the new Lazarus—and her need had thrown his own helplessness into relief. Hence the unusual earnestness, utterly free from any tinge of irony, of *An die Engel*, a poem which ends with a moving appeal to another world to afford Mathilde the protection that the new Lazarus is no longer able to give:

Bei allen Tränen, die ihr je
Geweint um unser Menschenweh,

Beim Wort, das nur der Priester kennt
Und niemals ohne Schauder nennt,
Bei eurer eignen Schönheit, Huld und Milde,
Beschwör ich euch, ihr Engel, schützt Mathilde.

No one at all sensitive to the rhythms of poetry can mistake the genuine urgency of that appeal.

In *Gedichte 1853 und 1854* the cares which animated *An die Engel* are voiced again. The poem *Babylonische Sorgen*, for instance, uses images familiar from *Das Sklavenschiff* to paint the dangers to which Mathilde will be exposed after the death of her (even now so inadequate) protector.

Mich ruft der Tod — Es wär noch besser
Müßt ich auf hohem Seegewässer
Verlassen dich, mein Weib, mein Kind,
Wenn gleich der tolle Nordpolwind
Dort peitscht die Wellen, und aus den Tiefen
Die Ungetüme, die dort schliefen,
Haifisch' und Krokodile kommen
Mit offnem Rachen emporgeschwommen —

* * *

Viel grimmere, schlimmere Bestien enthält
Paris, die leuchtende Haupstadt der Welt.

The horrors and dangers lurking beneath the glittering surface of the modern city are here suggested—as they so often are in Balzac's *Comédie Humaine*—by images of marine menace; and these in their turn are supplemented by images of German forests. Not, of course, the forests of Heine's earlier love-poetry, inhabited by harmless song-birds that tempt lovers into the pathetic fallacy; but rather the forests suggested in Caput XII of *Deutschland. Ein Wintermärchen*, inhabited by wolves, buzzards and wild boars. The poem then culminates in images—none the less terrifying for being presented with irony—of strange denizens of the human mind, half animal, half human; beings suggested by the flies that settle on a sick man's face.

Mit spöttischem Sumsen mein Bett umschwirrn
Die schwarzen Fliegen; auf Nas und Stirn

Setzen sie sich — fatales Gelichter!
Etwelche haben wie Menschengesichter,
Auch Elefantenrüssel daran,
Wie Gott Ganesa in Hindostan....

Beasts, men and gods are confounded in this almost surrealist presentation of mocking menace, of threats not only to a sick man who fears for his reason, but also to the defenceless wife he must leave behind.

Through its suggestions of howling wolves lying in wait for the unwary, *Babylonische Sorgen* prepared the way for another image in one of the last poems addressed to Mathilde.

Ich war, o Lamm, als Hirt bestellt,
Zu hüten dich auf dieser Welt....

This poem once again presents Mathilde as a helpless being in need of protection; and like *An die Engel* it ends with an appeal to higher powers—this time to God himself—to extend that protection. Yet it will be felt that the tone of this appeal differs from that of *An die Engel*:

O schütz ihr Vließ vor Dornenhecken
Und auch vor Sümpfen, die beflecken;
Laß überall zu ihren Füßen
Das allerbeste Futter sprießen;
Und laß sie schlafen, sorgenlos,
Wie einst sie schlief in meinem Schoß.

In the lines preceding those just quoted, Heine specifically disclaimed the pastoral tradition, renouncing 'die Schäferei, das Hirtenspiel' as no longer appropriate to his situation. Yet in his poem pastoral imagery seems to point to something real—seems to suggest that the relation described, the relation between a husband and his child-like wife, has something of the relation between a man and a cherished pet animal. There is love, but no intellectual respect; there are care and a sense of responsibility, but there is no communion of the spirit. 'Mein armes Lamm' could give to the new Lazarus a sense that he was still needed, that for one person at least he was more than simply an object to be pitied, to be feared or to be passed by; she could give him keen pleasure as he watched her gay gambollings—but she could give no more than that. The name 'Mathilde' still remained a pointer to all she lacked, for she was incapable of offering her lover the kind of communion that Novalis had described.

O dear Mathilde, it fairly tortures me that I cannot tell you everything at once, that I cannot give you all my heart at once. No thought, no feeling can I henceforth keep hidden from you: you must know everything. My whole being shall merge in yours. Only the most limitless devotion can suffice my love....It is a mysterious confluence of our most secret and particular being.[1]

His 'Blue Flower' Heine would have to seek elsewhere.

It is not surprising, therefore, that the deepest notes of Heine's last love-poetry are not sounded in his verses about Mathilde. We hear them instead in the poems he addressed, in the very last year of his life, to Elise Krinitz, a young woman who occasionally acted as his secretary and who aroused his last and in some respects deepest passion. Because of the emblem with which she sealed her letters, Heine called her his 'Mouche'; and it is under this name that she has entered the history of literature.

In the 'Mouche' poems Heine revives again the convention that had served him so often and so well in the *Buch der Lieder*—the convention of vegetable love, yearning lotus-flowers and amorous moons. He does so, however, with a new accent, a new awareness that it all is only a convention and not a very satisfactory one at that.

Sie sei eine Lotosblume,
Bildet die Liebste sich ein;
Doch er, der blaße Geselle,
Vermeint der Mond zu sein.

Die Lotosblume erschließet
Ihr Kelchlein im Mondenlicht,
Doch statt des befruchtenden Lebens
Empfängt sie nur ein Gedicht. (*Lotosblume*)

The sexual imagery is bold and unmistakable here—longing for physical sensations to supplement a spiritual bond is expressed with a nakedness that characterises many of these late poems.

[1] Novalis, *Heinrich von Ofterdingen*, Part I, ch. 8.

Worte! Worte! keine Taten!
Niemals Fleisch, geliebte Puppe,
Immer Geist und keinen Braten,
Keine Knödel in der Suppe!

But the paralysed body is for ever beyond these sensations; and the lover is reduced, at the end of the poem whose opening lines have just been quoted, to recommending 'eine Art Gesundheitsliebe' which does not depend on the body and is therefore less exhausting (but also, we are left to infer, less satisfactory) than the steeplechase of common love. The one communion of which he is still capable is precisely that which Heine had always refused to admit in his love-relationships. A poem which had originally formed part of *Lyrisches Intermezzo* but had been omitted from the *Buch der Lieder* because of its impropriety, reveals this earlier refusal with cynical openness:

Ich kann es nicht vergessen,
Geliebtes, holdes Weib,
Daß ich dich einst besessen,
Die Seele und den Leib.

Den Leib möcht ich noch haben,
Den Leib so zart und jung;
Die Seele könnt ihr begraben,
Hab selber Seele genung....[1]

In his relationship with his 'Mouche' Heine came to know, for the first time in his life, a communion of souls.

Mein Leib liegt tot im Grab, jedoch
Mein Geist, der ist lebendig noch,
Er wohnt gleich einem Hauskobolde
In deinem Herzchen, meine Holde!

* * *

Denn überall, wohin du reist,
Sitzt ja im Herzen dir mein Geist,
Und denken mußt du, was ich sann —
Dich fesselt mein Gedankenbann!

[1] *SW*, II, 10.

In this, the first poem addressed to the 'Mouche', the new Lazarus is weaving a spell, letting his spirit call to another in compulsive, incantatory rhythms that had never been heard in his work before:

Dich fesselt mein Gedankenbann,
Und was ich dachte, was ich sann,
Das mußt du denken, mußt du sinnen, —
Du kannst nicht meinem Geist entrinnen.

Repetitions, assonances and alliterations combine to make actual the compulsive spell woven about a beloved woman by a spirit imprisoned in a dying, paralysed body.

Very soon, however, this sense of having to dominate, to conjure in order to maintain an ascendancy, disappears and gives way to the still communion described in the most famous of this group of poems: the dream-vision which begins with the words 'Es träumte mir von einer Sommernacht' and which is generally entitled *Für die Mouche*.

In a manuscript of *Für die Mouche* preserved at the University of Harvard[1] there are clear indications that the colloquy between two strange lovers, a dead man and a passion-flower (which is now, in every sense, the centre of the poem), was an afterthought; that it did not originally form part of Heine's conception. The poem was to draw the sum of his existence—to show, in the guise of bas-reliefs on a dead poet's tomb, the Greek and Hebrew sources of Heine's inspiration and the irreconcilable conflicts between them. Amor, Apollo and Venus appear and so does the Wild Hunt led by Diana, familiar to all readers of *Atta Troll*; Herodias dances again, and the Children of Israel receive the Law before Mount Sinai in a stanza which the poet remodelled again and again but in which he left one constant: the characteristic rhyme

Ochsen
Orthodoxen.

After all these Greek and Hebrew sculptures have been described (some, it is important to notice, in ways which recall German

[1] Transcription and facsimiles in *Harvard Library Bulletin*, XIII (1959), pp. 414–43.

popular legend rather than classical or Biblical sources), the dreamer identifies *himself* with the dead man in his sarcophagus.

> Doch wunderbar! derweile solcherlei
> Bildwerke träumend ich betrachtet habe
> Ward plötzlich mir zu Sinn, ich selber sei
> Der tote Mann im großen Marmorgrabe.
>
> O weh! es schwand in diesem Augenblick
> Die süße, holde Totenschlafesruhe,
> Der Grabesstille ungestörtes Glück,
> Das ich genossen in der Marmortruhe, —
>
> Ein widerwärtig wüster Lärm erhob
> Sich draußen, ein Getümmel und Gekrächze,
> Ein Zanken, Stampfen, Fluchen, roh und grob,
> Dazwischen ein Gegreine und Geächze.[1]

The sculptured images come to life, and engage once again in that struggle which Heine had so often diagnosed in world-history, and more especially in the intellectual history of Germany: the struggle between Nazarenes and Hellenes, or—as Heine deliberately over-simplifies in *Für die Mouche*—between Barbarians and Hellenes. It was a battle which disturbed even the silence of the mattress-grave: for it was one which Heine had to fight out in his own breast.

The last two stanzas just quoted are, however, crossed out in the Harvard manuscript to make room for a second vision—that dream within a dream for which the poem is now best remembered. Above the dead man now grows a passion-flower, bearing within its chalice the instruments of torture that played a part in the passion of Christ. This flower—such is the strange logic of the dream—is also a woman with whom the dead man engages in mute colloquy.

> Wir sprachen nicht, jedoch mein Herz vernahm,
> Was du verschwiegen dachtest im Gemüte —
> Das ausgesprochne Wort ist ohne Scham,
> Das Schweigen ist der Liebe keusche Blüte.

[1] *Harvard Library Bulletin*, *loc. cit.*

Alfred Meissner, who first published the later and better-known version of this poem from which the stanza just quoted has been taken, omitted some lines through a sense of delicacy and some for reasons now unfathomable. Among those omitted is the following stanza:

Und wie beredsam dieses Schweigen ist!
Man sagt sich alles ohne Metaphoren
Ganz ohne Feigenblatt, ganz ohne List
Des Silbenfalls, des Wohllauts der Rhetoren.[1]

What is happening in these two clearly related stanzas is not difficult to see. A great poet is discovering, at the end of his life, the inadequacy of words. He is pointing to that *Sprachnot* which has been diagnosed in his work by Walther Killy[2]—to the frequent inadequacy of his language to his experience. He is pointing behind and beyond worn metaphors and rhetorical devices and words themselves to regions of experience where silence alone is eloquent.

The passion-flower is of course—as critics have recognised from the first—a stylisation of the 'Mouche'; but Elise Krinitz herself said with commendable modesty and much truth that it represented 'la patrie lontaine' Heine had sought throughout his life.[3] By this she did not mean Germany, but rather a Romantic Atlantis, a land of the Blue Flower. It is not, therefore, surprising to find the silence of love merging into another and intimately related silence:

O Tod! mit deiner Grabesstille, du,
Nur du kannst uns die beste Wollust geben;
Den Krampf der Leidenschaft, Lust ohne Ruh,
Gibt uns für Glück das albern rohe Leben.

The silent communion of soul with soul, a wordless colloquy of love, turns inevitably into communion with death. The sweetness of love and the sweetness of death are one. At the very end of his

[1] *Harvard Library Bulletin, loc. cit.*

[2] *Wandlungen des lyrischen Bildes* (Göttingen, 1958), p. 103.

[3] 'Camille Selden' (= Elise Krinitz), *Les derniers Jours de Henri Heine* (Paris, 1884), p. 83.

life, Heine seems about to enter those realms of experience which Novalis had opened up to an at once weary and hopeful generation.

At this point, however, the reader is dragged back to the vision with which Heine's poem had begun. The flower of love and death disappears, and what is left is the quarrelling of Hellenic and Nazarene phantoms, out-brayed by Balaam's ass: the noisy dispute of beauty and truth out-shouted by stupidity.

> Mit diesem I-A, I-A, dem Gewiehr,
> Dem schluchzend ekelhaften Mißlaut, brachte
> Mich zur Verzweiflung schier das dumme Tier,
> Ich selbst zuletzt schrie auf — und ich erwachte.

The ass often served Heine, in his last poems and letters, to symbolise the dulness and impotent malice of the world around him. To that world, as the end of *Für die Mouche* clearly shows, he could not close his ears. He could not gaze into the eyes of a beloved woman or meditate on death without becoming aware, sooner or later, of the claims of an intellectual and social world of which he might disapprove but which he could not ignore. The end of *Für die Mouche* has affinities with the justly celebrated *Seegespenst* in his early *Nordsee* cycle: for both poems show Heine's inability to be either a Parnassian or a *symboliste*. He could not fashion for himself a 'pure' world of poetry into which he might escape from that 'albern rohes Leben' to which he clung in despite of all.

That was his limitation—but it was also his greatness.

7. DOPPELGÄNGER

Jene seltsame Narrheit, in der das eigne Ich sich mit sich selbst entzweit, worüber denn die eigne Persönlichkeit sich nicht mehr festhalten kann. E. T. A. HOFFMANN

It has often been noticed that Heine's last poetry forms a perfect circle with his first;[1] that the *Traumbilder* whose often meretricious horrors open the *Buch der Lieder* are matched and surpassed by the dreams of *Nächtliche Fahrt*, *Vitzliputzli* and *Für die Mouche*, behind whose terrors and ardours we feel the pressure, not only of Heine's reading, but also of his life. When the poet now speaks of mythological or medieval or exotic tortures, he is speaking of pains his racked body knew only too well.

Laß mich mit glühnden Zangen kneipen,
Laß grausam schinden mein Gesicht,
Laß mich mit Ruten peitschen, stäupen —
Nur warten, warten laß mich nicht!

In the poem which begins with this stanza—a poem addressed to the 'Mouche'—images of hardly bearable physical pain are used to throw into relief a mental agony that outdoes the physical: the agony of *waiting*, experienced by a man for whom each moment has become, when not filled with the effort of composition or the presence of a beloved being, a dragging eternity.

Wie langsam kriechet sie dahin,
Die Zeit, die schauderhafte Schnecke!
Ich aber, ganz bewegungslos
Blieb ich hier auf demselben Flecke.

(*Zum Lazarus* 3)

Yet the truly remarkable feature of these last poems is the way in which the poet's mocking spirit can rise above the mental and physical torments he so terrifyingly presents. 'Laß mich mit glühnden Zangen kneipen', which begins with such earnestness of pain and impatience, soon modulates into a different tone.

[1] E.g. Charles Andler, 'L'Œuvre lyrique de Heine', *Études Germaniques*, II, 305: 'La dernière poésie de Heine dit d'une façon vécue ce que fut l'hallucination des poèmes les plus macabres de sa jeunesse.'

Du kamest nicht — ich rase, schnaube,
Und Satanas raunt mir ins Ohr;
Die Lotosblume, wie ich glaube,
Mokiert sich deiner, alter Tor!

How it was possible for Heine to see the amusing side of his own plight—to look at his own 'Rasen und Schnauben' and find it out of proportion to its immediate cause—will for ever remain a mystery of the human spirit. These verses to the 'Mouche', which begin with the earnest conjuration of the threefold 'Laß' at the beginning of successive lines and with the racked outcry of the repeated 'warten', end in a wry jest at the tortured lover's own expense; and they enable later readers to re-experience for themselves that resilience of spirit to which so many of Heine's visitors have testified. One caller found him reading a medical work about his own complaint: 'but', said Heine, 'what good this reading is to do me, I don't know, except that it will qualify me to give lectures in Heaven on the ignorance of terrestrial doctors about diseases of the spine'. Another visitor he assures that if his nerves were exhibited at the Paris 'Exposition' that was then taking place, they would be awarded the Gold Medal for Pain and Misery; and on being told to ask God's forgiveness he characteristically declared: 'Dieu me pardonnera; c'est son métier.'[1]

Such ability to suffer and at the same time to look down ironically on his own sufferings Heine had presented, in the *Buch der Lieder*, under the image of the 'Doppelgänger', the ghostly double of the twentieth poem of *Die Heimkehr*. The 'Doppelgänger' of that poem is a spirit of the *past*, which breaks into the present to mock present misery. It has all happened before—so why take suffering so seriously? Memories of the past are a parody of the present.

In Heine's middle period, the 'Doppelgänger' had reappeared in a new guise. Capita VI and VII of *Deutschland. Ein Wintermärchen* had shown him as the shadow of the *future*; a future brought about, ineluctably, by the thoughts and writings of the traveller

[1] *Gespräche*, pp. 902, 984.

to whom he appears; a future whose terrors would seem to be at least as great as its benefits.

Now, at the very end of his life, Heine presents once again his vision of that second self which haunted him as it had haunted the German Romantics. He finds once again that the 'Doppelgänger' motif is more adequate than any other to convey his recurrent experience—more adequate even than those 'theatre' and 'vaudeville' images that form, as Barker Fairley has shown,[1] so constant a feature of his work.

> Der Vorhang fällt, das Stück ist aus,
> Und gähnend wandelt jetzt nach Haus
> Mein liebes deutsches Publikum.... (*Der Scheidende*)

Such theatre images show Heine as the social being he was: show him presenting himself to his public in different guises and *personae*. The 'Doppelgänger', on the other hand, appears only in that more intimate theatre of the soul in which man is at once actor and spectator and in which the dramas that most nearly affect him are all played out. The vaudeville-actor is a figure of waking life, the 'Doppelgänger' a figure of dreams; and from the first Heine's best poems had tended to be dream-poems.

The unaccountably neglected lyric in which Heine returns, for the last time, to the figure of the 'Doppelgänger' begins with a powerful presentation of that chaos of the mind out of which most of Heine's last poems were born.

> Mir lodert und wogt im Hirn eine Flut
> Von Wäldern, Bergen und Fluren;
> Aus dem tollen Wust tritt endlich hervor
> Ein Bild mit festen Konturen.

In the opening image of a fiery flood Heine merges the tortures of the damned of which Dante and Shakespeare had spoken—

> Poco più oltre il Centauro s'affisse
> sopra una gente, che infino alla gola
> parea che di quel bulicame uscisse.
>
> (*Inferno*, Canto XII)

[1] Notably in his essay 'Heine's Vaudeville', *University of Toronto Quarterly*, III (1934).

> ...and the delighted spirit
> To bathe in fiery floods...
>
> (*Measure for Measure*, III, i)

—with the benumbed and yet feverishly active consciousness produced by opium drugs. The stanza suggests bright colour and constant motion, a shining flux in which remembered sights are caught up and whirled about in a giddying sway that is perfectly conveyed by the alternation of iambs with dactyls or anapaests. Only gradually do firm contours emerge—an emergence made actual by the line-division:

> ...tritt endlich hervor
> Ein Bild....

What presents itself to the consciousness is not, however, the contour of an actual, a present world, which had shrunk, for the later Heine, to the four walls of his sick-room. It is rather a *remembered* landscape.

> Das Städtchen, das mir im Sinne schwebt,
> Ist Godesberg, ich denke.
> Dort wieder unter dem Lindenbaum
> Sitz ich vor der alten Schenke.
>
> Der Hals ist mir trocken, als hätt ich verschluckt
> Die untergehende Sonne....

The dead metaphor 'im Sinne schweben' is given startling new life, a literal as well as metaphorical application; its usually forgotten associations of 'hovering' are clearly linked with suggestions of 'flowing' and 'whirling' in the previous stanza. It subtly suggests the trembling unreality that blurs even the 'firm contours' which have just emerged from the bright chaos of the mind. In the same way, the landscape suggestions of 'die untergehende Sonne' are linked with physical sensations, with a parched and burning throat—the sensation of a sick man rather than that of a thirsty wanderer. The image of the 'swallowed sun', which opens the third stanza, recalls that of the 'fiery flood' which had opened the first; but it is significant that the later image is introduced as a simile rather than a metaphor.

> *Als hätt* ich verschluckt....

The contours, it would seem, are growing more steady. A past self rises up, a young and vigorous wanderer by the Rhine, with a healthy thirst and an imperious way with landlords, who takes control of the poem and makes the reader almost forget the feverish chaos out of which his image emerged.

This past self, however, which now occupies the foreground of the poem is itself anything but simple. It is a self healthily appreciative of good landscapes and good wines; but in its speeches there is an element of self-parody that reveals itself in consciously *outré* adjectives—

> Ich sah hinauf nach dem Drachenfels,
> Der, *hochromantisch* beschienen
> Vom Abendrot, sich spiegelt im Rhein
> Mit seinen Burgruinen —

and in outrageous sound-combinations:

> Jetzt aber steck ich die Nase ins Glas,
> Und ernsthaft zuvor beguck ich
> Den Wein, den ich schlucke; manchmal auch
> Ganz *ohne zu gucken, schluck ich* [my italics].

We recognise here the authentic note of *Die Heimkehr*, in which self-parody had constantly broken in, conveying an impression of a second self mocking the feelings and attitudes of the 'lyric I'.

In 'Mir lodert und wogt im Hirn eine Flut', however, this divided past self is watched by yet another, a *third* self which had spoken in the first two stanzas; and this third self suddenly abandons its position as watcher and presenter to enter the past conjured up in the poem as a protagonist. In true dream-fashion, the word 'schlucken' suggests a complementary 'armer Schlucker':

> Doch sonderbar! Während dem Schlucken wird mir
> Zu Sinne, als ob ich verdoppelt,
> Ein andrer armer Schlucker sei
> Mit mir zusammengekoppelt.
>
> Der sieht so krank und elend aus,
> So bleich und abgemergelt.
> Gar schmerzlich verhöhnend schaut er mich an,
> Wodurch er mich seltsam nergelt.

The 'Doppelgänger' is now not past or future, but the unendurable *present* itself, confounding dreams of past happiness. The spectre is the actual, the real, the 'here and now', dispelling visions of a bliss that could never more be attained.

Nicht in der Schenke von Godesberg,
In einer Krankenstube
Des fernen Paris befänden wir uns —
Du lügst, du bleicher Bube!

What follows is an alarming presentation of a struggle between past self and present 'Doppelgänger', a struggle felt as physical pain, which leads to a return of those sensations of dryness and burning with which the vision had begun.

Bei dieser fatalen Balgerei
Ward wieder der Hals mir trocken,
Und will ich rufen nach Wein den Wirt
Die Worte im Munde stocken.

Mir schwinden die Sinne, und traumhaft hör
Ich von Kataplasmen reden,
Auch von der Mixtur — einen Eßlöffel voll —
Zwölf Tropfen stündlich in jeden.

The dream is shattered, the double's mockery justified. Parched throat, physical pain and mental anguish alone were real. As the Parisian doctor takes the place of mine host of Godesberg, clear outlines are once again blurred and the poem falls back into the chaos with which it had opened. The colours and the images of remembered landscape are no more—what remains is a drowsy numbness that is a foretaste of death.

There is no parallel in German literature for poems like 'Mir lodert und wogt im Hirn eine Flut'. Never has a German poet presented so vividly at once the visions of a dream and the clear consciousness that it all *is* a dream. Never has anyone painted so true and terrifying a picture of divided consciousness; of genuine emotions which are watched and ridiculed by a daemonic intellectual self. Nowhere outside Heine will we find so powerful a presentation of the terrors of life together with its beauty—and of the nullification of that terror through the detachment, the wit, with which it is transformed.

Vielleicht bin ich gestorben längst;
Es sind vielleicht nur Spukgestalten
Die Phantasieen, die des Nachts
Im Hirn den bunten Umzug halten.

Es mögen wohl Gespenster sein,
Altheidnisch göttlichen Gelichters;
Sie wählen gern zum Tummelplatz
Den Schädel eines toten Dichters. —

Die schaurig süßen Orgia,
Das nächtlich tolle Geistertreiben,
Sucht des Poeten Leichenhand
Manchmal am Morgen aufzuschreiben.

(*Zum Lazarus* 3)

Out of his opium dreams and nocturnal visions, out of his apprehensions of death and memories of life, out of his physical pain, mental anguish and spiritual resurgence Heine fashioned his greatest and truest poetry.

8. VOYAGE TO AVALON

Womb? Weary?
He rests. He has travelled.

JOYCE

IN the intervals of writing his memoirs—a work of which all but a fragment seems to be irrevocably lost to posterity—the dying poet worked out plans for longer poems that were never to come to fruition. Among these was a comic epic on the subject of *Till Eulenspiegel* of which Heine had spoken to Adolf Stahr and Fanny Lewald in 1850.

I wanted to give this work its form by pretending to travel about and collect information about Eulenspiegel — and I would have done this so thoroughly, that antiquaries might have mistaken it for a work of scholarship. But in between I would have said everything I had on my mind about God and the world. It would surely have been my best work![1]

Till Eulenspiegel would have been an ideal subject for the author of *Atta Troll* and *Deutschland. Ein Wintermärchen*—but the Heine of the *Romanzero* and the last poems had become too remote from the world to have risen fully to the opportunities for political and social satire it seems to offer. *Till Eulenspiegel*, therefore, was never written, and *Bimini*, the only longer poem of Heine's last years of which fragments have been preserved, has affinities with *Vitzliputzli* and *Jehuda ben Halevi* rather than with the 'versified travel-pictures' of his early Paris period.

Bimini begins with one of those obsessive repetitions of individual words that characterise Heine's later poetry. The word here is 'Wunder'; and it is not surprising to find the dying poet obsessed with the idea of a saving miracle. What is conjured up in the *Prolog* of *Bimini*, however, is not so much an age of actual miracles, as an age of *belief* in miracles.

> Wunderglaube! blaue Blume,
> Die verschollen jetzt, wie prachtvoll
> Blühte sie im Menschenherzen
> Zu der Zeit, von der wir singen!

The 'blue flower' of that opening line reminds us that the Romantics too, and notably Novalis, had looked back to an age of faith which they opposed to their own rationalising times. The wise Pope of the late middle ages, we read in Novalis's *Die Christenheit oder Europa*, checked the too curious enquiry of Copernican astronomy,

> for he knew well that once men lost their respect for their dwelling-place and terrestrial fatherland they would lose also their respect for their celestial home...and that they would then prefer limited knowledge to illimited faith and would accustom themselves to despise all that is great and worthy of admiration and regard it as the mere result of a [scientific] law.[2]

[1] *Gespräche*, p. 763.

[2] Novalis, *Gesammelte Werke*, ed. C. Seelig (Herliberg and Zürich, 1945), v, 13.

That kind of medievalism the later Heine found as impossible as the earlier had done. The age of miracles to which he appeals is rather that of artistic Renaissance, scientific and geographical Exploration and religious Reformation: the time which Hegel had characterised, in the fourth part of his *Philosophie der Geschichte*, as the rejuvenation of mankind. Heine's 'miracles' are achievements of the human spirit: the invention of the compass, of gunpowder and of printing, the rediscovery and translation of the literature of classical antiquity, the translation of the Bible into the vernacular, and the discovery and conquest of new worlds. In the repossessed classics and the repossessed Bible mankind explored those two realms which had shown their eternal incompatibility in *Für die Mouche*, but which here, in *Bimini*, are depicted as but two works written in different languages by the supreme author of the world:

Buch der Schönheit heißt das eine,
Buch der Wahrheit heißt das andre.
Beide aber hat Gott selber
Abgefaßt in zwei verschiednen
Himmelssprachen, und er schrieb sie,
Wie wir glauben, eigenhändig.

The image of a God writing in two different languages would commend itself to Heine, who had seen his own works appearing alternately in German and in French for a quarter of a century.

What attracted the author of *Bimini* most, in the history of the sixteenth century, was the exploration of new worlds. From the narrow room to which his body was for ever confined his spirit could take wing as he listened to the adventures of conquistadors that his secretaries read to him—adventures chronicled by Washington Irving, for instance, in *Voyages and Discoveries of the Companions of Columbus*.[1] In this volume he heard amongst other things of the adventures of Juan Ponce de Leon, who accompanied Columbus on three expeditions, conquered Porto Rico and became its governor, and who sailed to the Bahamas in 1512 in

[1] For Heine's reading in the last years of his life cf. my essay on the *Romanzero* in *The Germanic Review*, XXXI (1956), p. 299.

an effort to discover the mythical island of *Bimini*. This *voyage à Cythère* is the real starting-point of Heine's poem.

Don Juan Ponce de Leon is the last important *persona* of Heine's poetry. In one way he is an obvious wish-dream: he lived in a time of human greatness which contrasts most favourably with Heine's own age of 'sophisters, economists and calculators'.

In der Zeit des Wunderglaubens
Taten auch die Menschen Wunder;
Wer Unmögliches geglaubt,
Konnt Unmögliches verrichten.

Even crimes were then enormous, and through their colourful enormity throw into relief the pettiness of the nineteenth century.

Hei! Das waren große Spieler,
Große Diebe, Meuchelmörder,
(Ganz vollkommen ist kein Mensch.)
Doch sie taten Wundertaten....

The young Don Juan Ponce de Leon had been another Ali Bey, successful at once as a warrior and as a lover:

Rief der Reiter seinen Hunden,
Mit der Zung am Gaumen schnalzend,
Dann durchdrang der Laut die Herzen
Hocherrötend schöner Frauen.

Ist das Juan Ponce de Leon,
Der ein Schreck der Mohren war,
Und, als wären's Distelköpfe,
Niederhieb die Turbanhäupter?

The old Ponce de Leon has all that Heine himself conspicuously lacked:

Habe nun erlangt, wonach
Stets die Menschen gierig laufen:
Fürstengunst und Ruhm und Würden,
Auch den Calatrava-Orden.

Bin Statthalter, ich besitze
Wohl an hunderttausend Pesos,
Gold in Barren, Edelsteine,
Säcke voll der schönsten Perlen....

Yet the hero of Bimini represents not only his author's wish-dreams but also his reality. Memories of the conquests of youth and consciousness of honour and wealth cannot protect against the effects of age and time—the lament of the aged Ponce de Leon is Heine's own.

> Was er leidet, der vergänglich
> Arme Mensch, wenn seines Leibes
> Edle Kraft und Herrlichkeit
> Dorrt und hinwelkt bis zum Zerrbild!

Here the wealthy and conventionally happy hero shows himself in the same plight as the dying jester who so disconcertingly peeps into his world:

> Und ich fahre auf, erschrocken
> Meine kranken Glieder schüttelnd
> Also heftig, daß die Nähte
> Meiner Narrenjacke platzen.

The voyage to Bimini through which he hopes to escape his fate is therefore shown from the outset to be but a metaphor for the dying poet's own attempt, *in this very poem*, to escape into an Avalon of poetry:

> Sehr solide ist mein Schiff;
> Aus Trochäen, stark wie Eichen,
> Sind gezimmert Kiel und Planken.
>
> Phantasie sitzt an dem Steuer,
> Gute Laune bläht die Segel,
> Schiffsjung ist der Witz, der flinke.
> Ob Verstand an Bord? Ich weiß nicht!
>
> Meine Raen sind Metaphern,
> Die Hyperbel ist mein Mastbaum....

But for the poet no less than his creation such an escape was—as the *Romanzero* had demonstrated again and again—impossible in the long run. The *voyage à Cythère* is therefore doomed. Ponce de Leon cannot find his Bimini, or rather, he can find it only, like other men, in death. *Bimini* therefore ends on a prospect of the peace of death—its hero sails to a land that contrasts strangely with the exotic landscapes of the rest of the poem:

> In das stille Land, wo schaurig
> Unter schattigen Zypressen
> Fließt ein Flüßlein, dessen Wasser
> Gleichfalls wundertätig heilsam —
>
> Lethe heißt das gute Wasser!

'Gutes Wasser! gutes Land!' the last stanza proclaims, and *Für die Mouche* too had praised the peace of death at the expense of the garishness of life. But the adjective 'schaurig' suggests at least another possible attitude. The poet who had so exalted the human spirit in the *Prolog* of *Bimini*, who had presented in such glowing colours the world Ponce de Leon had to leave, could not become an unequivocal *laudator mortis*. The end of *Bimini* has to be read, not only in the context of the whole poem, but also in that of all Heine's last poems; and these include the sonnet 'Mein Tag war heiter' with its famous last lines:

> O Gott! wie häßlich bitter ist das Sterben!
> O Gott! wie süß und traulich läßt sich leben
> In diesem traulich süßen Erdenneste!

They include also *Der Scheidende*, which ends with a reference to a passage from the *Odyssey* which Heine had quoted before in the *Epilog* of *Gedichte 1853 und 1854*:

> Er hatte Recht, der edle Heros,
> Der weiland sprach im Buch Homeros':
> Der kleinste lebendige Philister
> Zu Stukkert am Neckar, viel glücklicher ist er
> Als ich, der Pelide, der tote Held,
> Der Schattenfürst in der Unterwelt.

That 'places' the praise of Lethe at the end of *Bimini*; but it 'places' no less, through its hilarious adaptation of Homer's lines, the poet's own desire for Philistine creature comforts.

Death is not the true Avalon. There is another, for poets at least—a land which the real Juan Ponce de Leon could not reach with his actual ships, but which the poet who speaks in the *Prolog* of *Bimini* could reach with his own apparently no less foolish expedition.

Schallende Fanfaren blasen —
Aber horch! da unten klingt
Aus der Meerestiefe plötzlich
Ein Gekicher und Gelächter.

Ach, ich kenne diese Laute,
Diese süß mokanten Stimmen —
Das sind schnippische Undinen,
Nixen, welche skeptisch spötteln

Über mich, mein Narrenschiff,
Meine Narrenpassagiere,
Über meine Narrenfahrt
Nach der Insel Bimini.

The scepticism of the water-sprites corresponds to Heine's recurrent doubts of his poetic mission. But such doubts did not last. Heine knew, deep down in his heart, that in his poetry he had created an imperishable world; a world which would withstand the ravages of time long after he himself was no more; an Avalon accessible to all who could listen and attend. That had been the burden of *Die Wahlverlobten*, the confident farewell of a love-poet who knew his work would long outlast the women that had on occasions inspired it:

Wir scheiden heut
Auf immerdar. Kein Wiedersehn
Gibt es für uns in Himmelshöhn.
Die Schönheit ist dem Staub verfallen,
Du wirst zerstieben, wirst verhallen.
Viel anders ist es mit Poeten;
Die kann der Tod nicht gänzlich töten.
Uns trifft nicht weltliche Vernichtung,
Wir leben fort im Land der Dichtung,
In Avalun, dem Feenreiche —
Leb wohl auf ewig, schöne Leiche!

The poem *Bimini* is itself the Avalon which its hero so vainly strives to reach.

Yet what a strange fairyland it is that Heine has here conjured up! The poet of *Prolog* presents himself alternately as Lazarus, as a Fool and as a fairground barker:

Leidet ihr am Zipperlein,
Edle Herren? Schöne Damen,
Habt ihr auf der weißen Stirn
Schon ein Rünzelchen entdeckt?

Folget mir nach Bimini,
Dorten werdet ihr genesen....

The world into which he takes his readers is filled with bright colours and sweet scents; but colours and scents become *too* bright, *too* overpowering, and suggest opium visions rather than an actual exotic landscape. In the end, the sixteenth-century world with which the poem began becomes a timeless world of the grotesque.

Selbst der Bischof schmunzelt freudig,
Freudig glänzen die Karbunkeln
Seiner Nase, und im Festschmuck
Wackelt er einher vergnüglich

Unterm Purpurbaldachin,
Eingeräuchert von Chorknaben,
Und gefolgt von Clericis,
Die mit Goldbrokat bedeckt sind

Und goldgelbe Sonnenschirme
Über ihre Köpfe halten,
Kolossalen Champignons,
Welche wandeln, schier vergleichbar.

That begins as anticlerical satire and caricature; but the vision soon acquires a life and colour of its own that cannot be referred to any satiric intention. The enormous walking mushrooms as well as the bright tints of the whole recall the grotesque paintings of Brueghel. From there the poem blossoms into one *grotesquerie* after another.

Rokoko-anthropophagisch,
Karaibisch-Pompadour,
Hebet sich der Haarwulstkopfputz,
Der gespickt ist mit unzählgen

Vögelein, die, groß wie Käfer,
Durch des prächtigen Gefieders
Farbenschmelz wie Blumen aussehn,
Die formiert aus Edelsteinen.

Diese närrische Frisur
Von Gevögel paßt vortrefflich
Zu der Kaka wunderlichem
Papageienvogelantlitz.

The opening compounds confound inextricably the most savage and the most civilised, annihilate all distinctions of space and of time. The categories of the actual world no longer obtain in this world of the grotesque—a world which appeals, as Wolfgang Kayser has reminded us,[1] to societies that have lost their belief in a firm universal order. Kaka is an amalgam of the mulatto nurse who frequented Heine's sick-room in his last illness, of Mathilde's parrot and of figures from books about the rococo world and about travel in foreign lands. Men and beasts, flora and fauna, past and present, Europe and the Indies all meet in this ridiculous and oddly disturbing creation; in this figure of Kaka which corresponds exactly with Edgar Alan Poe's definition of the grotesque:

Much of the beautiful, much of the wanton, much of the *bizarre*, something of the terrible, and not a little of that which might have excited disgust. (*The Masque of the Red Death*)

A comparison with Poe will, however, show up the peculiar quality of Heine's own dealings with the grotesque in this his final period. His *Fratzen*, from Vitzliputzli to Kaka and the aged Ponce de Leon, are genuine visions of the absurd, presentations of a mysterious unreality and often of horror breaking into the apparently solid world. But Heine, unlike Poe, rarely allows himself to be swept away by his own creations. He keeps his distance, and allows his readers to keep their distance through the urbanity, the humour and the occasional self-parody with which he presents

[1] *Das Groteske. Seine Gestaltung in Malerei und Dichtung* (Oldenburg, 1957), p. 202.

his vision. And even the absurd, the scabrous and the grotesque can give birth, in Heine's world, to simple beauty.

> Und er kneift die armen Saiten
> Seiner Laute, daß sie wimmern,
> Und mit altgebrochner Stimme
> Meckert er die Singsangworte:
>
> 'Kleiner Vogel Kolibri,
> Kleines Fischchen Brididi,
> Fliegt und schwimmt voraus, und zeiget
> Uns den Weg nach Bimini.'

Heine's image of the old Ponce de Leon dressed in the colours of youth and cavorting with forced gaiety anticipates similar images used, with horrifying effect, in Thomas Mann's *Tod in Venedig*. Yet when we actually hear the song Ponce de Leon sings, it has nothing of the goat-like accent, the *meckern* for which the previous verse had prepared us. With its many high, light vowels, this song has a melodious charm that transcends and contradicts the absurd vision within which it was born. Its unpretentious beauty is Heine's answer to the menace of time and the menace of the unknown which he so powerfully presented in his grotesques.

Heine did not live to complete and revise this poem; but even in its fragmentary form, *Bimini* is entirely characteristic of the poetry of his last period. It is written in those unrhymed 'Spanish' trochees the poet had first tried out, on a large scale, in *Atta Troll*: a four-line stanza capable, on occasions, of the terse, epigrammatic effects we associate with the *Buch der Lieder*, but much more accommodating than any rhymed stanza to the expansive and discursive mode favoured by the later Heine. Its rhythms keep close to natural speech; but they have a strangely hypnotic quality for which verbal analysis cannot fully account—a quality that can be put down in part to rich vowel-music and obsessive repetition of individual words and phrases. Heine's vocabulary remains simple, sometimes even trite, in its elements, but complex and powerfully individual in combination. He keeps his range of adjectives deliberately narrow ('lieblich', 'leidenschaftlich', 'üppig', 'blühend' recur frequently), but shows himself, as always, a master of significant variation. One need point only to the strange marriages of adjectives and nouns in his later poetry (gold is called, in *Bimini*, 'der gelbe Kuppler'); to unusual compounds of adverb and adjective (Ponce de Leon sings 'mit altgebrochner Stimme'); and to boldly amusing coinages like 'Großfliegenwedelmeisterin' and 'Oberhamakschaukeldame'. Often a word from a quite different level of speech will break into the verse, with distancing or disillusioning or parodistic effect:

> Cortez und Pizarro wälzten
> Gold*besoffen* sich im Golde;

or widely separated worlds of history will be brought together in such combinations as 'Karaibisch-Pompadour' and 'Donna Venus Aphrodite'. Historical re-evocations will be invaded by references to the present:

> Von dem großen Holofernes
> Bis auf Haynau und Radetzki;

there is even, in the *Prolog* of *Bimini*, a scarcely veiled attack on an obscure contemporary who played a part in Heine's life, the Hungarian doctor Gruby. And like so many other works of this period, the vocabulary of *Bimini* does not altogether conceal its author's long residence in France—the noun in the lines

> Und bemalt mit ganz vorzüglich
> Wohlgefirnißten Couleuren

is but one of several examples which explain (though their comparative infrequency invalidates) the complaint of Jules Legras: 'Le souvenir de notre langue devient ici vraiment insupportable.'[1]

There are other features of *Bimini* which will be familiar to all readers of Heine's last poetry. Its wish-dream revelling in images of wealth and in exotic sights and sounds; its nostalgic evocation of Jewish ceremonies such as that of building the *Succah* ('Laubhütte') before the Feast of Tabernacles:

> Einer Lauberhütte gleich
> Ist sie ausgeschmückt mit Maien,
> Blumenkränzen und Girlanden
> Und mit flatternd bunten Wimpeln;

[1] *Heinri Heine, Poète*, p. 351.

and its equally nostalgic harking back to the world of German Romanticism, the world of the Blue Flower which Heine always associated with his own beginnings as a poet. Characteristic, too, is the occasional deliberate assumption of a mountebank tone; and the veiled but unmistakable references, in the poem, to the hopeless situation within which it was composed. All this makes *Bimini* at once escape into helpful illusion and presentation of reality; at once garish dream-vision and acknowledgment that such dreams cannot be man's permanent home; at once quest for regression and brave admission that such quests can end only in death.

In retelling the stories of Ponce de Leon, Cortez and Bilbao, *Bimini* speaks of human injustice, human greed and human suffering; yet as always in Heine's last poetry, the final effect is neither depressing nor hopeless. Degradation and wickedness are balanced against the greatness and dignity that can co-exist with them; suffering and weakness are outweighed by the power of the human spirit, symbolised in this poem by the inventions and discoveries of the sixteenth century. As so often in his later period, Heine tries to look beyond nature and man and to find God—to find him in the Bible and in His works; but what he finds is only a reflection of himself, a divine author who writes—like Heine in Paris!—in two languages. Searching for lost youth he finds a beautiful world; searching for God, he finds man, fallen and tainted by sin and disease, yet with unquenchable signs of his pristine nobility; searching for Lethe, he finds a poetry which takes account of suffering and indignity and which yet enhances life.

Bimini, at once grotesque and beautiful, is not a comfortable work. Its frequent changes of tone demand alert readers that can respond immediately to the author's shifts of feeling; its mood at any one moment is as complex and difficult to analyse as its levels of speech; and just as its language combines simple and even hackneyed terms into new and original aggregates, so its often traditional motifs are fused into a whole that reflects faithfully a complicated state of mind. Poems like *Bimini* can be fitted into no known category—and in this, as Heine well knew, they resemble their author.

I could have achieved fame as a lyric poet—and Germany would have loved me; as a satirist it would have feared me, as a polemic writer it would have listened to me and would have hated me. But unfortunately I have been all these things, and now no one knows how to classify me....[1]

Heine said this to a visitor in 1850, at the very time when he first planned *Bimini*; and in the poem he drew the sum of his existence, exhibiting himself as the complex and unclassifiable being that he was. He showed himself here as a lyric poet, who could make the German language sing with melodies as sweet as any ever found by a Romantic poet; as a satirist, who scourged human wickedness and folly; as a mountebank and jester who could laugh at himself; as a polemic writer who conveyed 'felt thoughts' on world-history and on the relation between God and man. He showed himself capable, in his last poetry as in his first, of lapses of taste—the veiled reference to Dr Gruby might well have been omitted from *Bimini*, some passages might have been tightened up, some French words might, without loss, have been replaced by German; but he now spoke unmistakably with the voice of a great poet, whose sufferings had extended his range and had led him to discover new realms of feeling and new ways of making these accessible to his fellow-men.

Heine died in February 1856. His voyage to Bimini was over: it had ended in death, certainly, but it had ended also in a new world of poetry which he opened up not only for himself but for posterity and in which he will outlive all those changes of fashion that occasionally obscure his achievement.

[1] *Gespräche*, p. 730.

CONCLUSION

THE German Romantics had felt themselves the end of a long development, heirs of a great literary culture that was alive all around them and acted not only as a goad but also (paradoxically) as a brake. So much had already been written; there was so much to digest; the position of the sane individual in his world had been so thoroughly plotted, the German language so patently enriched and its possibilities so widely explored that the generation of Novalis, and even more that of E. T. A. Hoffmann, might well feel that it was difficult to be an heir. It is a measure of the greatness of these writers of the Romantic period that they did not allow themselves to be overwhelmed by the achievement of Goethe and that they produced, against all odds, a body of literature that is not dwarfed by the work of Goethe, Schiller, Herder and Wieland—yet it may well be felt that their concern with the darker side of nature and the human mind, their search for new *frissons*, their fruitful exploration of the frontiers of human consciousness and beyond, was dictated by necessity as much as inclination. They had to find new fields of activity that Goethe had not cultivated. They moved into realms where language fails, where the most that is possible (witness Novalis's fondness for words beginning with 'un-'!) is to gesture towards the inexpressible.

Heine was born in the very year that saw the inception of the Romantic movement in German literature. In 1797 Wackenroder–Tieck's *Herzensergießungen eines kunstliebenden Klosterbruders* and Tieck's *Volksmärchen von Peter Leberecht* were published; Novalis had in this same year the experience that led to *Hymnen an die Nacht*; Friedrich Schlegel published his essay *Über das Studium der griechischen Poesie* and mooted the plan of the *Athenäum*, which was to become the chief critical organ of the movement in its early phase.[1] The language that Heine inherited,

[1] Cf. Paul Kluckhohn's introductory lecture in Th. Steinbüchel (ed.), *Romantik. Ein Zyklus Tübinger Vorlesungen* (Tübingen, 1948), p. 13.

therefore, was even more 'charged' with literature than that inherited by Novalis, Tieck and the Schlegels. The language of the *Buch der Lieder* is a worn language—yet Heine manages to use it with surprising freshness, through sudden shifts of levels of speech, through the parodistic mingling of conventionally poetic, conversational and commercial terms, and through the rhythmic vitality that informs even his slightest lyrics. He rings the changes on a deliberately restricted vocabulary and range of experience and produces, in the *Buch der Lieder*, the greatest set of variations in German verse since the days of Reinmar von Hagenau.

After the dazzling success of his first collection Heine tried, not unnaturally, to work again in the mode he had there perfected. *Neuer Frühling*, in which he attempted this most consistently, was—on the whole—a failure; but in later collections the reader comes again and again upon fine poems which would not be out of place in *Lyrisches Intermezzo* or *Die Heimkehr*. 'Das ist eine weiße Möwe' is such a poem; so is *Bertrand de Born*; so is *Der Asra*. Yet gradually Heine's manner and his matter changed as he gained new interests and new insights during his long stay in Paris. He sought now to present in poetry relationships the German Romantics did not know: the metropolitan amours depicted, in different ways, in *Verschiedene*, *Der Tannhäuser* and *Ein Weib*; and he allowed his political and social interests to shape his poetry more and more directly. From the vantage-point of his Parisian Venusberg he looked back at the Germany he still loved and satirised its faults concretely, vigorously and wittily. Behind his satire is the nineteenth-century dream of an ideal society, of heaven brought down to earth through the removal of social injustice—the dream that inspired Enfantin and Fourier, Proudhon, Lassalle and Marx, the dream which Zola was later to present so powerfully in *Germinal*:

Since God was no more, it was the turn of justice to bestow happiness upon mankind and usher in the kingdom of equality and brotherhood. As happens in dreams, there grew up a new society in a single day and, shining like a mirage, a great city, in which each citizen lived by his own appointed task and shared in the joys of all. The old decaying world had crumbled into dust, humanity made young again and cleansed of its crimes was but a single nation of workers having for its motto: To each according to his worth, and each man's worth determined by his works.[1]

But the greatness of this poetry of Heine's middle years lies in its complexity: in Heine's true portrait, in *Zeitgedichte*, *Atta Troll* and *Deutschland. Ein Wintermärchen*, of a man between, a man outside, a man torn between allegiance to a juster future and allegiance to the past. The very language and metres of these poems reflect this conflict. Traditional images, a simple, 'folk-like' vocabulary and popular stanza forms are used to portray states of mind that are anything but simple and traditional and are frequently, in the satirical poems, turned against themselves, used to parody the very emotions with which they are traditionally associated.

In the poetry of Heine's last years the dream of a heaven built on earth is finally shattered. In *Romanzero* and *Gedichte 1853 und 1854* the reader is made to enter a world of suffering and of humiliation—a world presided over by a capricious God who wears in turn the features of Jehovah, of Hardy's 'President of the Immortals' and of Heine's uncle Salomon. The present has turned into a nightmare, the past into a torturing memory, the future into a vision of boredom or blank extinction. This is a world inhabited by grotesques, by creatures of real life transformed into ridiculous and horrible shapes by an imagination at once dulled and stimulated by opium. Yet somewhere at the centre there is always a weighing, rational mind that refuses to be subdued by suffering and mocks its own visions; a mind that clings to life and continues to acknowledge the beauty of this earth; a mind that knows of man's greatness as well as his indignity. The characteristic *personae* of these last poems are Lazarus, the Prodigal Son, Faibisch Apollo, Cortez, Ponce de Leon—tragic and ambivalent figures that have hardly any counterpart in Heine's earlier poetry. They may be grotesque or even villainous;

[1] *Germinal* (transl. R. W. Tancock), Part III, ch. 3.

but they acquire dignity and beauty under the stress of suffering. 'I cannot tell my own griefs', Heine had said in his *Buch der Lieder* period, 'without making them appear ridiculous.'[1] Now, in the last years of his life, he shows the ridiculous itself taking on a tragic dignity, and presents a complex vision of man and the world in poetry whose shifting tone and level of speech demand constant alertness and attention but reward the reader with a proportionately rich experience.

Heine's voice can be too loud and strident. He can rest too easily satisfied with verbal or emotional cliché and is too little adventurous, for many modern tastes, in his range of vocabulary and verse forms. Writing for an audience he at once courted and despised, he was inclined, occasionally, to keep his intelligence out of his poetry and give contemporary readers what they expected of him; or—worse still—he would try to have it both ways and write poems like 'Du bist wie eine Blume' which simple-minded readers could take one way and sophisticated readers another. He can be sentimental. He can be cynical. His satiric and lyric moods do not always blend happily. His earlier poetry sometimes sacrifices truth to a 'point', his later sometimes rambles on too loosely and too long. He fails occasionally to keep his distance and tries to nudge the reader into a response the poetry does not warrant. His *personae* disintegrate too easily into obvious portraits or idealisations of their creator. The parvenu, the journalist, the *artiste*, the conscious virtuoso all peep disconcertingly out of his work. Yet with all that, Heine is a great poet, the creator of mysterious lyrics and ballads like 'Still ist die Nacht', 'Das ist eine weiße Möwe', *Begegnung*, *Lebensfahrt*, *Schelm von Bergen*, *Gedächtnisfeier*, *Jehuda ben Halevi* and 'Mir lodert und wogt im Hirn eine Flut', and of satires like *Atta Troll* whose grace, lightness and accuracy have never been surpassed. He shows himself able, in poems such as these, to give his work a resonance beyond that of its ostensible subject; to convey in apparently simple lyrics the intricacy of life; and to transmute his personal struggles, as only true poets can, into generally

[1] Letter to Moses Moser, 28 November 1823 (*Briefe*, I, 125).

accessible and generally valid symbols. Nietzsche therefore came to see in Heine the lyric poet *par excellence*:

Den größten Begriff vom Lyriker hat mir Heinrich Heine gegeben. Ich suche umsonst in allen Reichen der Jahrtausende nach einer gleich süßen und leidenschaftlichen Musik.... Man wird einmal sagen, daß Heine und ich die ersten Artisten der deutschen Sprache gewesen sind.[1]

The young Rilke, whose own poetry was clearly under the sway of the *Buch der Lieder*, defended Heine the satirist even in his most unpopular work, *Deutschland. Ein Wintermärchen*:

Dem Franken selbst krümmt man kein Härchen,
Der offen über Deutschland spricht;
Allein das wahre 'Wintermärchen'
Verzeiht man einem Deutschen nicht.

Grüb jeder nur mit scharfem Stichel
Die Fehler alle frei herauf, —
Leicht gingen dann dem deutschen Michel
Die—blauen Augen endlich auf.[2]

Ezra Pound celebrated the same side of his genius, that mocking, light-hearted, superior annihilation of Philistine pretensions which had already delighted Matthew Arnold:

O Harry Heine, cursed be
I live too late to sup with thee!
Who can demolish at such polished ease
Philistia's pomp and art's pomposities![3]

And Hugo von Hofmannsthal, fastidiously repelled by Heine's occasional stridencies, found words that describe exactly the effect of Heine's later poetry: a poetry whose imperfections pale

[1] That was Nietzsche's final feeling about Heine; it is only fair, however, to quote also an earlier judgment: 'Bei Hegel ist alles nichtswürdiges Grau, bei Heine elektrisches Farbenspiel, das aber die Augen ebenso fürchterlich angreift, als jenes Grau sie abstumpft.' Nietzsche, *Werke* (Leipzig, 1900ff.), XIV, 173 and X, 246.

[2] Rilke, *Sämtliche Werke* (Wiesbaden, 1959), III, 433, where the poem is entitled 'Nochmals "Heine"'.

[3] Pound interpolated this poem (entitled 'Translator to Translated') in his 'Translations and Adaptations from Heine' (*Personae*, 1909).

before unforgettable images of the tragedy, the squalor and the splendour of human life.

Zerrissnen Tones, überlauter Rede
Verfänglich Blendwerk muß vergessen sein:
Allein den bunten schmerzverzognen Lippen
Entrollte, unverweslicher als Perlen
Und leuchtender, zuweilen ein Gebild:
Das traget am lebendigen Leib, und nie
Verliert es seinen innern feuchten Glanz.[1]

[1] Hugo v. Hofmannsthal, *Gesammelte Werke in Einzelausgaben*, ed. Steiner (Stockholm, 1946), I, 107–8. The poem is entitled 'Zu Heinrich Heines Gedächtnis'.

APPENDIX

THE MAKING OF A SATIRIC POEM

THE Heine archives of the Landes- und Stadtbibliothek Düsseldorf contain a work-manuscript[1] of three and a half pages which gives a unique insight into the poet's methods of composition. A few readings from this manuscript were first published, in woefully incorrect form, by Michael Salzer in the *Neues Wiener Journal* of 24 February 1929[2] and its first page has been reproduced in facsimile by Eberhard Galley in his centenary tribute: *Heinrich Heine: Aus der Werkstatt des Dichters*.[3] The manuscript does not contain all Heine's corrections, transpositions and amplifications—it would seem that the drafts for the final page have been lost; but enough remains to give us an unusually clear insight into the evolution of one of Heine's satiric poems.

The work is headed *Flottentraum* and dated May 1844. Title and date leave no doubt that Heine is here satirising the plan of an all-German navy mooted in the 1840's; a plan soon abandoned which inspired cloudy hopes and cloudier visions in many a German liberal.[4] Among the poems inspired by the as yet hypothetical navy was Georg Herwegh's *Die deutsche Flotte*, which has been well characterised by F. Th. Vischer:

I turned to this poem in the hope that I might find there an imposing vision of the German navy of the future, majestically cleaving the sea with the coloured pennants of the different states. My hopes were disappointed; a few beautiful comparisons, bombastic 'points', no

[1] MS. Düsseldorf, *Heine-Sammlung* 15.z.14.

[2] Of the few variants Salzer lists, nearly half are misread or misspelt. 'Kölle' appears as 'Jölle', 'Schiffprügel' as 'Schiffsrüppel', 'Wir rieben' as 'Wir reiben', etc.

[3] *Op. cit.* (Düsseldorf, 1956), Sheet 2.

[4] Cf. Petzet, *Die Blütezeit der politischen Dichtung*, pp. 143ff.; and M. F. Liddell, *German Sea Poetry* (Diss. Birmingham, 1925).

progression, a mere concatenation of abstract ideas, until at last, in the final verse, we read: 'Schon schaut mein Geist das nie Geschaute.' Now, I thought, it comes. But no. The expected vision is shuffled off with a few words: 'Schon ist die Flotte aufgestellt, / Die unser Volk erbaute'; then the poet *sees*; and he sees — himself.

> Schon lehn ich selbst, ein deutscher Argonaute,
> An einem Mast, und kämpfe mit der Laute
> Ums goldne Vließ der Welt.

Add to this the artificiality of form, these 'Garden–Kokarden–Leoparden' rhymes, and you have the whole of Herwegh: the kind of poet who is passionately excited by the idea of a political future, but whose depiction of that idea lacks clarity of definition, and whose enthusiasm is clouded by a perceptible trace of self-approbation and artificiality.[1]

The concrete vision of whose absence Vischer here complains was to be provided by Ferdinand Freiligrath, who had recently abandoned his allegiance to the desert and the fabulous Orient ('Wer besäng den Löwen besser', Heine had unkindly asked,[2] 'als sein Landsmann, das Kamel?') and had entered the lists as a political poet. A sonnet sequence in his collection *Ein Glaubensbekenntnis* (1844) is entitled *Flottenträume*. The following is a fair sample of these 'dreams' of an all-German fleet:

> Wie unsre mut'gen Orlogsmänner heißen?
> Komm mit aufs Meer, ich will es dir verkünden!
> Da drüben der mit sechzig Feuerschlünden,
> Das ist der 'Arndt'! du siehst die Goldschrift gleißen!
>
> Hier die Fregatte, bauschig rings von weißen
> Halbvollen Segeln, kämpfend mit den Winden —
> O Gott, ihr Name mahnt an alte Sünden! —
> 'Die Sieben' heißt sie! Mag kein Strick ihr reißen!
>
> Dort die Korvette, segelnd wie der Blitz,
> Es ist die 'Hansa'! Doch am Ufer diese,
> Stolz wie ein Schwan, die 'Königin Luise!'
>
> Der Dreimast drüben ist der 'Alte Fritz'!
> Und hier voll Zorns der schlagbereite Kutter,
> Du ahnst es schon, das ist der 'Doktor Luther'![3]

[1] *Kritische Gänge*, ed. R. Vischer, 2. Aufl. (München, n.d.), II, 120–1.

[2] *SW*, II, 365.

[3] *Freiligraths Werke*, ed. Zaunert, I, 339.

Here was an invitation to parody Heine would find it hard to resist. His first reaction to Freiligrath's political conversion had been two lines in 'Verkehrte Welt':

> Das arme Kamel, der Freiligrath,
> Macht eine Löwenmiene...,[1]

but feeling that this might wound his new ally,[2] he substituted a dig at Bettina von Arnim.[3] Freiligrath's *Flottenträume*, however, with their heavy rhythmic tread and their plethora of exclamation marks, with their visions of Ernst Moritz Arndt as a warship with sixty guns and Queen Louise of Prussia as a corvette hugging the shore 'proud as a swan', fairly cried out for the complementary pictures of Heine's comic imagination. In these, naturally, Freiligrath would himself figure, and a rather closer correspondence might be expected between the physical properties of the vessel described and the characteristics of those of Heine's butts whose name it was given.

The title *Flottentraum* clearly points to the connection between Heine's poem and Freiligrath's sonnet sequence. The mould, however, in which Heine chose to cast his parody was not that of the sonnet: he preferred the comfortable folk-song stanza, the rhymed 'Vagantenpaar', which had served him so well for his *Buch der Lieder* mode and which he had made, in *Deutschland. Ein Wintermärchen*, so effective a vehicle for his satire.

> Wir träumten von einer Flotte jüngst
> Und segelten schon vergnüglich
> Hinaus auf's balkenlose Meer;
> Der Wind war ganz vorzüglich.

The implied solidarity of that opening 'Wir' parodies Freiligrath's '*Unsre*...Orlogsmänner'; Heine uses it, as he had done earlier in poems like 'Zur Beruhigung', to mock the tone of the German Philistine and confound him, as it were, out of his own mouth:

> Wir schlafen ganz wie Brutus schlief—
> Doch jener erwachte und bohrte tief
> In Cäsars Brust das kalte Messer...[3]

[1] This is a MS. version of lines which appear in *SW* (I, 317) as: 'Der Häring wird ein Sansculott / Die Wahrheit sagt uns Bettine...'

[2] Cf. *SW*, II, 353–4.

[3] *SW*, I, 316.

The movement of the opening stanza of 'Flottentraum' has the same jauntiness as that of *Zur Beruhigung*, a jauntiness that goes well with the comfortable spirit of hearty 'good fellowship' which is being evoked. Is it perhaps just a little *too* brisk for these steady and comfortable *Bürger*? The manuscript shows Heine trying the second line in a different way:

Und schifften schon vergnüglich....

But no—the original 'segelten' went so much better that the reading is restored.

The adjectives of that opening stanza (left unchanged in the manuscript) bear further scrutiny. 'Balkenlos', for instance, in the second line, conveys vividly the speakers' sense of boldness and daring by conjuring up the negative co-presence of the solid floors on which they are wont to walk. Above all, however, it is the rhymes that drive home to us the inadequacy of these dreamers to the experience of which they dream. 'Vergnüglich' implies an attitude that goes with a pleasant family stroll in the country rather than a pioneering venture like the establishment of a fleet; while 'ganz vorzüglich', perfectly in place when applied to a good dinner, hardly seems the right term for the favourable winds that waft a noble fleet out to sea. And here it must be at once recalled that the establishment of a German navy had been made, by Herwegh, Freiligrath and many others, a symbol of the unification of Germany which would go hand in hand with constitutional government. Inadequacy in face of the one endeavour would imply an equal inadequacy in face of the other.

The second stanza of Heine's poem, it would seem from the Düsseldorf manuscript, had originally read as follows:

Wir hatten unseren Schiffen schon
Die stolzesten Namen gegeben;
Die eine Fregatte, die hieß Prutz,
Die andre hieß Fallersleben.

Here the parody of Freiligrath's 'name-giving' sonnet begins in earnest. Robert Prutz is given pride of place because he seems to have been the most obvious sheep in wolves' clothing among the liberals of those years; a man full of his own daring and 'stolzer Mut'—

Habe, während ihr noch euer Kindersüppchen habt gegessen,
Brust an Brust und Aug in Auge mich mit der Gewalt gemessen.[1]

—who was apt to write letters to the king of Prussia disavowing all subversive intent.[2] Next comes Hoffmann von Fallersleben, whose 'dangerous' poetry Heine had satirised in the second Caput of *Deutschland. Ein Wintermärchen* and—more overtly—in his letter to Julius Campe of 28 February 1842:

The poems of Hoffmann von Fallersleben, which have been the immediate cause of your troubles, are ridiculously poor, and from an aesthetic standpoint the Prussian government was quite right to be annoyed with them: bad jokes fit only to amuse Philistines at their beer and tobacco.[3]

Hoffmann therefore joins Prutz among the frigates of the new navy, for whose speed and manœuvrability these two names would seem a poor guarantee.

Reading his stanza over, Heine was not, however, satisfied with it. He toyed for a moment with the idea of substituting for the name 'Prutz' that of Gustav Schwab, whose surname made him the ideal representative of those Swabian poets who had always seemed to Heine the last word in idyllic pedestrianism. But the projected line

Die eine Fregatte hieß Gustav Schwab

did not seem to improve matters: on the contrary, it weakened the comic contrast between the spluttering brevity of the name in the third and the sonority of that in the fourth stanza. Here, of course, lay the solution. The mere juxtaposition of these two names could produce an irresistibly comic effect if nothing weighty was allowed to interpose between them. The word 'Fregatte' is therefore transferred from the third to the first line, and the whole of the fourth is given up to Hoffmann's sonorous name.

[1] Prutz, *Confiteor*, quoted Petzet, *op. cit.* p. 181.

[2] Prutz himself quotes such a letter in *Vorlesungen über die deutsche Literatur der Gegenwart* (Leipzig, 1847), pp. liv–lv.

[3] *Briefe*, II, 420.

Wir hatten unseren Fregatten schon
Die stolzesten Namen gegeben;
Prutz hieß die Eine, die Andre hieß
Hoffmann von Fallersleben.

The expectant pause after 'hieß' makes the final line, with all its associations, the more amusing.

Now comes the turn of Freiligrath himself—words Heine crossed out appear in square brackets:

Da [schwammen] schwamm ein [hölzerner] großer Freilichrath;
Am Steuer prangte als Puppe
Ein Mohrenkönig; [ihm folgte] er schleppte am [Thau] Tau,
Den Geibel, die lecke Schaluppe.

The 'Mohrenkönig' is there by virtue of Freiligrath's poem *Der Mohrenfürst*,[1] satirised throughout *Atta Troll*; and Geibel follows because like Freiligrath he had been offered, and had accepted, a pension from Frederick William IV of Prussia, for which both had been bitterly derided by Herwegh in a poem entitled *Duett der Pensionierten*.[2]

The chief objection to this stanza of 'Flottentraum' was, as on second thoughts Heine was bound to realise, that Geibel and Freiligrath were no longer linked in this way. Freiligrath had publicly renounced his pension, while Geibel was retreating ever more definitely to the conservative and reactionary camp:

Doch dir, o Fürst aus edlem Stamme,
Der treu vor Gott sein Volk regiert,
Den schöner noch des Geistes Flamme
Als seiner Väter Krone ziert,
Auf den, wenn sich die Wolken schwärzen,
Als Leuchtturm schauet Deutschlands Kern,
Wie dank ich dir aus tiefstem Herzen,
Wie dank ich alles dir so gern!

* * *

Fern von dem Schwarm, der unbesonnen
Altar und Herz in Stücke schlägt,
Quillt mir der Dichtung heil'ger Bronnen
Am Felsen, der die Kirche trägt.[3]

[1] *Freiligraths Werke*, ed. cit. I, 44. [2] *Herweghs Werke*, ed. Tardel, pp. 122–3.

[3] Quoted Petzet, *op. cit.* p. 250. The poem was written in 1842.

Geibel, then, had to go, and Freiligrath would have the stanza to himself:

> Da [schwamm] kam geschwommen ein Freiligrath
>   [woran]
> [Als] [Woran] Woran als Puppe grüßte
> Wie ein verfinstert schwarzer Mond
> Des Mohrenkönigs Büste.

By referring once again to that absurd image of a 'black' moon already ridiculed in *Atta Troll*,[1] Heine glances back, not only at Freiligrath's desert poetry, but also to the whole context of *Atta Troll.* This is an important point: Heine's satires form a corpus in which a comic figure is gradually constructed out of some obscure German figure. Work after work adds details to the caricature, which gradually assumes a life of its own and can be enjoyed by posterity independently of its model.

The stanza of 'Flottentraum' as we left it did not, however, seem to add sufficient life to the caricature of Freiligrath already given in *Atta Troll.* Heine tried again, going back to a characterising adjective he had earlier rejected

> Da schwamm ein hölzerner Freyligrath
> Worauf als...;

and at last, remembering the ridiculous final rhyme ('Kutter'–'Doktor Luther') of the sonnet from Freiligrath's *Flottenträume* that has already been quoted, he arrived at this:

> Da schwamm der Kutter Freyligrath
> Darauf als Puppe die Büste
> Des Mohrenkönigs, [wie] der wie ein Mond
> Versteht sich ein schwarzer, grüßte.

That brings together, inimitably, Freiligrath's desert and political poetry; the line-endings 'Büste'–'grüßte' mock Freiligrath's own more venturesome excursions into rhyme; and the 'versteht sich' of the final line speaks volumes of Heine's opinion of the imaginative power of his butt and the taste of his audience.

From the liberal and the exotic poets Heine now turns his eyes

[1] See above, p. 83.

to Swabia, home of the opportunist Wolfgang Menzel who had denounced 'Jung Deutschland' as treasonable, irreligious and immoral and who had jeered at Heine's poetry as 'französische Affenschande';[1] home of the idyllic poets Gustav Schwab and Karl Mayer, who had refused to be associated with an almanack that bore a portrait of Heine as its frontispiece;[2] and home too of *Legationsrat* F. K. von Kölle, who had published in the first number of the *Deutsche Vierteljahrsschrift* he helped to found a virulent attack on Heine's 'writings and tendencies' from the pen of Gustav Pfizer.[3] Here they come, impressed into the new German navy of 'Flottentraum':

> Da schwamm der Pfitzer, der Gustav Schwab,
> Der Wolfgang Menzel, der Flegel,
> Schiffprügel von schwäbischem Eichenholz,
> Hochaufgebläht die Segel.

Hatred of Menzel seems to be weakening Heine's grip on his comic creation here: the speakers whose tone Heine ostensibly adopts would hardly refer to the respected editor of Cotta's *Literaturblatt* as a 'Flegel'. That word, which literally of course means a flail, brings with it the strange image of the next line—rude, rough ships, hollowed out of oak-trees and looking like clubs. Another version, scribbled like the first one on to the margin of the manuscript, removes the offending 'Flegel' but leaves the image it brought with it:

> Da schwamm ein Menzel, ein Gustav Schwab, —
> Ein Pfitzer, ein Kölle, ein Mayer —
> Schiffprügel von Holz, sehr schön verziert
> Mit einer schwäbischen Leyer.

[1] Menzel's attack on Gutzkow and the 'Jung Deutschland' movement opened in the Stuttgart *Literaturblatt*, 11 and 13 September 1835. His reference to 'diese französische Affenschande, die im Arme von Metzen Gott lästert' was generally understood to glance at Heine; cf. A. Strodtmann, *H. Heines Leben und Werke* (Berlin, 1869), II, 369.

[2] Cf. *SW*, II, 221.

[3] Gustav Pfizer, *Heines Schriften und Tendenz*, *Deutsche Vierteljahrsschrift* (Stuttgart, 1838), I, 167f.

That third line won't do—'sehr schön verziert' is deplorably weak, and the force of 'Schiffprügel' is not easily understood now that 'Flegel' has disappeared. So Heine tries again—and the many corrections bear witness that this is the most refractory stanza yet:

Da schwamm ein Menzel, ein Gustav Schwab
[Auf jedem prangt ein] [ein schwäbischer Wasser] [Apoll]
[Mit einer hölzernen Leyer]
[Ein jeder] Auf jedem [ein hölzernes] stand ein Schwabengesicht
Mit einer hölzernen Leyer.

That still did not sound right. Heine tried again: 'Da schwamm ein Menzel...'; but thinking, perhaps, that it was his too profound hatred of Menzel which was impairing his satiric powers, he threw his name out of the poem altogether and arrived at his final version:

Da kamen geschwommen ein Gustav Schwab,
Ein Pfitzer, ein [Pfitzer] Kölle, ein Mayer,
Auf jedem stand ein Schwabengesicht
Mit einer hölzernen Leyer.

The bust of the 'Mohrenfürst' on the prow of the good ship Freiligrath now has its counterpart in the 'wooden lyres' on the prows of these Swabian vessels.

After the tame poetry of provincial Philistia Heine turns his attention to the no less tame though superficially more exciting diet of the German stage. This is represented here, as in Caput XI of *Deutschland. Ein Wintermärchen*,[1] by Charlotte Birch-Pfeiffer; and as always when Heine comes to talk of Birch-Pfeiffer, his humour becomes broad, obvious and (to some of us) irresistible. At first this stanza too would not come:

Birch-Pfeiffer hieß ein Kutter der trug
Am Fokmast das edle Wappen....

Heine tries again:

Da schwamm [ein Kutter] eine Brigg Birch-Pfeiffer genannt
[Der] die trug....

[1] *SW*, II, 453.

From then onwards the only check is a copying mistake:

> Da schwamm die Birch-Pfeiffer, eine Brigg
> Die trug am Fokmast das Wappen
> Der deutschen Admiralität
> Auf schwarz-roth-goldnem [Wappen] Lappen.

The naming of the ships is now completed and Heine can return to the 'We' of the opening, the dreamers who had been so incongruously turned into sailors.

> Wir kletterten [kek] keck an Bugspriet und Rah'n,
> Und trugen uns wie Matrosen:
> Die Jacke kurz, der Huth betheert,
> Und weite Schifferhosen.
>
> Gar mancher, der [früher] früher nur Thee genoß,
> Als wohlerzogener Eh'mann,
> Der soff jetzt Rhum und kaute Tabak
> Und fluchte wie ein Seemann.
>
> Seekrank ist mancher geworden sogar,
> Und auf dem Fallersleben,
> Dem wackelnden Kasten, hat mancher sich
> Gemüthlich [sich] übergeben.

The main point here is incongruity—the kind of incongruity that crystallises in the contrast between the last-quoted verb and its adverb. At the same time, however, there is a characteristic link between the dream and the waking life of those who have it. The features of a sailor's existence that are here isolated—drinking, swearing, chewing tobacco—are precisely those that would appeal to coarse natures whom love of comfort has made into 'well brought-up husbands'. As so often in Heine's satire, we have here the feeling that the vision is at once incongruous and appropriate, at once absurd and logical.

Only one detail disturbs us in this version. The words 'der wackelnde Kasten' seem to sort ill with the dreamers' pride in their navy, to smack too much of invective for so oblique a poem. Heine appears to have felt this; he deleted the offending words and revived instead that strange coinage which he had been forced to omit from an earlier stanza:

Und auf dem Fallersleben
Dem alten Schiffprügel...

This reading remains the final one in the Düsseldorf manuscript. But Heine clearly had doubts about it later, and in the printed version the neologism disappears and is never used again.

The stanzas that follow bear not a single correction in the manuscript—but this is of course no guarantee that they came to the poet as a single inspiration. It seems, in fact, probable that his sketches for this whole fourth page of the manuscript (beginning at 'Gar mancher, der früher nur Thee genoß...') have been lost.

Wir träumten so schön! Wir hatten fast
Schon eine Seeschlacht gewonnen!
Doch als die Morgensonne kam,
Ist Traum und Flotte zerronnen.

The line-division forces the reader to dwell, with ironic emphasis, on the word 'fast'; and then, in the lines that speak of inevitable disillusion, the reader will catch a note familiar from other, very different Heine poems:

Ach! jenes Land der Wonne,
Das seh' ich oft im Traum;
Doch kommt die Morgensonne,
Zerfließt's wie eitel Schaum.[1]

The search for comforting illusions and its disappointment, the clash between aspirations and reality—these are of course central themes in Heine's work: and sure enough, the 'Ach' with which the poet of *Lyrisches Intermezzo* greeted this recurrent and painful experience is echoed within the comic context of 'Flottentraum'.

Wir rieben uns aus den Augen den Schlaf,
Und ach! wir sahen mit Zagen,
Daß wir noch immer im heimischen Bett
Ganz ruhig vor Anker lagen.

[1] *SW*, I, 82.

For these dreamers, however, unlike those of the *Buch der Lieder* —the contrast is significant and intentional—an easy consolation is possible.

Wir trösteten uns: die Erde ist rund,
Und auch der Wirklichkeits Welle [*sic*]
Bringt jeden Weltumsegler am End'
Zurück auf dieselbe Stelle.

The mock logic of this, and the controlled stress that falls on 'zurück', make up one of Heine's happiest inventions. But did not the 'ach' of the penultimate stanza beg the question? Was it not the point of the whole poem that however pleasant the dream of an all-German navy and of German unification might be, the German 'Bürger' was perfectly happy even *without* it all, and that he would awake from his dream with a sigh (or a yawn) of contentment and relief? Heine therefore put a stroke through the last two stanzas and substituted two others which he wrote in on a previous page:

Wir lagen noch immer im heimischen Bett
Mit ausgestreckten Knochen
Wir rieben uns aus den Augen den Schlaf
Und haben gähnend gesprochen:

Die Welt ist rund; es nützt nicht am End'
Zu schaukeln auf müßiger Welle....

Here he again had second thoughts—it would surely be more effective to turn these last lines into a rhetorical question or exclamation, which would show up the inability of these Philistines to conceive of any view other than their own.

Die Welt ist rund; was nützt es [wohl] am End'
Zu schaukeln auf müßiger Welle!
Der Weltumsegler kommt zuletzt
Zurück auf dieselbe Stelle.

Now the poem was complete. It circulated among Heine's friends,[1] but was never published in book form before the pirated

[1] Cf. Galley, *Heinrich Heine: Aus der Werkstatt des Dichters*, p. 5: 'Das Gedicht kursierte schnell handschriftlich unter Freunden und Bekannten in Paris, und die Nachricht davon drang bald nach Deutschland. So meldet z. B. die

Philadelphia edition of his works.[1] Here it had the title by which it is now known; a title which draws our attention away from Freiligrath's sonnet sequence. Freiligrath's *Flottenträume* had done its work by providing a starting-point, an initial idea—that of giving names to ships which showed as yet no sign of coming into existence; it had suggested the form of a dream-vision, so congenial to Heine in any case; and it had suggested the idea of a plurality of speakers with whom the dreamer identified himself. Out of this germ Heine's poem had grown to self-sufficient life. The cord that bound it to Freiligrath could now safely be cut.

Unsere Marine

(Nautisches Gedicht)[2]

Wir träumten von einer Flotte jüngst,
Und segelten schon vergnüglich
Hinaus aufs balkenlose Meer,
Der Wind war ganz vorzüglich.

Wir hatten unsern Fregatten schon
Die stolzesten Namen gegeben,
Prutz hieß die eine, die andre hieß
Hoffmann von Fallersleben.

Da schwamm der Kutter Freiligrath,
Darauf als Puppe die Büste
Des Mohrenkönigs, die wie ein Mond
(Versteht sich ein schwarzer) grüßte.

Da kamen geschwommen ein Gustav Schwab,
Ein Pfitzer, ein Kölle, ein Mayer;
Auf jedem stand ein Schwabengesicht
Mit einer hölzernen Leier.

Düsseldorfer Zeitung vom 4. Januar 1845 aus Paris: "Heines neuestes Gedicht 'Unsere Marine' cirkuliert hier handschriftlich und macht bei allen Freunden der deutschen Flotte großes Glück.'' This passage shows that the original title *Flottentraum* was soon replaced by the now familiar one.

[1] It did, however, find its way into German newspapers, including the *Kölnische Zeitung*, in 1845. Elster's claim that it appeared in *Vorwärts* is incorrect (*SW*, II, 512).

[2] The text reprinted here is that prepared by Jonas Fränkel (Insel edition, III, 360–1) from the Philadelphia edition of 1855.

Da schwamm die Birch-Pfeiffer, eine Brigg,
Sie trug am Fockmast das Wappen
Der deutschen Admiralität
Auf schwarz-rot-goldnem Lappen.

Wir kletterten keck an Bugspriet und Raan
Und trugen uns wie Matrosen,
Die Jacke kurz, der Hut beteert,
Und weite Schifferhosen.

Gar Mancher, der früher nur Tee genoß
Als wohlerzogner Ehmann.
Der soff jetzt Rum und kaute Tabak,
Und fluchte wie ein Seemann.

Seekrank ist mancher geworden sogar,
Und auf dem Fallersleben,
Dem alten Brander, hat Mancher sich
Gemütlich übergeben.

Wir träumten so schön, wir hatten fast
Schon eine Seeschlacht gewonnen —
Doch als die Morgensonne kam
Ist Traum und Flotte zerronnen.

Wir lagen noch immer im heimischen Bett
Mit ausgestreckten Knochen.
Wir rieben uns aus den Augen den Schlaf,
Und haben gähnend gesprochen:

'Die Welt ist rund. Was nützt es am End
Zu schaukeln auf müßiger Welle!
Der Weltumsegler kommt zuletzt
Zurück auf dieselbe Stelle.'

SELECT BIBLIOGRAPHY

I. BIBLIOGRAPHIES

Wilhelm, G. and Galley, E., *Heine-Bibliographie*. Weimar, 1960–1.

Arnold, A., *Heine in England and America. A Bibliographical Check-List*. London, 1959.

Meyer, F., *Verzeichnis einer Heinrich Heine Bibliothek*. Leipzig, 1905–10.

Elster, E., *Die Heine-Sammlung Strauß. Ein Verzeichnis*. Marburg, 1929.

II. EDITIONS

Heinrich Heines Sämtliche Werke, ed. E. Elster. Leipzig and Wien, 1887–90. (Quoted as *SW*.)

The same, second revised edition of first four volumes only, without variant readings. Leipzig, 1925.

Heinrich Heines Sämtliche Werke, ed. O. Walzel, J. Fränkel and others. Leipzig, 1911–15 (Index volume 1920).

Heinrich Heines Sämtliche Werke, ed. H. Herrmann and others. Berlin and Leipzig, 1921.

Heines Werke in Einzelausgaben, ed. G. Bogeng and others. Hamburg and Berlin, 1921–6.

Heinrich Heine: Deutschland. Ein Wintermärchen. Faksimiledruck nach der Handschrift des Dichters, ed. F. Hirth. Berlin, 1915.

Heinrich Heine: Aus der Werkstatt des Dichters. Faksimiles nach Handschriften..., ed. E. Galley. Düsseldorf, 1956.

Heinrich Heine: Briefe. Erste Gesamtausgabe, ed. F. Hirth. Mainz, 1950–6. (Quoted as *Briefe*.)

Heinrich Heines Briefwechsel, ed. F. Hirth. Berlin, 1914–20.

Gespräche mit Heine, ed. H. H. Houben. Frankfurt, 1926. (Quoted as *Gespräche*.)

III. GENERAL WORKS

Bieber, H., *Der Kampf um die Tradition*. Stuttgart, 1928.

Butler, E. M., *The Saint-Simonian Religion in Germany*. Cambridge, 1926.

—— *The Tyranny of Greece over Germany*. Cambridge, 1935.

Closs, A., *The Genius of the German Lyric*. London, 1938.

Demetz, P., *Marx, Engels und die Dichter*. Stuttgart, 1959.

Doerk, B., *Reiseroman und -Novelle in Deutschland von Hermes bis Heine*. Münster, 1925.

Ermatinger, E., *Deutsche Dichter, 1700–1900*, vol. II. Bonn, 1949.

Heusler, A., *Deutsche Versgeschichte*, vol. III. Leipzig and Berlin, 1925.

Höllerer, W., *Zwischen Klassik und Moderne*. Stuttgart, 1958.

Houben, H. H., *Verbotene Literatur von der klassischen Zeit bis zur Gegenwart*. Berlin, 1924–8.

Junk, V., *Der Tannhäuser in Sage und Dichtung*. München, 1911.

Kayser, W., *Geschichte der deutschen Ballade*. Berlin, 1936.

—— *Das Groteske. Seine Gestaltung in Malerei und Dichtung*. Oldenburg, 1957.

Killy, W., *Wandlungen des lyrischen Bildes*. Göttingen, 1958.

Kleinmayr, H. v., *Welt- und Kunstanschauung des jungen Deutschland*. Wien, 1930.

Korff, H. A., *Geist der Goethezeit*, vol. IV. Leipzig, 1953.

Müller, G., *Geschichte des deutschen Liedes*. München, 1925.

Mustard, H. M., *The Lyric Cycle in German Literature*. New York, 1926.

Petzet, C. *Die Blütezeit der deutschen politischen Lyrik, von 1840 bis 1850*. München, 1903.

Prawer, S. S., *German Lyric Poetry*. London, 1952.

Spoerri, Th., *Der Weg zur Form. Dasein und Verwirklichung des Menschen im Spiegel der europäischen Literatur*. Hamburg, 1954.

Tymms, R., *Doubles in Literary Psychology*. Cambridge, 1949.

v. Wiese, B., *Politische Dichtung Deutschlands*. Berlin, 1931.

—— (ed.), *Die deutsche Lyrik*, vol. II. Düsseldorf, 1956.

IV. BIOGRAPHIES

Atkins, H. G., *Heine*. London, 1929.

Bianquis, G., *Henri Heine, l'Homme et l'Œuvre*. Paris, 1948.

Bieber, H. and Hadas, M., *Heine. A Biographical Anthology*. Philadelphia, 1956.

Bottacchiardi, R., *Heine*. Torino, 1927.

Brinitzer, C., *Heinrich Heine. Roman seines Lebens*. Hamburg, 1960.

Brod, M., *Heinrich Heine*. Amsterdam, 1934. (New revised edition, Berlin, 1956.)

Butler, E. M., *Heinrich Heine. A Biography*. London, 1956.

Hirth, F. *Heinrich Heine. Bausteine zu einer Biographie*. Mainz, 1950.

Lehrmann, C. C., *Heinrich Heine. Kämpfer und Dichter*. Bern, 1957.

Marcuse, L., *Heinrich Heine. Ein Leben zwischen Gestern und Morgen.* Berlin, 1932.

—— *Heinrich Heine in Selbstzeugnissen und Bilddokumenten.* Hamburg, 1960.

Strodtmann, A., *Heines Leben und Werke.* Berlin, 1867–9.

Untermeyer, L., *Heinrich Heine.* London, 1938.

Uyttersprot, H., *Heinrich Heine en zijn Invloed in de Nederlandse Letterkunde.* Oudenaarde, 1953.

Walter, H., *Heinrich Heine. A Critical Examination of the Poet and his Works.* New York, 1930.

Wendel, H., *Heinrich Heine. Ein Lebens- und Zeitbild.* Dresden, 1916.

Wolff, M. J., *Heinrich Heine.* München, 1922.

V. MONOGRAPHS, ARTICLES, THESES

Adorno, T. W., 'Die Wunde Heine', in *Noten zur Literatur*, Berlin and Frankfurt, 1958.

Andler, C., 'L'Œuvre lyrique de Heine', *Études Germaniques*, I–II, Paris, 1946–7.

Arnold, Matthew, 'Heinrich Heine', in *Essays in Criticism*, London, 1865.

Atkins, S., 'The First Draft of Heine's *Für die Mouche*', *Harvard Library Bulletin*, XIII (1959).

Balser, C., 'Heine und Campe', *Börsenblatt für den deutschen Buchhandel* (Frankfurt), XII (1956).

Becker, H., *Der Fall Heine–Meyerbeer.* Berlin, 1958.

Belart, U., *Gehalt und Aufbau von Heines Gedichtsammlungen.* Bern, 1925.

Betz, L. P., *Heine in Frankreich.* Zürich, 1894.

Beyer, P., *Der junge Heine.* Berlin, 1911.

Birkenbihl, M., 'Die orientalischen Elemente in der Poesie Heines', in *Analecta Germanica für Hermann Paul*, Amberg, 1906.

Brandes, G., *Ludwig Börne und Heinrich Heine.* Leipzig, 1896.

Brauweiler, E., *Heines Prosa. Beiträge zu ihrer Wesensbestimmung.* Berlin, 1915.

Chiles, J. A., *Über den Gebrauch des Beiwortes in Heines Gedichten.* Diss. Illinois, 1908.

Clarke, M. A., *Heine et la Monarchie de Juillet.* Paris, 1927.

Dresch, J., *Heine à Paris, 1831–56.* Paris, 1956.

Eckertz, E., *Heine und sein Witz.* Berlin, 1908.

Eliot, George, 'German Wit', in *Essays and Leaves from a Note-Book*, London, 1884.

Fairley, B., 'Heine's Vaudeville', *Univ. of Toronto Quarterly*, III (1934).

—— *Heinrich Heine. An Interpretation.* Oxford, 1954.

Feise, E., 'Heinrich Heine. Political Poet and Publicist', *Monatshefte für den deutschen Unterricht*, XL (1948).

—— 'Heine's *Unterwelt*', *Germanic Review*, XXI (1956).

Feuchtwanger, L., *Heinrich Heines Rabbi von Bacharach.* München, 1907.

Fränkel, J., 'Studien zu Heinrich Heines Gedichten', *Euphorion*, XIX (1912).

Friedemann, H., *Die Götter Griechenlands von Schiller bis Heine.* Berlin, 1905.

Galley, E., 'Heine und der Kölner Dom', *Deutsche Vierteljahrsschrift*, XXXII (1958).

Gautier, Théophile, *Tableaux de Voyage. Précédé d'une Étude sur Heine.* Paris, 1895.

Gebhard, H., *Interpretation der 'Historien' aus Heines* 'Romanzero'. Diss. Erlangen, 1956.

Gilbert, R. W., 'The Scope of Heine's Reading', *Susquehanna University Studies*, 1 and 2 (1945–6).

Gowa, F., *Heines Ästhetik.* München, 1923.

Hamburger, M., 'Heinrich Heine', in *Reason and Energy*, London, 1957.

Hammerich, L. L., *Heine: 'Deutschland. Ein Wintermärchen.* København, 1921.

Hammerich, L. L., *Heinrich Heine som Politiske Digter.* København, 1957.

Herrmann, H., *Studien zu Heines* 'Romanzero'. Berlin, 1906.

Holzhausen, P., *Heine und Napoleon I.* Frankfurt, 1903.

Hüffer, H., *Heinrich Heine. Gesammelte Aufsätze.* Berlin, 1906.

Iggers, G. G., 'Heine and the Saint Simonians. A Re-examination', *Comparative Literature*, X (1958).

Kaufmann, H., *Politisches Gedicht und klassische Dichtung. Heinrich Heine: Deutschland. Ein Wintermärchen.* Berlin, 1958.

Kieft, P., *Heine in westeuropäischer Beurteilung.* Amsterdam, 1938.

Kraus, Karl, *Heine und die Folgen.* München, 1910.

Legras, J., *Henri Heine, Poète.* Paris, 1897.

Lichtenberger, H., *Henri Heine, Penseur.* Paris, 1905.

Liptzin, S., *The Weavers in German Literature* (*Hesperia*, XVI). Göttingen and Baltimore, 1926.

Liptzin, S., *The English Legend of Heinrich Heine*. New York, 1954.

Lucács, G., 'Heinrich Heine als nationaler Dichter', in *Deutsche Realisten des 19. Jahrhunderts*. Berlin, 1951.

Luther, A., *Studien zur deutschen Dichtung*. Kuppenheim-Murgtal, 1948.

Mayer, H., 'Die Ausnahme Heine', in *Von Lessing bis Thomas Mann*. Pfullingen, 1959.

Maione, I., *La Poesia di Heine*. Firenze, 1926.

Melchior, F., *Heinrich Heines Verhältnis zu Lord Byron*. Berlin, 1903.

Meyer, R. M., 'Heine's *Romanzero*', in *Gestalten und Probleme*. Berlin, 1905.

Mücke, G., *Heinrich Heines Beziehungen zum deutschen Mittelalter*. Berlin, 1908.

Pache, A., *Naturgefühl und Natursymbolik bei Heinrich Heine*. Leipzig, 1904.

Paul, A., 'Atta Troll', *Zeitschrift für dt. Philologie*, LVI (1931).

Pfeiffer, H., *Begriff und Bild. Heines philosophische und ästhetische Ansichten*. Rudolstadt, 1958.

Politzer, H., 'Heinrich Heine', *Die Neue Rundschau*. December, 1948.

Prawer, S. S., *Heine's 'Buch der Lieder'*. London, 1960.

—— 'Heine's "Return"', *German Life and Letters*, N.S. IX (1956).

—— 'Heine's *Romanzero*', *Germanic Review*, XXXI (1956).

Pützfeld, C., *Heinrich Heines Verhältnis zur Religion*. Berlin, 1912.

Rose, W., *Heinrich Heine. Two Studies of his Thought and Feeling*. Oxford, 1956.

Schmohl, E., *Der Streit um Heinrich Heine. Darstellung und Kritik der bisherigen Heine-Wertung*. Diss. Marburg, 1956.

Schnapp, F., *Heinrich Heine und Robert Schumann*. Hamburg and Berlin, 1924.

Seeger, H., *Der Erzähler in Heines Balladen und Gedichten*. Diss. Bonn, 1953.

Silz, W., 'Heine's Synaesthesia', *Proc. Mod. Lang. Ass.* LVII (1942).

Stamm, F., 'Die Liebeszyklen in Heines *Neuen Gedichten*', *Euphorion*, XXIII (1921).

Steinberg, W., 'Unbekannte Autographien Heinrich Heines', *Die Kultur*, IV (1956).

Sternberg, K., *Heines geistige Gestalt und Welt*. Leipzig, 1929.

Strich, F., 'Goethe und Heine', in *Der Dichter und die Zeit*. Bern, 1947.

Tabak, I., *Judaic Lore in Heine*. Baltimore, 1948.

Taillandier, S.-R., *Henri Heine*. Paris, 1861.

Uhlendahl, H., *Fünf Kapitel über Heinrich Heine und E. T. A. Hoffmann*. Münster, 1919.

Vontin, W. B., *Die Darstellung der Landschaft in den Werken Heinrich Heines*. Hamburg, 1923.

Wadepuhl, W., *Heine-Studien*. Weimar, 1956.

Walzel, O., 'Heine, Goethe und die Antike', *Die Zeit*, I (1896).

Weckmüller, A., *Heines Stil*. Breslau, 1934.

Weidekampf, I., *Traum und Wirklichkeit in der Romantik und bei Heine* (*Palaestra*, 182). Leipzig, 1932.

Weigand, H. J., 'Heine's Return to God', *Modern Philology*, XVIII (1920).

—— 'Heine in Paris', *Orbis Litterarum*, XI (1956).

Weinberg, K., *Henri Heine, Romantique défroqué, Héraut du Symbolisme Français*. Yale and Paris, 1954.

Werner, H. G., *Heine. Seine weltanschauliche Entwicklung und sein Deutschlandbild*. Bukarest, 1958.

Wood, F. H., *Heine as a Critic of his own Works*. New York, 1934.

Wormley, S. L., *Heine in England*. Chapel Hill, 1943.

INDEX

(a) PROPER NAMES

(*b*) TITLES OF HEINE'S WORKS